International Nietzsche Studies

Richard Schacht, series editor

Nietzsche's Revaluation of Values

Nietzsche's Revaluation of Values

A STUDY IN STRATEGIES

E. E. Sleinis

University of Illinois Press URBANA AND CHICAGO

This book is printed on acid-free paper.

Library of Congress Cataloging-in-Publication Data

Sleinis, E. E. (Edgar Evalt), 1943–
  Nietzsche's revaluation of values : a study in
strategies / E. E. Sleinis.
      p.   cm. — (International Nietzsche studies)
  ISBN 0-252-02090-1 (cloth). — ISBN 0-252-06383-X (paper).
  1. Nietzsche, Friedrich Wilhelm, 1844–1900. 2. Values.
I. Title. II. Series.
B3318.V25S57   1994
121'.8'092—dc20   93-40385
                                                          CIP

Contents

International Nietzsche Studies

Nietzsche has emerged as a thinker of extraordinary importance, not only in the history of philosophy but in many fields of contemporary inquiry. Nietzsche studies are maturing and flourishing in many parts of the world. This internationalization of inquiry with respect to Nietzsche's thought and significance may be expected to continue.

International Nietzsche Studies is conceived as a series of monographs and essay collections that will reflect and contribute to these developments. The series will present studies in which responsible scholarship is joined to the analysis, interpretation, and assessment of the many aspects of Nietzsche's thought that bear significantly upon matters of moment today. In many respects Nietzsche is our contemporary, with whom we do better to reckon than to ignore, even when we find ourselves at odds with him. The series is intended to promote this reckoning, embracing diverse interpretive perspectives, philosophical orientations, and critical assessments.

The series is also intended to contribute to the ongoing reconsideration of the character, agenda, and prospects of philosophy itself. Nietzsche was much concerned with philosophy's past, present, and future. He sought to affect not only its understanding but also its practice. The future of philosophy is an open question today, thanks at least in part to Nietzsche's challenge to the philosophical traditions of which he was so critical. It remains to be seen—and determined—whether philosophy's future will turn out to resemble the "philosophy of the future" to which he offered us a prelude and foretaste, by both precept and practice. But this is a possibility we do well to take seriously. International Nietzsche Studies will attempt to do so, while contributing to the understanding of Nietzsche's philosophical thinking and its bearing upon contemporary inquiry.

—Richard Schacht

Acknowledgments

I would like to thank the Cambridge University Press, Cambridge, U.K., and R. J. Hollingdale for permission to quote from their translations of Nietzsche's *Untimely Meditations, Human, All Too Human,* and *Daybreak.*

Many persons have helped in this enterprise either by discussing ideas, reading and correcting drafts, or otherwise assisting in the production of this work. Among those I am indebted to are Bill and Gwen Harwood, Frank White, Moira Nicholls, Susumu Okada, Leila Shotten, Diane Boyle, Louie Simon, and Sally Sleinis. However, my greatest debt is to Richard Schacht both for his encouragement and for his instructive observations at earlier stages of this work.

Abbreviations

BT	*The Birth of Tragedy*
UM	*Untimely Meditations*
HAH	*Human, All Too Human*
D	*Daybreak*
GS	*Gay Science*
Z	*Thus Spoke Zarathustra*
BGE	*Beyond Good and Evil*
GM	*On the Genealogy of Morals*
CW	*The Case of Wagner*
TI	*Twilight of the Idols*
A	*The Anti-Christ*
NCW	*Nietzsche contra Wagner*
EH	*Ecce Homo*
WP	*The Will to Power*

Introduction

The Approach

Nietzsche's principal concern was with values. From the beginning of his productive life to its end, questions of value predominate. The focus becomes sharper, the questioning more incisive, the projects more ambitious, but issues of value are always at the core or close to it. *"In what do you believe?—*In this, that the weights of all things must be determined anew" (GS 269). The task that he set himself as his philosophy matured was the *revaluation of all values* and, especially, the *revaluation of the highest values*. At the end of the late *Twilight of the Idols* Nietzsche goes so far as to assert that even his first book, *The Birth of Tragedy,* was a part of the enterprise of revaluing all values. Even if we allow for the element of afterthought in this, it still reveals the unity he saw in his own work, and not entirely without reason. Already in the works immediately following *The Birth of Tragedy,* namely the *Untimely Meditations,* there is a self-conscious opposition to the values of his time.

The enterprise of revaluing all values initially appears exciting, challenging, and both practically and theoretically important. Yet, only a moment's reflection reveals an apparently overwhelming difficulty. How can one reassess what is absolutely basic to, and exhaustive of, our value system? With a little reflection, the enterprise rapidly begins to appear impossible. In fact, it was never completed the way Nietzsche originally intended, but what there is of it raises issues of real importance and deserves serious consideration. The immediate difficulty raised by his quest is this: *What* do you use when you revalue *all* values? If you do not use values, how can you *revalue?* If you do use values, then all values are not being revalued. How *can* all values be revalued? Similar difficulties arise from the formulation in terms of the highest values. *What* do you use when you revalue the highest values? By assumption, you cannot have recourse to even higher values. Yet, it is surely inconceivable that lower values could form the basis for a revaluation of the highest values. Can someone as undeniably incisive as Nietzsche simply have blundered into supposing that this apparently impossible task is really possible? Or, is a revaluation as extreme and comprehensive as the one he intended really possible after all? This issue forms the core of this study.

Although central aspects of Nietzsche's philosophy will be dealt with, this study is not a balanced and comprehensive account of his philosophy. The focus is specific, and even within this restricted scope selection is unavoidable. I concentrate on the problems raised by the projects of the mature years, namely the revaluation of all values and the revaluation of the highest values, and in particular on the theoretical feasibility of such an enterprise. There are three main reasons for this specific orientation. First, given that the enterprise appears impossible, a consideration of whether things are as they appear raises basic theoretical questions about the structure and status of systems of value, and the degree to which they are subject to appraisal and change. Second, quite apart from the previous meta-issue, the pursuit of the project of revaluation is of interest in its own right. The overall goal of the revaluation of all values is to replace life-denying values with life-affirming values. Nietzsche has made important contributions here, and these contributions deserve attention. Third, the question of what methods and strategies Nietzsche employs in his philosophizing warrants further investigation.[1]

Within this context, it is my intention to be selective, and to focus on those revaluation strategies that are central to the most radical aspect of Nietzsche's enterprise, namely, the revaluation of the highest values. After all, these are the most problematic and theoretically interesting cases. Thus, I do not plan an exhaustive coverage of his investigation of values. As he himself says, "The most valuable insights are the last to be discovered; but the most valuable insights are *methods*" (A 13), and it is indeed methods to which most attention will be paid.

Nietzsche among Philosophers

Fortunately, even in the English-speaking world, it is no longer necessary to argue a case for taking Nietzsche seriously as a philosopher, but there are still points worth making. In the past there has been a curious disparity in the positions assigned to him. Artists and writers have considered him to be a philosopher of the first rank, and his influence on them has been enormous. Among philosophers, at any rate in the English-speaking world, many have regarded him as a significant philosopher, but not as central. The view is often of an idiosyncratic thinker forging his own way beside the mainstream but not in it, and certainly not as important as those who are.[2] Stimulation, incisiveness, and interest are conceded, but centrality is denied. This slight is undeserved; it has lost ground steadily over the years, and arguably, has already been put to rest. However, in the final analysis the issue can only be settled by showing that his ideas matter, and I hope this study contributes to that end.

Undoubtedly, some of the past neglect was due to misconceptions about Nietzsche's political and racial views, and some of the unflattering estimates of the past are in some measure due to a style that philosophers have not been accustomed to. But even knowledgeable sympathizers have on occasion not been helpful. Jaspers[3] contends that Nietzsche contradicts himself on virtually every point; a claim so extreme that, to my knowledge, no one has made the like about any other philosopher. An apparently authoritative claim like this, by a Nietzsche expert, hardly constitutes an invitation to analytically inclined philosophers to pursue Nietzsche studies. While the substance of the matter can hardly be regarded as uncontroversial, I take the claim to be unwarranted. There are things about which Nietzsche changed his mind; there are things about which he did not change his mind; there are things about which he vacillated, and there are things on which he contradicted himself. When everything is taken into account, the level of contradiction may be a little greater, but I doubt that it is much greater than that of most other philosophers. Even such a monument in the history of modern logic as Bertrand Russell might well invite a similar condemnation under interpretative principles that see Nietzsche contradicting himself on every point. Such extreme views no longer dominate, although this is not to say that no one holds them. In any event, tolerance for different philosophical styles has increased, as is shown by Wittgenstein's reception, whose style is closer to Nietzsche's than to that of traditional philosophers.[4]

Let me add to the case that the philosophical tasks Nietzsche undertook and the way he undertook them warrant locating him as a central figure among the major philosophers. It is common to regard Descartes as the father of modern philosophy. Descartes sought to subject "knowledge" to the severest critical scrutiny in order to arrive at claims that are indubitably true.[5] These would constitute a solid foundation upon which the true view of the world could be built. Two issues are fundamental here: What are the genuine items of knowledge? and, What is the world like? The preoccupation is with epistemology and metaphysics, in that order. The Method of Doubt is intended to furnish a bedrock from which the construction of the true world view can confidently proceed. This is the Cartesian agenda, and much of modern Western philosophy has followed it, at any rate as far as the first part of the agenda is concerned.

But there is a glaring gap here. The *value* of knowledge, the *value* of truth is simply taken for granted. Indeed, the very nature of truth is taken for granted. The hunt is directly for the ultimate "truths." The severest critical scrutiny is *not* applied to the question whether knowledge is valuable or whether truth is valuable. Indeed, no critical scrutiny is applied to them at all. The Method of Doubt as applied leaves these questions of value entirely untouched. Equally seriously, it leaves questions of value as a whole hardly considered at all. There are occasions on which it would be unfair to criticize a thinker for not doing everything he might have done. Here the situation is different. The very spirit of the Cartesian enterprise, the underlying impetus that gives the enterprise the significance it has, is to not admit anything that does not pass the severest tests. It is of the essence of the enterprise to be exhaustive. Yet at the very basis of Descartes's philosophy lie untested assumptions about the value of knowledge and truth and a notable failure to pursue the Method of Doubt in the realm of value in general. To be sure, Descartes devotes some attention to moral values in the third discourse of the *Discourse on Method*,[6] but by no stretch of the imagination could this be called either a critical investigation or an extensive investigation. Had the attention to knowledge about the world been as perfunctory, Descartes's position in philosophy would be quite other than it is.

One reason why Nietzsche ought to be regarded not only as a major but also as a central figure in the Western philosophical tradition is precisely because he is prepared to take to its logical conclusion the critical scrutiny of beliefs that is such a focal point in this tradition. He seeks to challenge all assumptions, and in particular those assumptions that other philosophers have ignored, although it is true that his emphasis is heavily on values. We can justifiably say that while Descartes is the great proponent of the need for doubt as a starting point in the realm of fact, Nietzsche is the great proponent of the need for doubt as a starting point in the realm of value.[7] In relation to Descartes, he is quite specific concerning the neglect of values. "The question of values is more *fundamental* than the question of certainty: the latter becomes serious only by presupposing that the value question has already been answered" (WP 588). To be sure, many philosophers have been interested in the nature of truth, but few have questioned the value of truth. Nietzsche seizes on this crucial omission and makes it central to his mature philosophizing. "The problem of the value of truth stepped before us—or was it we who stepped before this problem? . . . And, would you believe it, it has finally almost come to seem to us that this problem has never before been posed—that we have been the first to see it, to fix our eyes on it, to hazard it?" (BGE 1).

The conception of truth that emerges forms a pivotal role in Nietzsche's philosophy.[8] Accept his conception of truth, and challenging questions immediately arise about the most cherished values. Reject his conception of truth, and his critique of values, although stimulating, would be significantly diminished. For this reason, after an initial ground-setting chapter on Nietzsche's theory of value and his higher-order values, the study proceeds directly to his investigations into the nature and value of truth. But there is another reason for beginning the consideration of specific values with truth. The revaluation of truth poses the greatest difficulties for the enterprise of revaluation. How can an apparently key instrument of intellectual inquiry itself be subject to an impartial and non-question-begging intellectual inquiry? If revaluation is possible in the case of truth, then its feasibility in other cases must be less problematic. However, before delving into these issues, it is useful to have an outline of the scope of this inquiry.

The Scope of the Inquiry

Five great questions dominate Nietzsche's critical scrutiny of values. First, what is the value of knowledge? Second, what is the value of morality? "Thus nobody up to now has examined the *value* of that most famous of all medicines which is called morality; and the first step would be—for once to *question* it. Well then, precisely this is our task" (GS 345). Third, what is the value of religion? Fourth, what is the value of art? Finally, what is the value of the state? Since the last question raises less fundamental issues, I will not deal with it directly.[9]

Bound to each of these questions is a cluster of values and further questions. The first question raises the following issues: What is the value of truth? What is the nature of truth? What is the nature of knowledge? What is the value of reason? What is the nature of reason? What is the value of objectivity? What is the value of impartiality? What is the value of science? What is the value of history? Is truth attainable? and so on. The second question leads to the following issues: What is the value of goodness? What is the nature of goodness? Is goodness an objective characteristic? What is the value of altruism? What is the value of happiness? What is the value of freedom? What is the value of justice? What is the value of punishment? and so on. Of course, these questions are only representative and do not exhaust the respective clusters. Naturally, parallel questions arise in the other clusters.

The very existence of these *separate* clusters raises an acute question of values. Namely, according to what values are the clusters themselves to be ranked? How is the matter to be settled whether morality takes precedence over art, or whether knowledge takes precedence over morality? Indeed, how are any questions of ranking between these clusters to be decided? It is one of Nietzsche's undoubted merits that he both gives a comprehensive scrutiny to the values in each cluster and also makes important claims concerning the relations between these clusters. The case will be put that, for him, the most important values lie outside these traditional clusters.

In the past these five clusters of values have formed the substance of valuation in the Western tradition. They have appeared to exhaust the landscape. To be sure, other values have been suggested, but even if we accept there are others, their role has been peripheral. Two reasons arise from this for taking special note of Nietzsche. First, the scope and detail of his interest in values exceeds that of all other modern philosophers. He may not cover everything, but he covers a great deal. Second, he is unique in the seriousness, fearlessness, and penetration with which he pursues the task of critical appraisal. He is not afraid to come to the conclusion that cherished values are not merely baseless, but even pernicious.[10] He may or may not be right, but he is one of the few who have ventured to say such things, and it makes the issue of how these conclusions are arrived at all the more intriguing.

This study concentrates on the issue of the intelligibility of the enterprise of revaluing *all* values and the intelligibility of the enterprise of revaluing the *highest* values. While I am interested in the success of the revaluation in practice, I am just as interested in the possibility of success in principle. There is a greater methodological emphasis here than in Nietzsche's own work. Thus this study does not aim at the same comprehensive treatment of values he provides, but it aims to deal with what is most important.

The Structure of Revaluation

Let me identify the main elements in the revaluation. Naturally, the values targeted for revaluation stand at the forefront of the enterprise, but the means used to effect the revaluation are also of crucial importance. These means fall into two categories. On the one hand there are Nietzsche's own specific values, his higher-order values, and his theory of value. On the other hand there is a range of strategies that do not themselves presuppose values but that are deployed against the target values. Revaluation is sometimes confronting specific values with other specific values; it is sometimes confronting specific values with higher-order values; but frequently it is neither. Indeed, I aim to establish that the number of strategies Nietzsche uses to challenge values without in turn presupposing values is both extensive and varied.

The status of the specific values, higher-order values, and theory of value Nietzsche uses in his revaluation is crucial to the theoretical feasibility of the enterprise of revaluing *all* values, and of revaluing the *highest* values. The key issue is whether his own values are capable of being revalued. There are three considerations indicating that this is indeed the case. The first arises from his conception of truth; the second arises from his conception of value; the third arises from the fact that there are strategies for challenging values that do not themselves presuppose values. For him no values are immune from revision, not even his own. The issue is taken up at the end of chapter 1 and throughout this study, especially in chapter 7.

The next element of note is the value situation that exists after the revaluation has taken place. Here complexity sets in on a number of levels. Some of the target values are rejected outright; some undergo a downward displacement; some are elevated; while others stay where they are. Metaphors of philosophizing with a hammer notwithstanding, it is a misconstruction to suppose that the revaluation of values leads only to outright rejection. In addition to the repositioned target values there are also the specific values and higher-order values he brings to the revaluation. The principal complicating factor is the value vacuum he conceives to exist, created by the outright rejection of some values and the independent disintegration of others. To be sure, some of the values find replacements in the process of revaluation, others are discarded without need of replacement, but for all that, a significant value vacuum remains, and for him it is vital that new values be created to fill this vacuum.

Nietzsche furnishes a positive contribution to the filling of this value vacuum through his conceptions of the Eternal Recurrence and the *Übermensch*. But there are several complications. One problem arises from the relation between the Eternal Recurrence, the *Übermensch*, and the values that survive revaluation. For example, some interpreters see the Eternal Recurrence as furnishing an individually centered but nevertheless completely general principle governing all choice. On this view, even values that survive revaluation appear superfluous, or raise the possibility of conflict between themselves and the purported rule furnished by Eternal Recurrence. An analogous problem arises in the case of the *Übermensch*. The conception of the *Übermensch* cannot just be a construct from the values that survive revaluation. As such it would be superfluous and incapable of filling the value vacuum left after the outright rejection of some values and disintegration of others. The *Übermensch* must either embody new values or create new values. But this raises the problem of how these newly embodied or newly created values relate to the values Nietzsche brings to the revaluation and the values that survive it.

My view is that the values utilized in the revaluation and the values that survive it in substantial measure serve to define the conceptions of the Eternal Recurrence and the *Übermensch*. While not determining them in a narrow way, they shape their outer boundaries. Thus the prospect for conflict is diminished and perhaps eliminated entirely. The key point is that the higher-order values invoked in the revaluation form a stable background. These higher-order values not only define the boundaries for the Eternal Recurrence and the *Übermensch*, they also define the boundaries for additional new values. The new values required are specific values that give effect to the fundamentals already in place.

Allowance must be made for flexibility in the ordering of the elements identified. In *Ecce Homo*, Nietzsche conceived of *Thus Spoke Zarathustra* as the positive component of the revaluation and the books that came later as the negative component: "Now that the affirmative part of my task was done, it was the turn of the denying, the No-saying and No-*doing* part: the revaluation of existing values themselves, the great war—the evocation of a day of decision" (EH X:1). Yet the critical enterprise started before *Thus Spoke Zarathustra* in *Human, All Too Human, Daybreak,* and *Gay Science,* even if these lack some of the intensity of the later works. In any event, Nietzsche built in addition to destroying. Certainly he did not think of himself as just a "problem-thinker," to use the term Kaufmann favored. He undoubtedly had a constructive contribution to make. But he also had a marked preference for brevity—consequently, an element of conjecture in the reconstruction of arguments is unavoidable, "For I approach deep problems like cold baths: quickly into them and quickly out again" (GS 381).

Nietzsche's Revaluation of Values

ONE

Value and Power

The Theory of Value

A grasp of Nietzsche's theory of value is required to understand its role in revaluation and also to understand why he takes revaluation to be so vital and the outcome he expects from it. It is crucial to distinguish an account of the nature of value from a listing of what is valuable. However closely the two may be linked, they are not identical. First some general observations are in order. For Nietzsche, value does not arise from outside life, nor is value to be understood in terms of ontologically distinct axiological properties that are additional to or supervenient upon the natural world. Put another way, there are no values without valuing beings. There are values just insofar as there are beings who value things. Clearly, this constitutes a reversal of one common conception of the matter. According to this conception we value things *because* they are valuable; valuing is seen as the appropriate response to something that is valuable independently of that response. For Nietzsche, things are valuable *because* we value them; it is valuing that makes things valuable. The source of value lies within valuing beings.

Contrary to appearances, there is an important sense in which Nietzsche is not a noncognitivist. Neither merely feeling something to be valuable, nor merely judging something to be valuable, nor merely being favorably disposed to something constitute either necessary or sufficient conditions for something being valuable. Such subjective responses are not the source of value; they neither define value, nor do they constitute value, and actual value varies independently of them (WP 707). His view combines individual variability with a naturalistic conception of value. Further, conscious subjective states themselves are not ultimately valuable. Neither pleasure, nor happiness, nor contentment, nor inner peace, nor merely subjective feelings of increased power constitute ultimate values. Conscious states are peripheral both to what it is to be a value and to what is actually valuable.

A key to understanding Nietzsche's theory of value is furnished by his highest value—the maximally affirmative attitude toward life. Life as a whole is valuable to the degree that this attitude is attained. What this means is that the greater the inner power is that draws to life, the greater the inner power is that can surmount the pain, suffering, and terror of life, the greater the inner power is to celebrate life no matter what, the greater is the value of life. The very power that draws to life is constitutive of the value of life. The passage "What is the objective measure of value? Solely the quantum of enhanced and organized power" (WP 674) is also crucial. Four points need to be noted. First, it asserts that there is an *objective* measure of value. Second, it asserts that power is the objective *measure* of value. Third, there is no other source of value besides power. Fourth, it relates value to *increased* power and to *organized* power. The challenge is to flesh out the theory in a way that it will accommodate these points. I believe that the challenge can be met.

Individuals

In valuing, the basic situation consists of a valuer and what is valued. The valuer is an individual, and let me call what is valued "the goal."[1] What ingredient in the situation containing the individual and the goal makes it a value relation? What distinguishes a basic value relation from a spatial relation, or a temporal relation, or a size relation, and so on? What makes it a value relation is that there is an inner power in the individual that draws the individual to the goal, or else there is an inner power in the individual that repels the individual from something. The inner power that attracts and the inner power that repels are each the basis for positive and negative values. Variations in the strength of the inner powers that attract and the inner powers that repel ground the possibility of variation in positive values and negative values. Attainment of what is attracted may ground a positive value, nonattainment of what is attracted may ground a negative value. Nonattainment of what is repelled may ground a positive value, attainment of what is repelled may ground a negative value. The power to repel what threatens to destroy is as much the basis of positive value as is the power to attract.

There are several points to note. First, at this stage of analysis the conception of value does not assert or imply that it is the inner power itself that is valuable. To be sure, without power there would be no value, but this does not of itself entail that power is valuable. Second, this conception of value does not claim that the value of the goal is in strict linear proportion to the inner power of attraction or repulsion. The additional factor is the role that the attainment of the goal plays in the general economy of power of the individual. Goals whose attainment increase the individual's overall power are of a higher value than goals whose attainment decreases the individual's overall power even where the inner power drawing the individual to each goal is equal in strength. The strength of the drive is one dimension at the foundation of value, the place of the drive in the individual's network of drives is the other.

A concrete example may help. Persons being attracted to other persons constitute the basis for fulfilling human relationships. If persons were in no way attracted to each other, there would be no possibility of fulfilling human relationships. The greater the attraction, the greater the potential is for a fulfilling human relationship. But it is notorious that even some strong mutual attractions do not yield fulfilling relationships; the two broader networks of drives do not mesh. It is equally notorious that a strong attraction on one side matched with an equally strong repulsion on the other side does not yield much that is valuable; the potential for such a situation to be debilitating is obvious. Thus, while there is no strict linear relation between the strength of the inner power that attracts or the strength of the inner power that repels and the actual value of the goals in question, there is nevertheless an important relation between the two.

The strength of the inner power that attracts an individual to a goal determines the *propensity* of the goal to be valuable for the individual; an additional factor needs to interfere to prevent the goal yielding its value. Only where the general economy of power of the individual is unfavorably affected by the attainment of the goal will its attainment not yield a value strictly proportional to the strength of the inner power that draws the individual to the goal. In other words, when one comes to attain a goal to which one is drawn to by one's inner power, then one attains something of value for oneself unless there are countervailing factors. The theory has a noteworthy consequence. Nothing can guarantee that a goal will remain of constant value to an individual even when the inner power of attraction or repulsion remains constant. The arrival or departure of countervailing factors or the intensification or attenuation of power in other parts of an individual's network of drives can always lead to a variation of value for the individual. In an important sense, values are contextual; change the context and you change the value. No goal has a fixed value independently of other goals. Thus, assessment of values is essentially holistic; values cannot be assessed in isolation. But it is vital to note that the context itself consists of a network of power relations.

Let me illustrate this contextual aspect of value. Suppose an individual's inner power attracts him or her to a solitary goal. The individual attains the goal and there are no countervailing factors to undermine the value; that is, the attainment of the goal does not lessen the overall power in the individual's network of drives. Here there is a positive value, and it is not only the *highest* value that the individual has, it is *all* the value that the individual has. Suppose now that the individual's inner power, in addition, draws him or her to another goal with twice the force. The goal is attained and there are no countervailing factors to undermine the value. The new value is now the highest value while the original value is only a second best. Further, whereas the original value was all the value the individual possessed, it is now only a fraction of the value that the individual possesses. The value of the original value has changed through other changes in value, although the power that grounds it remains constant (WP 1006). Thus while values are grounded in the inner power to attract and repel, and there are no other sources of value, there is still a significant looseness between the specific inner power that draws an individual to a goal and the actual value of the goal for the individual. Value is a function of both the intensity of the drive and the place of the drive in the individual's network of drives.

There is an aspect of this conception it is important to be clear about. Power is not a means to value for an individual; it is not the cause that has value as an effect; it is not an instrument that leads to value that then exists independently of the instrument; nor is it an ontologically supervenient feature to the power. Rather, where a positive value obtains,[2] the inner power of the individual that draws the individual to the goal is constitutive of the positive value. What makes the positive value *a positive value* is precisely the existence of the individual's inner power, drawing the individual to the goal. Put generally, the individual's attracting and repelling power is the essential ingredient in a value; the only other requirement is that the background setting be right. Nevertheless, care must be taken not to make the connection between power and value too general. Power ranges beyond an individual's inner power to attract and repel, and it would be a mistake to generalize that whenever a power is active it is constitutive of a value. For example, the power active in nonliving things is not constitutive of value.

This theory of value carries with it a natural criterion of how valuable goals are both *intra*personally and *inter*personally. For a single individual the value of the goal increases the more strongly the individual is drawn to it. For two individuals, other things being equal, there is more value for the individual who is the more strongly drawn to a goal. Imagine an individual A who is strongly drawn to a particular goal and is not drawn to or repelled by anything else. Next, imagine an individual B who is drawn to the same goal as A but with only half the strength with which A is drawn to it, and is also not drawn to or repelled by anything else. For Nietzsche, there is more value *for* those who are more strongly drawn to goals rather than *for* those who are less strongly drawn to goals. Thus, there is more value *for* A, than *for* B. But also, there is more value *in* the world to have those who are more strongly drawn to goals rather than those who are less strongly drawn to goals. Consequently, if only one of A and B could exist, there would be more value in the world if A existed rather than B.

Let me turn to another aspect of the basic situation. How a goal is conceived of by the individual, and how the individual conceives of himself or herself can affect the strength of the inner power that draws the individual to the goal or repels the individual from something, and hence can influence the value of the goal to the individual: "Man first implanted values into things to maintain himself—he created the meaning of things, a human meaning!" (Z I:15). There are two ways new values can be created. First, we can change an individual's conception of himself or herself in such a way that the inner power directed at goals is either augmented or diminished or redirected, thus furnishing the basis for new values for that individual. Second, we can change an individual's conception of the world in such a way that the inner power directed at goals is either augmented or diminished or redirected, thus furnishing the basis for new values. Of course, there are other ways. Directly changing persons and directly changing the world also furnish the basis for variation in the inner power to attract and repel, and hence furnish the potential for new values. Combining these points, we can see that effecting change and exercising power is essential to the creation of new values. Those with the greatest capacity to change the world or to change conceptions of the world, or to change us or our conceptions of ourselves have the greatest capacity to create new values. Value creation is not for the weak. Creating new values is not merely thinking up new sentences of the form "X is good."

The basic theory of value deals with what it is to be a value, but it does not propose anything specific as valuable, and it is compatible with anything whatever being valuable for an individual. Further, this conception of value is not restricted to human beings; it is applicable to life forms in general. In addition, it is a theory of value that does not differentiate between aesthetic value, moral value, cognitive value, or any other kind of value; it is a general theory of value basic to all areas. However, the theory embraces more than an account of value for individuals alone.

Groups

Value for an individual may be basic, but it does not exhaust the realm of valuation. There are also values that pertain to collections of individuals. Of course, mere aggregates of individuals do not introduce anything new, but there are modes of relating, modes of organization, modes of structuring collections of individuals that give the collection an identity, a possibility of common purpose, common interest, and common action that cannot readily be reduced to the individual identities, individual purposes, individual interests, and individual actions of members that constitute it. Let me call such collections groups. Groups are more than the sum of their separate parts, and it is this that generates the possibility of values beyond the mere aggregation of the values of the individuals that make them up. This distinction is required to make sense of conceptions like the slave morality and the herd morality.

Value for a group is formally parallel to value for an individual. If the power of the group draws it to a goal, then the attainment of the goal is valuable in proportion to the power that draws the group to that goal provided that there are no countervailing factors. As in the case of an individual, the countervailing factors are also to be understood in terms of power. What is at issue is the general economy of power of the group. If the attainment of the goal diminishes the power of the group, then the attainment of the goal lacks the value it would have if it left the power the same or increased it. Thus group values are also contextual. In any event, the power that draws a group to a goal is constitutive of the value of the goal to the group.

An example may help to clarify these points. Suppose that there are two football teams, one with a powerful drive to win the championship, the other with no strong drive to win it—they are there for the fun. Suppose that each team wins the championship in successive years. Other things being equal, the championship is of more value to the team with the stronger drive to win. Of course all things need not be equal. The team with the strong drive to win may feel after their win that they have reached a peak they cannot maintain, and subsequently sink into decline. For them the value of the win decreases from what it would otherwise be, given the strength of their original drive. On the other hand, the team that won the championship with no great desire to do so, may be invigorated by the taste of victory and acquire a real drive for a repeat victory. For them the value of the win increases from what it would otherwise be, given the strength of their original drive.

Just as in the case of individuals, there are two dimensions to the value a group derives from the attainment of its goals. First, there is the strength of the drive that draws the group to the goal, and second, there is the effect of the attainment of the goal on the general economy of power of the group. The position can be formulated as follows. The strength of the power that draws a group to a goal determines the *propensity* of the goal to be valuable for the group. The only thing that can prevent the attainment of the goal yielding an actual value directly proportional to the strength of the drive is the adverse impact the attainment of the goal may have on the general economy of power of the group. This is an important qualification and means, as previously noted, that no goal has a fixed value independently of other goals.

One consequence of additional value at the level of groups is that it introduces new possibilities for conflict. Not only is there the possibility of conflict among individuals and between groups, there is also the possibility of conflict between groups and individuals. Thus, life is a vast arena where striving individuals and groups are drawn to their goals, sometimes in conflict and sometimes not. The outcome is either value or disvalue depending on the success or failure of the striving individuals or groups. Value is right there in the fabric of life as it is lived, and further, it is there without any normative principles or rules of conduct.

This theory of value warrants serious consideration as it has a number of advantages over available alternatives. First, it is a theory of value for all life forms, and as such it fits naturally with the life sciences. Second, it does not countenance an ontologically dubious realm of mind-independent axiological characteristics.[3] Third, it does not require the postulation of a special mental faculty for becoming aware of values. Fourth, it furnishes a unified account for all human value. Fifth, it does not require ad hoc explanations for conflict of values, indeed, it serves in considerable measure to explain them. In short, its scope is broad; it is ontologically modest; it does not need an extravagant epistemology; it fits with the life sciences, and it can explain rather than having to explain away conflict of values. However, while this furnishes an account of what it is to be a value, it does not furnish an account of what is valuable, and it is to this that we need to turn.

The Ultimate Value

Nietzsche has a clear thesis about *what* it is that is valued, and *what* it is that is valuable. At the most fundamental level, individuals, groups, life forms, all seek to increase their power: "what man wants, what every smallest part of a living organism wants, is an increase of power" (WP 702). Ultimately, it is power that is valued, and it is power that is valuable. Thus there is a double occurrence of power in valuation. The inner power that draws individuals and groups to a goal is constitutive of the value of the goal, but the goal itself is the increase of power. Increase of power is the ultimate value for individuals, groups, and indeed all living things. However, it is vital to recognize that the two parts of the doctrine are logically independent, and that the tenability and plausibility of either can vary independently of the other. In essence, what makes an increase of power valuable is *being drawn to* an increase of power.

The doctrine immediately faces a seemingly powerful objection that needs to be dealt with. The objection is this. The only function that an increase in power could serve for any being is to furnish increased means to attain what really matters to that being. In other words, power can only intelligibly be construed as a means; power cannot intelligibly be construed as an ultimate end. Underlying this objection, there is a model of power and its increase that needs to be made explicit. The model appears to commit Nietzsche to the following picture. One undertakes an action whose goal is the increase of power. After the successful completion of the action, the reservoir of power in the individual has been increased and the contents of this reservoir are now available to pursue further goals. The model centers on the possibility of a static reservoir of power from which power can be drawn to fuel the further pursuit of goals, and such a model certainly renders the view that power is an ultimate value either incoherent or highly implausible.

But not only is Nietzsche not committed to such a conception of power, he is flatly opposed to it. For him, power is essentially activity (GM I:13). He regards the idea of a static reservoir of power in general as nonsense. Increased power is not the static consequence of some action. *To desire an increase in power is to desire an increase in activity,* it is not to desire the attainment of a static state that follows the cessation of activity. "A living thing desires above all to vent its strength—life as such is will to power" (BGE 13). Of course more needs to be said about the kind of activity that is desired when an increase of power is desired. To be drawn to an increase of power is to be drawn to activities in which one masters more, controls more, dominates more, overcomes more. The actual activities of mastering more, of controlling more, of dominating more, of overcoming more are the increasings of power. Increase of power is not the effect or consequence of these activities; it is these activities themselves (GM I:13). For example, increasing one's power over opponents at chess or tennis *is* more convincingly outplaying them in chess or tennis games; it is not some state that ensues after the games are over.

Nietzsche's contention that all beings strive for an increase in power cannot be rejected simply on the grounds that it incoherently or implausibly turns a mere means into an ultimate end. He rejects the conception of power that the objection rests on. Of course this shifts the issue to another level. Which theory of power is the correct one? Is it Nietzsche's theory that power is essentially active? Or is it the theory of power that sees it as capable of storage in some static reservoir—to be drawn on when required? To my mind Nietzsche has the better of the debate here. The latter conception immediately invites the question, What must be added to the static stored power to turn it into an active fueler of our actions? This is an embarrassing question, since it appears to require the postulation of a power that turns static power into active power. Suddenly there is a nasty regress to hand. Unless some power is essentially active, no power can be activated. At the most basic level, power must be essentially active.

Nietzsche and Mill

To clarify both Nietzsche's theory of value and his ultimate value, it is useful to contrast them with another view. Superficially, his view has a structure parallel to John Stuart Mill's version of utilitarianism. Mill argues from the claim that everyone desires happiness to the conclusion that happiness is the ultimate value—that happiness is desirable, that happiness is good, that happiness is what ought to be pursued. There are intermediate goals: one can seek to become healthy, or well-educated, or to contemplate art, or to become wealthy, and so on, but the ultimate goal is happiness. So too for Nietzsche, one can pursue the same kinds of intermediate goals, but the ultimate goal is power. However, there are differences between the two views. For Mill, happiness is a state logically independent of the activities or objects that give rise to it. For Nietzsche, increase of power just is certain kinds activity. The activity itself is the goal, and not some state that obtains after its completion.

Crucial aspects of Mill's position require note to bring out the differences fully. The desire for happiness is not constitutive of the value of happiness; if the desiring was absent but the happiness remained, then the value would still remain. The universal desire for happiness is taken merely as *evidence* for its being valuable, which is something beyond its being desired.[4] Put another way, the value claim is *justified* by appeal to the claims about desire, it is not equivalent to those claims. Further, the claim that happiness is the ultimate value is held to justify normative claims, namely, that happiness is what ought to be pursued and maximized. To summarize Mill's position, value statements are epistemically justified by appeal to facts about people, but are not reducible to such facts, and value statements either embody or justify claims about how we ought to act.[5]

The structure of Nietzsche's position differs from Mill's in two respects. First, the inner power that draws an individual to a goal is not mere *evidence* for a value claim about the goal. Rather, the inner power that draws an individual to a goal is *constitutive* of the value of the goal. If the power that draws an individual to a goal is removed, then, other things being equal, the attainment of the goal ceases to be of value. We do not have an inference from a fact to a value; if the power of attraction is there, then the value is there, provided only that countervailing factors are absent. There are direct value facts about the world that are not derived from or dependent on nonvalue facts. Second, the connection is severed between value and rules of conduct. If an individual's or group's power draws them to a goal and a positive value ensues from the attainment of the goal, no conclusion follows about whether anyone else ought to pursue that goal. In these cases there is value, but there are no rules of conduct. Similarly, if all people are ultimately drawn to an increase of power, then to the degree they attain it there is positive value for them (again, subject to the qualifications noted), and it is correct to say that power is their ultimate value. But this in no way entails that anyone ought to pursue power.

For Nietzsche, value statements at this level do not entail statements of obligation or rules of conduct. This may invite the objection that statements of value that do not have normative force are not really value statements at all. There are two points to be made. First, the thesis that there is an analytic tie between value and obligation is unsustainable. The principal countercase arises from aesthetic values. From the warranted ascription of the highest aesthetic value to an artwork we cannot deduce any obligation to contemplate it. We can confidently claim that persons will miss something of value if they fail to contemplate it, but that is as far as it goes. Here as elsewhere, Nietzsche has views on values that appear puzzling at first but that become more intelligible if we take aesthetic value as a model. Second, Nietzsche's value system as a whole has normative force, but the normative force does not come in at this level of analysis, and in any event, is not specifically directed at the actions of individuals. The normative force in his value system is embodied in his higher-order values and is principally directed at the formation of value systems applying to the whole of an individual's life, or the whole of some group, or the whole of society, or the whole of life.

The Higher-Order Values

Nietzsche's theory of value and thesis about ultimate value raise two related questions. First, why is a revaluation of values required? The account appears to imply that values take care of themselves in the natural course of events. Second, why are any new values required besides those that are already furnished by the drawing and repelling power of individuals and groups? The key to these questions lies in the fact that overall value is capable of quantitative variation; it may either increase or decrease. To take a simple case, if the inner power that draws to goals is increased for all individuals and all groups, then, other things being equal, overall value in the system increases through an increase in value for the individuals and groups that attain their goals. On the other hand, if, other things being equal, the inner power that draws to goals is decreased for all individuals and all groups, then overall value in the system is decreased through a decrease in value for the groups and individuals that attain their goals.

Revaluation is required to eliminate from the system those artificial value constructs and those modes of organizing and directing life that have been taken to embody genuine values, but that in fact operate to diminish real value overall. The situation is critical because of the widespread deleterious impact that such value constructs and modes of organizing and directing life have had and continue to have. New values are required to add to the system new value constructs or new modes of organizing and directing life that will operate to increase real value overall. The acceptability of specific value systems will itself be determined by Nietzsche's own higher-order values, which in turn arise organically from the theory of value and his conception of reality.

The problem of where Nietzsche's value system has normative force can be clarified by drawing a distinction in his thinking parallel to the distinction drawn in economics between macroeconomics[6] and microeconomics. His value system does not have normative force at the micro-value level and does not of itself furnish rules governing the specific actions of individuals. There is simply no place for such rules given his theory of value. However, his value system has normative force at the macro-value level and furnishes rules for the optimization of value at the aggregate level.[7] In essence, the criteria embodied in his higher-order values constitute such prescriptions. Certainly, the higher-order values may justify rules governing individuals and groups, but this will depend entirely on particular circumstances and be determined by the contribution to overall value. "'Thou shalt obey someone and for a long time: *otherwise* thou shalt perish and lose all respect for thyself'—this seems to me to be nature's imperative, which is, to

be sure, neither 'categorical' as old Kant demanded it should be (hence
the 'otherwise'—), nor addressed to the individual (what do individuals matter to nature!), but to peoples, races, ages, classes, and above
all to the entire animal 'man,' to *mankind"* (BGE 188). The basic warrant for the higher-order values themselves is simply that they are the
most plausible way of optimizing value at the aggregate level given
Nietzsche's theory of value.

The Enhancement of Life

For Nietzsche, a principal requirement of values is that they enhance life (WP 354). All more specific values are subordinate to this
requirement: "Art, knowledge, morality are *means"* (WP 298). Two
closely related aspects are involved in the enhancement of life. On the
one hand, there is the increase in the health, strength, vitality, and
activity of life itself. In other words, an increase in the thriving and
flourishing of life, and thus an increase in the power with which life
forms are drawn to their goals, and hence to an increase in value. This
is the more directly biological aspect of the principle. On the other
hand, there is the increase in the products of creative activity. In other words, there is the addition to life of knowledge, art, new modes of
group oganization, and so on, and thus an increase in "objects" to
which people can be powerfully drawn, and hence to an increase in
value. This is the more directly cultural aspect of the principle. To differentiate the two aspects, I will call the first the invigoration of life,
and the second the enrichment of life.

A close connection exists between the two aspects and in ideal
circumstances they are mutually reinforcing. The greater the invigoration of life is, the greater the enrichment of life that is to be expected, and the greater the enrichment of life is, the greater the invigoration of life that is to be expected. But these must not be misconstrued
as a means and ends relationship—both the invigoration of life and the
enrichment of life, intertwined as they may be, are to be promoted in
their own right. It needs emphasis that these two aspects are intimately
connected to Nietzsche's theory of value. Invigoration furnishes the
basis for an increase in the power that draws individuals and groups
to their goals. Enriching creations furnish new goals to which individuals and groups may be drawn. In either case, the potential for value
is increased. The general principle combining the two aspects, the requirement that values enhance life, is the centerpiece of his higher-

order values. Certainly both individual life and group life are intended, but the concept of life that he is operating with extends beyond this and includes all living phenomena.

A Set of Criteria

Nietzsche regards it as important that an order of rank be established among values (GM I:17). In other words, values form a hierarchy and there is a need to establish what that hierarchy is. Naturally, the higher a value is in that hierarchy the greater the enhancement of life it furnishes. Clearly, the key issue is what principles serve to determine this hierarchy of values and what relation these principles have to the demand for the enhancement of life.

There are five closely interlocking principles determining such a hierarchy. First, there is the position of the value relative to the mere survival of the individual, the group, or the life form.[8] Let me call this the *post-survival* criterion. Something that merely keeps alive neither invigorates nor enriches life. Imagine two individuals, one whose inner power draws him or her to a goal the attainment of which serves only to keep the individual in existence, the other whose survival is already assured and who is drawn with *equal power* to a goal beyond survival; the value is greater in the second case. In the first case the individual is struggling to reach the starting line from which genuine invigoration or enrichment can begin. In the second case the value constitutes either a genuine invigoration or a genuine enrichment of life. What merely keeps in existence is formally a value, but it is only the beginning of value, and the point applies just as much to groups. This criterion is directly related to power; it takes more power to proceed beyond the starting line than merely to reach it.

One important addition is required. The post-survival values of the strong, the healthy, and the well-constituted rank more highly than the post-survival values of the weak, the sick, and the ill-constituted. Again the contribution to the invigoration and enrichment of life is decisive. Although what merely leads to survival is not as important, what contributes to the survival of the strong, the healthy, and the well-constituted ranks higher in value than what contributes to the survival of the weak, the sick, and the ill-constituted. Here we need to look not at what the value contributes to the individual but what the individual contributes to life. Other things being equal, the survival of the strong, the healthy, and the well-constituted invigorates and enriches life to a greater degree than the survival of the weak, the sick, and the ill-constituted, and hence what contributes to the survival of the strong, the healthy, and well-constituted ranks higher.

Second, there is the sheer quantity of power that draws life forms to goals. Let me call this the *intensity* criterion. The greater the inner power that attracts to goals, the greater the value is when the goals are attained. Those with the greatest inner power have the greatest potential for value. Other things being equal, it is better for goals pursued with the greatest intensity to be attained. To the extent that the overall intensity with which goals are pursued can be increased, to that extent the potential for value is increased. While this principle arises naturally from the theory of value itself, it is not simply equivalent to it, since it embodies a normative element furnishing a guide for situations at aggregate levels of value. It is a guide to preferring systems that increase the intensity of power over those that diminish it.

Third, there is coherent multiplicity. Let me call this the *coherent multiplicity* criterion. Naturally, coherent multiplicity has two dimensions, multiplicity and coherence: "a philosopher, assuming there could be philosophers today, would be compelled to see the greatness of man, the concept 'greatness,' precisely in his spaciousness and multiplicity, in his wholeness in diversity: he would even determine value and rank according to how much and how many things one could endure and take upon oneself, on how *far* one could extend ones responsibility" (BGE 212). Maximizing coherent multiplicity requires a coordinated increase along each dimension. Multiplicity is certainly important (WP 655). Uniqueness and number are vital to increasing multiplicity, but the embrace of multiplicity must not be construed as either unconditional or limitless. Nietzsche does not favor an undiscriminating welcoming of anything and everything. While a value system may well contain values that are in tension and conflict, it must also be the product of shaping, controlling, incorporating, excluding, mastering, and discipline—in short, it must form a coherent whole (BGE 230). Conflict and tension are desirable so long as they lead to growth. Value systems that contain mutually annihilating values or value systems that permit anything and everything dissipate the intensity of power and constitute a bar to its accumulation. Value can only be maximized in a coherent structure, however much dynamic tension there may be within it.

Fourth, there is the fecundity of value. Let me call this the *fecun-*

dity criterion. Suppose that an inner power draws to a goal, the goal is attained, there are no countervailing factors, and hence there is a positive value. Suppose also that the attainment of the goal increases the inner power. Let me call such a value a *fecund* value. Now consider a situation that is identical to the former, but with the following exception. The attained goal leaves inner power at the same level as before, thus leaving the potential for value at that same level. Let me call such a value a *static* value. Now consider a situation that is identical to the former, but with the following exception. The attained goal decreases inner power, thus leaving the potential for value diminished. Let me call such a value a *debilitating* value. Even if the inner power that draws to one goal is equal in strength to the inner power that draws to another goal, if the attainment of the goals yields either a static value or a debilitating value in the one case but yields a fecund value in the other, the fecund value ranks above the static or the debilitating value, with the debilitating value ranking the lowest. This applies not only to individuals but also to groups and life forms in general.

Finally, there is no doubt that the unconditional embrace and celebration of life are of paramount importance in Niezsche's value system. This is the maximally affirmative attitude toward life previously referred to. Let me call this the *affirmative attitude* criterion. This introduces something new. While the previous principles concerned changes in life contents that constitute an increase or decrease of value, this ideal embodies the conception that value can be found in life irrespective of specific life contents, indeed, that value can be found in life despite the most trying life contents. This constitutes an ideal in its own right, and is, of course, directly related to power. It requires power to resist suffering and misfortune and still have power to spare for the positive embrace and celebration of life. Indeed, this value takes its place at the core of Nietzsche's value system—it is the Dionysian affirmation. The more individuals or groups approximate to this attitude the more value in life there is for them. This can be seen as a special case of the intensity criterion, with life itself as the goal.

It is now possible to state what the enhancement of life consists in. Enhancement embraces the two aspects of invigoration and enrichment, and these are further elaborated in terms of the five criteria given. A value system will rank higher to the degree that it is post-survival, tends to increase intensity, coherent multiplicity, fecundity, and affirmative attitude. To foreshadow one application, the relative worth of the master morality, slave morality, and herd morality is essentially determined by these criteria. However, there is more to be said about the warrant for these higher-order values.

The Will to Power

The will to power has a special role to play in Nietzsche's philosophy; it furnishes the ontological grounding for his thought on value. Will to power is what the world is ultimately composed of.[9] "The world seen from within, the world described and defined according to its 'intelligible character'—it would be 'will to power' and nothing else" (BGE 36). There are six fundamental aspects of the will to power that need to be taken account of. First, there is a "raw energy" aspect, the sheer capacity to effect change irrespective of whether the change increases order or chaos (WP 1067). Second, there is a shaping, or structuring, or form-generating aspect (ibid.). Third, there is the tendency of concentrations of power to increase the concentration of power (WP 689). Fourth, there is the tendency for concentrations of power to increase the range of their influence (ibid.). Fifth, power is variously concentrated and variously distributed (WP 1067). Finally, there is the aspect of incessant dynamic change (ibid.). The two principles introduced in *The Birth of Tragedy,* the Dionysian and the Apollinian, become transformed into the two aspects of the will to power cited first; thus furnishing, by the way, an instructive example of the fundamental continuity in Nietzsche's thinking.

Key aspects of Nietzsche's reflections on value fit neatly with the realist conception of the will to power. First, power is constitutive of all value, and the increase in power all beings seek is the ultimate value. On the realist conception of the will to power, value is embedded in the very fabric of reality. Second, focusing on the higher-order values, there is a clear connection between the post-survival criterion, the intensity criterion, the coherent multiplicity criterion, the fecundity criterion, and the characteristics of the will to power cited above. Third, the possible existence of the *Übermensch,* the high valuation of the *Übermensch,* and the will to power are clearly complementary conceptions. Finally, Nietzsche is opposed to the view that a static, unchanging set of moral rules must be obeyed by all persons, in all places, at all times. The opposition is partly grounded in his conception of reality as the will to power.

To take the last point, the will to power expresses itself in different ways and to different degrees in different individuals and different groups. Some will exemplify more of the "raw energy" aspect; some will exemplify more of the form-generating aspect; some will exemplify a greater combination of both; some will have a greater capacity to control others; some will change more rapidly than others; some will have greater creative capacities than others, and so on. Not only are these possible variations at one time, but the whole mix is in constant flux over time. To seek to regulate such a diversity with one set of rules is bound to be unproductive. Provided we accept his position that morality must make a positive contribution to life and that a morality is better to the extent that its positive contribution is greater, then it is far more plausible to suppose that a better outcome could be obtained from rules adapted to specific circumstances rather than from rules that must do for all persons in all circumstances.

Consider three possible circumstances. Suppose, in the first instance, that the survival of the human species is threatened by massive overpopulation; in the second instance, that it is threatened by extreme underpopulation; and, in the third instance, that there is no threat to the survival of the species from either of these directions. Moral rules that work well for the third case may well be deleterious for the other cases. Indeed, rules that give the optimal result for the second case may well be fatal in the first case and vice versa. To seek to apply the same rules in each of these circumstances is to invite an inferior outcome at best, and complete disaster at worst. To put it negatively, there is no uniformity in the world either at a given time or over time that would warrant the application of a single set of rules to all cases. That a single set of rules could furnish the maximal positive contribution no matter what the circumstances is quite implausible. The underlying variability of the world as conceived by the doctrine of the will to power makes the warranted variability of moral rules inevitable.

One problem concerning the will to power and value needs special attention. Given that the amount of power in the world is fixed, something assumed in the defense of eternal recurrence, and given Nietzsche's theory of value, why is there not just as much value in the world if power is equally distributed as opposed to occurring in varying concentrations? In a world that contains both high concentrations of power such as the *Übermensch* and low concentrations of power, we can see in the light of his theory of value that there is more value *for* high concentrations of power than there is *for* low concentrations of power. However, there is no overall increase of value for the world as a whole, only an uneven distribution of value. There is no doubt that Nietzsche's higher-order values dictate that high concentrations of power are more valuable in a sense beyond that conceded above, but why are they more valuable? Why not distribute the same power over as many individuals as possible in as equal amounts as possible? He clearly thinks that there is more value in the world if power is differentially distributed, but how can that be grounded in the nature of reality as will to power given his theory of value?

The question has answers on several levels. First, it is an essential characteristic of the will to power that it operates against uniform distributions of power. Second, according to his theory of value, increased power is what all beings value, thus high concentrations of power are more valuable than low concentrations of power because that is what all beings are drawn to—even if it is only in their own case. Third, a strong additional case exists in favor of valuing greater concentrations of power more highly than lower concentrations of power, but this case requires appeal to assumptions that go beyond the basic characteristics of the will to power. There are two key assumptions involved. The first assumption is that even if the overall quantity of power in the world is fixed, the quantity of power that is marshalled to yield value can either increase or decrease. The second assumption is that unequal distributions of power tend to increase the quantity of power marshalled to yield value, and uniform distributions of power tend to decrease the quantity of power marshalled to yield value.

It is precisely the presence of high concentrations of power that makes value systems in which they are embedded productive of new value. Thus it is not just that there is more value *for* high concentrations of power; it is also that there will be more value *from* high concentrations of power. Other things being equal, the higher the concentration of power the greater the creative capacity. To promote a leveling of power is to promote a leveling of creative capacity. Average concentrations of power will only have an average capacity to invent plans or projects and only an average capacity to bring them to fruition; they will have as little creativity about means as they have about ends, and they will have only an average capacity to surmount obstacles. At least in a relative sense, they will not have the power to create objects to which we can be strongly drawn, they will not have the power to transform our vision of the world or ourselves such that we might be more strongly drawn to the world. Any significant enhancement of life positively requires a differential distribution of power.

While the core of Nietzsche's specific values, theory of value, and higher-order values is grounded in the will to power, this by no means extends to everything he has to say on values. To mention a specific case, he was an adamant opponent of judicial punishment (TI VI:7); but whatever the quality of his arguments against it, it is difficult to see any direct grounding for his opposition to it in the will to power. However, there is an additional major factor at work in the formation of his specific values, theory of value, and higher-order values, and that is their capacity to account for and accommodate the phenomena of valuation in general. This independent constraint lends a richness to his theorizing about value that cannot always be traced to features of the will to power in any simple way.

The Rationality of Revaluation

Nietzsche has his own specific values, higher-order values, and theory of value. Naturally, these are brought to bear in the process of revaluation, but their employment raises the issue of what grounds or rational warrant he has for them, and indeed, whether his own positions are subject to revaluation as well. There are two factors at work here. On the one hand, his specific values, his higher-order values, and his theory of value are grounded in his general conception of reality as consisting of the will to power. On the other hand, his specific values, higher-order values, and theory of value are tested by the phenomena of human and nonhuman valuation. How clearly, how comprehensively, how simply, how convincingly his own views and values can accommodate, order, and explain the phenomena of valuation is vital to their acceptability. It is crucial to recognize that both the support and test for his views come from two separate directions: the will to power on the one hand and the phenomena of valuation in general on the other. Thus, for example, his theory of value fits well with the will to power, but it deserves to be taken seriously as a theory of value even if it transpires that the will to power is untenable as metaphysical doctrine. Indeed, I have already argued that the theory has considerable independent merit.

However, there is a problem in conceiving the matter this way.

The phenomena of valuation in general are not all of a piece. Not only is there a long record of what has been valued and what has been condemned, there have been conflicting values, values have changed, frequently there have been condemnations by some of the values of others; there have been endless proposals about what ought to be valued; there have been extensive speculations about the nature of value. The phenomena of valuation, when taken together, are vast in extent, chaotic, complex, confused, conflicting, and already riddled with theory and theoretical presuppositions. The phenomena that comprise human and nonhuman valuation need to be sorted, tested, ordered, weighed, sifted, and so on, before they can seriously be used as a basis for theorizing.

An apparent dilemma arises here. If the only tools to perform these tasks are an antecedently espoused theory of value and an antecedently espoused set of values, then the sorting, testing, ordering, weighing, and sifting of the phenomena of valuation is guaranteed to leave behind "evidence" that will support the antecedently espoused theory of value and the antecedently espoused set of values. But of course the support is entirely sham. Theories or claims can neither be supported nor tested by the "evidence" that they themselves create. Such support could only be circular and hence worthless. If a theory of value and a set of values are to receive support from the phenomena of valuation, or be tested by them, then there must be some methods of sorting, testing, ordering, weighing, and sifting the phenomena of valuation that do not have recourse to an antecedently espoused theory of value or antecedently espoused values. One aim of this study is to show that Nietzsche utilizes an extensive array of strategies for investigating the phenomena of valuation that do not rely on the antecedent embrace of a theory of value or substantive values.

Let me cite one example. According to Nietzsche, the absolute theory of truth is incoherent, it collapses from its own unintelligibility. Hence, no appeal to values or a theory of value is required in its overthrow. But its overthrow profoundly transforms the phenomena valuation. Certain conceptions of the nature of value are immediately ruled out. Certain ways of dealing with issues become pointless. New questions and approaches become relevant. The phenomena of valuation become purified of numerous misconceptions, making them a more suitable basis for testing theories of value and values. Yet in this instance the result has been brought about without relying either on specific values or a specific theory of value. The existence of such strategies is vital to the rationality of revaluation, and considerable attention will be paid to them in the chapters that follow. In general terms, Neurath's metaphor—cited with approval by Quine[10] in a parallel context—is appropriate here. It is a matter of rebuilding the boat plank by plank while still at sea, but to do the job, we need some tools in addition to the planks of which our boat consists.

TWO

Cognitive Values

The Place of Truth

Truth and knowledge are at the peak of the cognitive values. Not only are they the most important in their own right, but they also form ideal test cases for the intelligibility of the enterprise of revaluing all values. Further, given that knowledge has the idea of truth at its core, it is convenient to focus on truth. Obviously, an investigation into the value of truth must begin with the question of what truth is, or at any rate, what truth is taken to be. According to Nietzsche, what truth has been taken to be is not in fact what truth is. Consequently, his views on truth fall into two parts.[1] First, there is the rejection of what he takes to be the prevailing view of truth; and second, there is the articulation of his own positive view of truth. What he takes to be the prevailing view of truth, and indeed the wrong view, is the absolute theory of truth. What he substitutes for it is his doctrine of perspectivism.

What is this absolute theory of truth that Nietzsche is opposed to? Although he never explicitly states it, his discussions enable us to frame a fairly comprehensive view of it. The following are its central features.

Uniqueness. There can only be one true and complete characterization of the world.

Objectivity. If something is true, then it is so independently of its presence to the consciousness of any being, excepting, of course, truths that are about the contents of the consciousness of some being.

Unrevisability. What is true cannot cease to be true and become false. Belief and opinion may change, the world may change, but truth cannot change.

Unconditionality. Truth is independent of the conditions of the knower, the nature of the knower, the placement of the knower, the conditions of knowing, and the processes of coming to know.

Impartiality. Truth is independent of the interests, needs, wants, and aversions of any individual, group, or animal kind.

Universality. If something is true, then it is not only true for me, but it is also true for you and for everybody else. It is true for animals, whether they are capable of coming to know that truth or not, it is true for extraterrestrial life forms, gods and angels, if there are any.

This theory of truth is inextricably linked to a complementary ontological and epistemological doctrine. Namely, the world has a fully articulated, fully determinate nature and structure independently of any awareness of it. Mind-independently, there is a way the world is down to the finest detail. The function of the mind that seeks to know the world is to uncover this nature and structure without any addition, contribution, coloring, or interference from its own nature. It requires a pure knowing subject that makes internal representations of the independent world without its own constitution making any contribution to that representation. This theory of truth requires a definite conception of the nature of the knower, the nature of the known, and the nature of the process of knowing.

Nietzsche took this to be the prevailing view of truth, and in this he was no doubt right. Whether he would still be right today is another matter.[2] In any event, the nature and status of truth has become more problematic, and, arguably, this is a state of affairs on which he himself had an influence. In any event, he rejects the absolute theory of truth. He is in disagreement with it on each of its major points, and these include its ontological and epistemological implications. Indeed, his own theory of truth, the doctrine of perspectivism, can most simply and directly be stated as a denial of the central features of the absolute theory of truth. According to Nietzsche's doctrine of perspectivism, the following conditions obtain.

Denial of Uniqueness. It is not the case, even in principle, that there is only one true and complete account of the world. In principle, there is no single, uniquely best account. "There are many kinds of eyes. Even the sphinx has eyes—and consequently there are many kinds of 'truths,' and consequently there is no truth" (WP 540). "No truth" is clearly meant to be taken as no unique truth.

Denial of Objectivity. The way things are can only be known through interpretations formed by various kinds of beings. Different beings will put different interpretations on the way things are, and there is no characterizable or articulatable way things are independently of such interpretations. No being can be aware of things independently of some interpretation it places on them. "'Truth' is therefore not something there, that might be found or discovered—but something that must be created and that gives a name to a process, or rather to a will to overcome that has in itself no end—introducing truth, as a *processus in infinitum,* an active determining—not a becoming-conscious of something that is in itself firm and determined" (WP 552).

Denial of Unrevisability. In whatever way the world is interpreted, there must always be either a better way or at least an equally good alternative way for it to be interpreted by some beings or other. "Among a higher kind of creatures, knowledge, too, will acquire new forms that are not yet needed" (WP 615).

Denial of Unconditionality. No interpretation of the world can free itself entirely from the nature or the condition or the position of the knowing being. All interpretations of the world, without exception, are at least in part conditional on the nature of the being that seeks to know it. "Coming to know means 'to place oneself in a conditional relation to something'; to feel oneself conditioned by something and oneself to condition it" (WP 555).

Denial of Impartiality. Every interpretation of the world is framed to serve the interests of a certain kind of being. Every interpretation of the world is framed to increase the mastery, power, or control that a certain being has over the world. "The apparent world, i.e., a world viewed according to values; ordered, selected according to values, i.e., in this case according to the viewpoint of utility in regard to the preservation and enhancement of the power of a certain species of animal" (WP 567).

Denial of Universality. An appropriate way of interpreting the world for one being may be totally inappropriate for another being. An eagle that knew the world *only* the way a worm knows it would doubtless not be an eagle for long. "It is obvious that every creature different from us senses different qualities and consequently lives in a different world from that in which we live. Qualities are an idiosyncrasy peculiar to man; to demand that our human interpretations and values should be universal and perhaps constitutive values is one of the hereditary madnesses of human pride" (WP 565).

These denials capture the nature of perspectivism. All interpretations of the world are from the point of view or perspective of a certain kind of being. In confronting the world as a knower, one must be a being of a certain kind; and hence, one cannot help but be influenced by one's nature in interpreting the world. Nevertheless, an important point remains to be clarified. The position is clearly relativist, but just how extreme is this relativism? Is any perspective or point of view as good as any other? It is plain Nietzsche does not hold this. For him, there are better perspectives and there are worse perspectives. The key is the notion of power. One perspective is better than another if it increases power compared to the other. "The criterion of truth resides in the enhancement of the feeling of power" (WP 534). He puts it in terms of increasing the feeling of power, but clearly he does not mean merely that it increases only our subjective feeling of power irrespective of the effects on actual power. He means it is a better perspective, if we can feel the actual increased power it furnishes.

The natural response is that this is merely another crude version of pragmatism. But this is a mistake. If we regard what a perspective gives power or control over as being exclusively limited to the physical world, then we only have a crude pragmatism here.[3] However, if we think of a perspective as furnishing power or control not only over the physical world but also over the realm of thought and ideas, in other words the cognitive realm, then Nietzsche's criterion becomes more subtle, and there is little doubt that he had this more subtle version in mind. With truth specifically in mind he writes, "From the stand-point of thought—: that which gives thought the greatest strength" (WP 533). Thus for one perspective to be better than another it must not only increase our power or control over the physical world, but it must also increase our power or control over the cognitive realm.

In furnishing greater power or control over the cognitive realm, the better perspective will enable us to answer more questions, to solve more intellectual problems, to have less unresolved difficulties than its inferior alternatives. The better perspective will enable us to rebut more objections; it may be the source of objections to other perspectives that they cannot readily meet. The better perspective will more simply, clearly, coherently, and comprehensively order the material we are interested in. Once we take into account that perspectives must be assessed not only in terms of the power or control they furnish over the physical world, but also in terms of the power or control they furnish over the cognitive realm, then Nietzsche's view can be seen to be much more formidable and not open to the simple objections sometimes urged against it. Perspectives that furnish us with no power or control over the physical world, perspectives that cannot rebut the simplest objections, perspectives that crumble at the slightest critical scrutiny are not the equals of perspectives without these defects.

Clearly, on Nietzsche's view, one is not entitled to accept something as true simply because it makes one feel good:

> would blessedness—more technically, *pleasure*—ever be a proof of truth? So little that it provides almost the counter-proof, at any rate the strongest suspicion against "truth," when feelings of pleasure enter into the question "what is true?" The proof by "pleasure" is a proof *of* pleasure—that is all; when on earth was it established that *true* judgements give more enjoyment than false ones and, in accordance with a predetermined harmony, necessarily bring pleasant feelings in their train?—The experience of all severe, all profound intellects teaches *the reverse*. Truth has had to be fought for every step of the way, almost everything else dear to our hearts, on which our love and trust in life depend, has been sacrificed to it. Greatness of soul is needed for it: the service of truth is the hardest service.—For what does it mean to be *honest* in intellectual things? That one is stern towards one's heart, that one despises "fine feelings," that one makes every Yes and No a question of conscience!—Belief makes blessed: *consequently* it lies. (A 50)

What furnishes the greatest power over the world and the realm of ideas will not arise from idleness or wishful thinking; what furnishes the greatest power will require the greatest expenditure of power to attain. Perspectivism offers no easy path to truth.

Perspectivism, then, is a highly qualified form of relativism. There are better perspectives and there are worse perspectives, but there is no unique best perspective. It is in principle possible that two different perspectives will furnish the same power or control over both the physical world and the cognitive realm. Further, perspectives do not satisfy the conditions of objectivity, unrevisability, unconditionality, impartiality, and universality. None of this implies that it is easy or even practically possible for us to shake off every aspect of our current perspective, or that we can always devise alternatives that are just as good.

There is a natural tendency to suppose that if perspectivism is the correct view, then it must be easy to frame viable alternatives to any of our views. When it is recognized that it is not at all easy to do, there is the temptation to take this as evidence against perspectivism. But this reasoning is unsound. Take our current physics as an example. It is extremely difficult to invent an alternative that is as good. But the current perspective furnished by physics is the product of thousands of brilliant minds working over hundreds of years. That any individual could easily, on his or her own, invent an alternative that is just as effective is pure fantasy. The probabilities are that the invention of an alternative that is just as effective would require just as many brilliant minds working for just as long as our physics took to develop. The difficulty of individuals inventing viable alternatives is no argument against perspectivism. It is sometimes argued that Nietzsche could not be a relativist on truth, for this would constitute a self-disqualification from having either his positive views or his criticisms of other views taken seriously. Given that he wanted his ideas to be taken seriously, he must not have espoused relativism. This argument would have merit if there were only one kind of relativism, and that was of the most extreme form. But the argument gains no grip once it is conceded that there can be qualified forms of relativism of the kind outlined, and to which he can plausibly be seen to be committed. This point will be taken up again later.

In characterizing the view of truth Nietzsche rejects and the view of truth he accepts, nothing has been said about the value of truth, except by way of the trivial implication that he values what he accepts more highly than what he rejects. It is to this problem that I now turn. Specifically, the issue is this. If absolute truth constitutes, or is accepted as the peak cognitive value, then how can it be revalued? Surely, any attempt to replace it as the peak cognitive value must fail, for in mounting a case against absolute truth we must either use claims that are absolutely true, or, if they are not absolutely true, then they must be ineffective. Nietzsche's principal strategy in the campaign to displace absolute truth as the peak cognitive value is to argue that it is an incoherent or contradictory notion. This is a theoretically important case in the enterprise of revaluing all values. The initial puzzle is over what could be used to displace or revalue peak values. Here is a reply. What has commonly been taken as a peak cognitive value is, in fact, no more than a tissue of incoherencies. No higher values are required to dislodge it as the peak value, for closer inspection reveals there is literally nothing there to dislodge; there are only contradictions and confusions to expose. Consequently, of course, absolute truth has no value; it is not even the kind of thing that could have value.

Let me highlight several points concerning the intelligibility of revaluing all values and of revaluing the highest values. The claim of incoherence might arise in one of two ways. The value we focused on might on close inspection simply reveal itself to be incoherent. No argument may be required to show this; it may become obvious when pointed out. Naturally, should this occur there would remain the puzzle of how those who supposed themselves to have espoused this value did not notice its incoherence. That such a puzzle would remain does not rule out the theoretical possibility of the case even though it suggests its improbability. On the other hand, the value may be shown to be incoherent by various arguments; thus the claim of incoherence may rest on numerous assumptions.

Each possibility invites a challenge. Does it not still have to be absolutely true that the notion of absolute truth is incoherent? And what possible conviction can an argument carry whose conclusion is that the notion of absolute truth is incoherent, if it is immediately conceded that the premises cannot be absolute truths? What is at issue is the *status of the claim* of incoherence, and the *status of the case* for the claim of incoherence, and whether or not non-absolute truth is adequate here. Nietzsche believes he can adequately meet these challenges. However, the main point is that one notable device in the revaluation of all values is to seek to show that some value is incoherent, contradictory, conceptually contentless, and not even a candidate for possible human pursuit. Whether he has established this for the notion of absolute truth, or whether it is even theoretically possible to do so in *this* case has not been settled and will shortly be addressed in greater detail.

In addition to the claim that the absolute theory of truth is incoherent and that perspectival truth is the best that knowing beings can attain, there are other issues relevant to the valuation of truth that Nietzsche is interested in. There are questions such as: Why was this conceptual fiction invented? Why was it held in such esteem? Whose interests does it serve to propound it? Further, once the kind of truth that is attainable has been understood, what is the value of knowledge that embodies it? What is its place among other values? and so on. The last of these issues will be taken up at the end of this chapter. Others will be given greater attention when other values are being considered; not because they are less interesting here, but because I take the essential case for the revaluation of truth to be the arguments against the intelligibility of the absolute theory of truth and in favor of perspectivism, and it is to these arguments that I now turn.

The Case for Perspectivism

Four main arguments will be considered because of their centrality to Nietzsche's case and because of the variety of the problems they raise in the context of revaluation.

The Impossibility of Self-Validation

Nietzsche argues that the intellect is incapable of establishing that it can attain the absolute truth. The core of the argument can be put as follows. Our perceptual systems and cognitive apparatus generate representations of the world. Whether these representations relate to the world in the way required by the absolute theory of truth could only be established by stepping outside our perceptual systems and cognitive apparatus and determining how the world is *in-itself*, and comparing this with the way the world is rendered by our perceptual systems and cognitive apparatus. Obviously, this is not something we can do:

> The intellect cannot criticize itself, simply because it cannot be compared with other species of intellect and because its capacity to know would be revealed only in the presence of "true reality," i.e., because in order to criticize the intellect would have to be a higher being with "absolute knowledge." This presupposes that, distinct from every perspective kind of outlook or sensual-spiritual appropriation, something exists, an "in-itself.'—But the psychological derivation of the belief in things forbids us to speak of "things-in-themselves." (WP 473)

One would have to know what *being* is, in order to decide whether this or that is real (e.g., "the facts of consciousness"); in the same way, what *certainty* is, what *knowledge* is, and the like.—But since we do not know this, a critique of the faculty of knowledge is senseless: how should a tool be able to criticize itself when it can use only itself for the critique? It cannot even define itself! (WP 486)

Let me use an analogy. Human beings can determine whether a camera is giving distorted pictures of reality by comparing the pictures it furnishes with our own independent view of reality. Could a camera, so to speak, do it for itself? Certainly not; all it can do is to take further pictures, each of whose relation to the world is as problematic as any other. The human intellect is essentially in the same position as the camera. It can add as much as it likes to the representations of the world furnished by the human perceptual systems and cognitive apparatus, but the problematic character of these representations cannot be diminished by simply adding to their number.

This is not just a limitation of the *human* intellect, it is a limitation of any conceivable intellect. Once an intellect reaches its optimal representation of the world it is powerless to settle the question whether its optimal representation of the world relates to the world as is required by the absolute theory of truth. The issue concerns the status of an intellect's optimal representations, and there is in principle no information available to that intellect that could settle the matter. The intellect's best information is in the selfsame optimal representations whose status is in doubt.

If we leave aside the problematic cases of introspection and self-awareness where the distinction between representation and what is represented may not be able to be drawn so readily,[4] then the argument as applied to the extra-mental world is of considerable weight. But this point does not settle the argument's role in the case for perspectivism. Indeed, it could be claimed that its role is rather minimal. One can argue that, at best, all it could establish is that we can never have adequate warrant for claiming that we have arrived at the absolute truth. But it does not follow from this that the absolute theory of truth is incoherent, or that the perspectival theory is the only rational alternative.

There is a strong and a weak interpretation of the argument. On the strong interpretation, the argument amounts to this: given that no conceivable intellect can determine whether its optimal representations of the world conform to the requirements of the absolute theory of truth, then this notion of truth is completely vacuous. A condition that in principle cannot be determined is no condition at all. The verificationist element in this interpretation is obvious, but that constitutes no ground for taking it less seriously. There is a point to verificationism, even if its advocates have overplayed it. On the weak interpretation, the argument is simply that it is impossible for any being to establish that it has arrived at the absolute truth, leaving the issue of the coherence or intelligibility of the notion untouched.

However, even the weak interpretation furnishes a pragmatic case against the absolute theory of truth. If it is in principle impossible to determine whether we have arrived at the absolute truth, then the concept is completely idle. A more reasonable strategy for managing our intellectual affairs would be to replace this idle concept by one that actually does some work or whose application can definitely be determined. This is certainly a strong point, but it is not my concern to settle the issue of the acceptability of this argument in either its strong or weak form. Nevertheless, we are surely entitled to conclude that the argument in either form loosens the grip of the absolute theory of truth to some degree. Having a serious case to answer is already a significant change of status, even if the case is eventually met.

The next argument is one directly in favor of perspectivism and directly against the conception of knowing involved in the absolute theory of truth.

The Impossibility of Unconditioned Knowing

This argument claims that all knowing is an interaction between the *knower* and the *known*.[5] What results from this interaction cannot help but be influenced by the *nature* of the knower. The very same "world" interacting with knowers of different kinds will of necessity furnish different views of the world as products of those interactions. There is no knowing without interacting: there is no unconditioned knowing. "Against the scientific prejudice.—The biggest fable of all is the fable of knowledge. One would like to know what things-in-themselves are; but behold, there are no things-in-themselves! But even supposing there were an in-itself, an unconditioned thing, it would for that reason be unknowable! Something unconditioned cannot be known! Coming to know, however, is always 'placing oneself in a conditional relation to something'" (WP 555).[6]

A natural response to the argument is that we can discount the contribution our own nature makes to the view of the world we frame.

Subtract our own contribution and you have the world as it is in-it-self. But a moment's reflection reveals that we are in the grip of a cir-cle we cannot escape. What contribution the knower's nature makes to its representation of the world cannot be determined, unless we in-dependently know the way the world is *in-itself*. Put another way, only if there were unconditioned knowing that revealed things as they ac-tually are *in-themselves*, would it be possible to discount for conditions in conditioned knowing. Nor can we approach the problem from the standpoint of the knower alone. There is no way of fully determining the knower's nature without determining what contribution it makes in knowledge acquiring interactions. We have two sides of one equa-tion: if only we could fully determine the nature of one side we could determine the nature of the other, but neither side is independently determinable. There is in principle no way of discounting the contri-bution that the knowing mind makes to its awareness of the world. No doubt, this inability in principle to discount for the way the know-er's mind conditions what it takes as knowledge is what gives rise to the pervasive illusion that knowledge is unconditioned. In any event, Nietzsche claims that knowing is an interaction, that it is inconceiv-able as anything else, and the nature of the interacting participants cannot be known independently of the interaction. Even in knowing we cannot escape what we are.

The fundamental premise is no mere empirical generalization that all knowing beings that science has encountered frame their represen-tations of the world as a result of interacting with it. Rather, it is that no mode of knowing is *conceivable* or *intelligible* in which there is no interaction between the knower and the known. The world is only *ever* knowable in relation to a knowing being of a certain kind. This is flatly counter to the kind of knowing that is required for the absolute theo-ry of truth. Here is a conceptually based case for the unintelligibility of the model of knowing required by that theory. But the case is not merely negative in its import, it is framed in such a way that it also furnishes positive support for perspectivism.

The next argument is closely linked to, and complementary to the previous one.

The Actual Conditioned Nature of Knowing

While this case dovetails with the previous one, it has indepen-dent significance. Nietzsche, although a critic of Darwin's specific version of the theory of evolution, was nevertheless an adherent to some generic form of the theory (TI IX:14). This adherence furnishes the basis for two related claims. On the one hand, humankind is a natural object in the world, and as such is just as much embroiled in the world and all of its activities as any other natural object. On the other hand, the perceptual systems and cognitive apparatus of evolved animals, of which humans are one, are there in service of the interests of these animals. As these animals differ and as their interests differ, so too will their perceptual systems and cognitive apparatus:

> The meaning of "knowledge": here, as in the case of "good" or "beautiful," the concept is to be regarded in a strict and narrow anthropocentric and biological sense. In order for a particular species to maintain itself and increase its power, its conception of reality must comprehend enough of the calculable and constant for it to base a scheme of behavior on it. The utility of preservation—not some abstract-theoretical need not to be deceived—stands as the motive behind the development of the organs of knowledge—they develop in such a way that their observations suffice for our preservation. In other words: the measure of the desire for knowledge depends upon the measure to which the will to power grows in a species: a species grasps a certain amount of reality in order to become master of it, in order to press it into service. (WP 480)

> To what extent even our intellect is a consequence of conditions of existence—: we would not have it if we did not *need* to have it, and we would not have it *as it is* if we did not need to have it *as it is*, if we could live *otherwise*. (WP 498)

There are two points here, one general and the other specific. First, human beings as natural objects cannot escape the conditions that all natural objects are subject to. Expressly, human beings do not stand outside of nature as "pure knowing subjects." As natural objects they have a nature that will make its contribution in knowledge-seeking interaction with the world. Second, the specific nature human beings have, including their perceptual systems and cognitive apparatus, will be a product of processes within the natural world. They are the way they are because of their contribution to the success of an animal of *this kind*. Human knowledge can only be arrived at by a natural object interacting with other natural objects. The only materials we ever have available are the products of such interactions; we only know in relation to our own specific nature.

Now, even if the conceptually based argument for the *impossibility of unconditioned knowing* failed, this third argument could still stand, as its claims are more modest. It does not seek to establish that all conceivable knowing beings must have a nature that makes a contribution to what they regard as knowledge. Rather it merely maintains that all knowing beings that we are acquainted with in this world are of this kind. Thus whatever the pure possibilities may be, we human beings can only arrive at a view of the world that is conditioned by the specific forms of our perceptual systems and cognitive apparatus. Whatever the purely theoretical possibilities may be, human knowing is perspectival. Of course if this third argument is sound, it provides an additional measure of support for the stronger position in the second argument, but it is quite capable of standing on its own.

For Nietzsche the contention that human beings are simply natural objects in a world of natural objects is supported by more than whatever empirical evidence there is in favor of some generic form of the theory of evolution. He has independent considerations against the coherence and acceptability of alternative conceptions of human nature. However, I am interested in the case *here* only insofar as it rests on empirical evidence or well-supported scientific claims. In the second argument, the case rests on *conceptual considerations* and obviously it is also important to consider cases that rest on *empirical considerations*. While these differences—between the conceptual and the empirical—may only be differences of degree, even differences of degree are differences.

Let me take the final argument that introduces a new aspect to the case.

Concepts as Simplifications

According to Nietzsche, all concepts are simplifications of, distortions of, schematizations of, and abstractions from what they designate. Of necessity, concepts cannot capture the full richness of the realities they are employed to characterize. Concepts are general while the world is not, the one cannot in principle fully represent the other. "The entire apparatus of knowledge is an apparatus for abstraction and simplification—directed not at knowledge but at taking possession of things" (WP 503).

To adapt an example from Nietzsche. If I say that there is a tree in my garden, there is an indefinitely large number of actual states of affairs in the world that would render the claim true. Even if the description is made more detailed, mentioning characteristics such as size, shape, location, species, coloring, and so on, then although some states of affairs that would previously have been allowed to count would be ruled out, there would still be an indefinitely large number of different states of affairs that would be compatible with this new more detailed description. Further, there is no description, no matter how elaborate we make it, that can uniquely select a single world condition to satisfy it. The generality inherent in concepts is to blame. Our characterizations of the world can never capture the full richness of the world.

Suppose Nietzsche is right; there is still the question of how this can be used to support perspectivism. It can be argued that while it may not be possible to render the full richness of reality linguistically or conceptually, nevertheless, what is so rendered is capable of being absolutely true. It may be absolutely true that there is a tree in my garden even allowing for the impoverished nature of the information. His case needs fleshing out if it is to support his substantive view of truth. To flesh out the argument, for him, all concepts are human creations. They are not necessarily conscious creations and they are not necessarily creations for which we can readily invent viable alternatives. There may be a biological inevitability in some of the concepts that the human species has created (WP 493). Nevertheless, in an important sense, concepts are creations or inventions, they are not "things" that one reads off reality as one reads the words of a text. They are created "devices" that are imposed on reality, but not in a way that captures its full richness.

The nature of concepts as creations yields an argument in favor of perspectivism in its own right, but a stronger argument emerges if we combine this with the claim that concepts are essentially simplifications of the reality they represent. For there is absolutely no reason to believe that simplifications must be unique even when dealing with the same matters. If we produce simple representations of complex states of affairs there may be differences merely in terms of the degree of simplicity of the representations. Nevertheless, for any specific degree of simplicity, alternative representations must surely always be possible. Suppose that one sets out to do a piano reduction of an orchestral score. We can specify a level of simplicity in the piano reduction by requiring that it contain no more than a specified number of notes. Within this constraint a large number of different piano reductions are still possible, all containing the same number of notes, and hence, in at least one sense, equally simple. Nietzsche's case can be bolstered along the following lines. Simplification is at the core omission, and there are no independent mandatory constraints on what must be left out. While in concept formation it is necessary to leave out something, it is not necessitated what that something is.

What is of interest about the argument is that it claims there is a *deficiency relation* between concepts and the world. The question immediately arises of how this claim could be established unless we had *knowledge* of the world independently of concepts. The argument appears to presuppose that we can have definite knowledge of the way the world is in itself, and this immediately raises difficulties of compatibility with perspectivism. Nor is this the only argument to raise such a difficulty; there are other troublesome cases. He repeatedly asserts that the world is constantly "becoming," constantly changing, constantly in flux, and that neither static concepts nor conceptions of the world as static and unchanging capture reality as it is (WP 517, 520). Leaving aside the issue of the capacity of static concepts to represent change, it appears that absolute claims are made about reality that his position on truth debars. My plan is to deal with the charge that Nietzsche's view of truth is self-refuting and that the arguments for it are self-defeating. If such a charge could be sustained it would lend strong support to the viewpoint that, at least here, revaluation is indeed impossible.

Problems of Self-Refutation

There are a number of objections to both Nietzsche's arguments and his conclusions, clustering around the notion of self-refutation.[7] The underlying strategy driving these objections is that either in the statement of his own positive doctrine of perspectivism or in the arguments for it, he is forced to resort to the very notion he regards as incoherent, namely the absolute truth. First to be considered will be problems for the doctrine of perspectivism itself; this will be followed by a consideration of the problems that arise in assessing the status of the arguments in its favor.

A typical response to perspectivism is this: If perspectivism is what we are *rationally compelled to accept*, then it follows from its acceptance that any view is as good as any other view. If any view is as good as any other view, then the view that there is absolute truth is as good as perspectivism. Hence, we are not rationally compelled to accept perspectivism. Thus, simply from the assumption that we are rationally compelled to accept perspectivism, we deduce the conclusion that we are not rationally compelled to accept perspectivism. Whatever the internal coherence of perspectivism may be, the moment we claim that we are reason bound to accept it we appear to be led into a blatant contradiction. The argument appears automatically to negate any basis for espousing perspectivism, irrespective of what arguments may have led to it.

Let me call this the *crude self-refutation argument*. The answer to this argument is straightforward. The crucial point is that perspectivism does not maintain any view is as good as any other view. Perspectivism allows for better views and worse views. One would hardly think it necessary to make such a point, except for a persistent misapprehension that there is only one kind of relativism, namely, one that holds any view is as good as any other. But it simply does not follow from Nietzsche's version of perspectivism that if we are rationally compelled to accept perspectivism, then we are also rationally compelled to accept the absolute theory of truth, or that the negation of perspectivism is just as good as perspectivism. A perspective that contains the metatheory of perspectivism as a part may be superior to any other perspective that we can currently devise. Thus it is possible to be rationally compelled to accept perspectivism without at the same time being rationally compelled to not accept it, or also being rationally compelled to accept some alternative to it.

Naturally the dialectic does not cease at this point and the previous reply invites an attempt to bolster the argument. Let me call this the *strengthened self-refutation argument*. It can be developed as follows. It is not required for any perspective to be as good as any other perspective for serious difficulties to arise for perspectivism. If the absolute theory of truth can form the metatheory of some perspective, then it is coherent. Now, if the absolute theory of truth is coherent, then we can *sensibly* ask of any view that is advanced whether or not it is absolutely true. In particular, we can apply it to perspectivism itself. If perspectivism is absolutely true, then we have a straightforward case of self-refutation, for perspectivism maintains that there are no absolute truths. If, on the other hand, perspectivism is absolutely false, then it will be absolutely true that perspectivism is not true. Again, we would have an example of an absolute truth whose existence is sufficient to constitute a refutation of perspectivism. It appears that if the mere coherence of the absolute theory of truth is admitted, then perspectivism is refuted.

On the other hand, if the absolute theory of truth cannot form the metatheory of any perspective, then it must be absolutely incoherent. That is, it must be true independently of any possible perspective that it is incoherent. Thus once again we are faced with at least one absolute truth whose existence constitutes a refutation of perspectivism. Note the utter simplicity of the assumptions that generate the problem. The only assumptions are that *either* the absolute theory of truth is coherent *or* the absolute theory of truth is not coherent, and that there are no absolute truths.

It is not so obvious that there is an adequate reply to this argument. Nevertheless it is my view that there is. Let me consider more carefully each horn of the dilemma from this *strengthened self-refutation argument*. The first horn of the dilemma is that the absolute theory of truth is coherent. This can be put in a way more congenial to perspectivism as follows. It is possible for the absolute theory of truth to form the metatheory of at least one coherent perspective. What is crucial here is the sense in which the proponent of perspectivism must admit that *it is possible* for the absolute theory of truth to be the metatheory of at least one coherent perspective.

The proponent of perspectivism can reply as follows. First, it can be maintained that by *possibility* is meant only that the coherence of the absolute theory of truth has not been *absolutely* excluded. That is, the proponent can consistently deny that he or she is committed to the view that the absolute theory of truth is demonstrably coherent; all that one need be committed to is that its coherence is not absolutely excluded. Second, it can be maintained that the case against the coherence of the absolute theory of truth is so strong that we cannot currently even imagine how it could be made coherent. In other words, the proponent of perspectivism can distinguish between *possible* coherence and *actual* coherence, and argue as follows. All that is meant by admitting the possibility of the coherence of the absolute theory of truth is that its coherence has not been absolutely excluded, in other words, that its incoherence has not been *absolutely* demonstrated. At the same time, it can be maintained that the case against the *actual* coherence of the absolute theory of truth is overwhelmingly strong. But for the advocate of the *strengthened self-refutation argument* what is required to generate the difficulties in the first horn of the dilemma is the *actual* coherence of the absolute theory of truth. Its mere *possible* coherence is not enough. Thus it does not follow that perspectivism must be either absolutely true, or it be absolutely true that it is not true, given that all we are entitled to maintain about the absolute theory of truth is that it is *possible* that it is coherent.

This reply, if adequate, as it appears to be, robs the dilemma of its force since the first horn can safely be embraced by the proponent of perspectivism. Nevertheless, it is useful to consider whether the second horn of the dilemma can be rendered equally harmless. The second horn of the dilemma is the claim that the absolute theory of truth is incoherent. Or, to put it more in the perspectival way of thinking, the absolute theory of truth cannot form the metatheory of any coherent perspective. Would such an admission be fatal to perspectivism by implying that there is at least one absolute truth? Surely, the proponent of perspectivism also has an adequate answer here. To begin, the point can be made that there is nothing about perspectivism that prohibits generalizations about perspectives. Generalizations about perspectives are undoubtedly permissible. The crucial issue is the status of such generalizations. That the absolute theory of truth cannot form the metatheory of any coherent perspective is a claim about all perspectives. The issue really is whether remarks can be made about *all* perspectives without either utilizing or implying the utilization of the absolute theory of truth.

There is no reason why the proponent of perspectivism cannot maintain the following. The claim that the absolute theory of truth is incoherent, or that the absolute theory of truth cannot form the metatheory of *any* coherent perspective is no more than the currently rationally best warranted view. In other words, the claim simply forms part of the best perspective currently available. Put directly, there is no reason why a proponent of perspectivism cannot maintain that the claim that the absolute theory of truth is incoherent is no more than a perspectival truth, that it is simply part of the currently best available perspective. All one need maintain is that the claim is a perspectival claim that is rationally better warranted than any of its alternatives.

Naturally, opponents of perspectivism will not give up so easily. An immediate challenge is likely to follow the previous argument. What about the meta-claim that "the absolute theory of Truth is incoherent" is a perspectival truth? Does not this meta-claim itself have to be an absolute truth if the defense is to work? It does not. It is sufficient if the meta-claim is a perspectival claim that is rationally better warranted than its alternatives. And what about this meta-meta-claim? This, too, need only be a perspectival claim that is simply rationally better warranted than its alternatives. There is no reason why this ought not to be an adequate reply at each stage as we move up the linguistic hierarchy. Those who find no problem with "true" iterated in this way through ascent in a linguistic hierarchy should not find difficulty in "is a perspectival claim rationally better warranted than its alternatives" iterated similarly in linguistic ascent. Thus the second horn of the dilemma is as freely embraceable as the first, and the dilemma is rendered harmless.

The attacks on perspectivism, and indeed relativism in general, are typically governed by a single underlying strategy. This strategy is to argue that either the doctrine of perspectivism itself, or the arguments for it, entail, presuppose, or require recourse to claims that are absolutely true, thereby rendering the doctrine self-refuting and the arguments self-defeating. Clearly, the defensive strategy not merely is, but must be, that both the doctrine of perspectivism and the arguments in its favor can be stated by utilizing claims that are no stronger than those permitted by perspectivism, that no absolute truths are required to state the doctrine or to state the supporting arguments. The case of the statement of the doctrine itself has just been dealt with, so let me turn to the problem of the status of arguments in favor of the doctrine.

The first two arguments centered around the claims of the *impossibility of self-validation* and the *impossibility of unconditioned knowing*. Since the principal difficulty raised by the two arguments is the same, they can be considered together. A key feature of these arguments is that their premises cannot be regarded as empirical claims. The conclusions that no intellect can validate itself and that there can be no knower whose nature does not affect what is known need something stronger than mere empirical claims to rest on. What yields these conclusions are conceptual investigations into the nature of intellect and knowledge. In other words, the arguments turn on conceptual claims. But, of course, conceptual claims, and these include logical claims, are for Nietzsche no more absolute claims than any other kind of claim. "Behind all logic too and its apparent autonomy there stand evaluations, in plainer terms physiological demands for the preservation of a certain species of life" (BGE 3); "The world seems logical to us because we have made it logical" (WP 521). Human beings create or invent concepts. To any set of concepts that are forged to deal with the world, there is in principle always an alternative set that could be employed. Thus, for Nietzsche, conceptual "truths" or claims can be rejected not just by being denied, but simply by the concepts that warrant them being replaced by other concepts that warrant other claims. Of course this does not imply it would be easy to do so. Indeed, our biology may make it forbiddingly difficult, but we are dealing here with possibilities in principle, and not with practicalities.

Given these understandings, the first move against Nietzsche is to claim that if perspectivism were to be adopted then the doctrine itself would undermine the arguments advanced in its favor. Specifically, it could be argued that for a different choice of concepts a conceptually based case could be made for the intellect's ability to validate itself and for the possibility of unconditioned knowing. There are several replies. First, while other perspectives containing other concepts of the intellect and knowers must be possible, there is no guarantee that there is a perspective as good as the perspective Nietzsche adopted in which his conclusions are reversed. Second, we are rationally constrained to adopt the best perspective currently available; the possibility of alternative perspectives cannot alter the case. Finally, the proponent of perspectivism must insist that it is not rational to believe that there are claims capable of having greater force than those permitted by perspectivism, and this includes claims about perspectivism and the arguments for it.

Neither the premises of the *impossibility of self-validation* or *impossibility of unconditioned knowing* arguments nor their conclusions can be regarded as unrejectable, unrevisable, unreplaceable absolute conceptual truths. An essential point about perspectivism is the claim that the very notion of such truths is incoherent. The proponent of perspectivism can point out that his or her opponent is requiring the proponent to formulate arguments and conclusions with a strength of claim that it is impossible to attain. The proponent of perspectivism must concede that the claims embodied in the premises of his or her arguments and in their conclusions are "weaker" or "softer" than the status that claims could attain if the absolute theory of truth were correct. But it is difficult to see this as a source of real embarrassment. All that the defender of perspectivism needs to maintain is that the premises of his or her arguments are what it is currently most rational to believe. No one can do better than that, nor can anyone sensibly be required to do better than that. What may or may not be most rational to believe in the future, when people have thought up "things" that they have no conception of at the moment, is not relevant to current rational choice in any other way than to caution against dogmatism.

If we turn to the *actual conditioned nature of knowing* argument, the considerations are formally similar. The opponent of perspectivism will point out that the argument, insofar as it relies on empirical evidence embedded in *current* science, relies on something to which, according to perspectivism, alternatives are always possible. The proponent of perspectivism does, and indeed must, allow that alternatives are possible, but he or she can point out that we are rationally constrained to base our beliefs on the *currently best available* evidence and not on merely possible evidence. The proponent of perspectivism need not be embarrassed by *possible* alternatives to the current scientific views; only *actual* alternatives that are better need move him or her. The proponent can maintain that his or her case stands on current scientific grounds. It is always in principle possible that the case could be undermined, but a *possible* undermining is not an *actual* undermining.

To be sure, from the standpoint of perspectivism all arguments and all conclusions will have to be considered "weaker" or "softer" than they would be if the absolute theory of truth was in force, and this includes perspectivism and the arguments for it. But surely these arguments can have currently compelling rational force even when adjustment is made for their more modest nature. Certainly the arguments in favor of perspectivism must themselves be seen in the light of perspectivism, but there appears to be no compelling ground for supposing that this cannot be done both consistently and coherently.

The next argument may be thought to furnish even greater difficulties for perspectivism. Take the *concepts as simplifications* argument. At the core of the argument is the claim that there is a deficiency relation between our concept-utilizing characterizations of the world and the world itself, and that this arises, not fortuitously, but necessarily and unavoidably due to the simplifying nature of concepts. What this argument appears to presuppose is that there is *a way of knowing* the world that is independent of our concept-utilizing characterizations of the world, *a way of knowing* that gets it right about the way the world is, and by reference to which the adequacy of the concept-utilizing characterizations can be assessed. The argument seemingly maintains that there is knowledge of a kind that perspectivism itself declares to be impossible. This is an important argument and needs to be taken seriously. But it can be dealt with as follows. We need to distinguish between perception and thought, and hence between a perceptual perspective and a conceptual perspective. Thus, for human beings, the relation of deficiency between "the world" and their conceptual perspective is *in fact* a deficiency relation between their *perceptual* perspective and their *conceptual* perspective. But the human perceptual perspective has no privileged status among actual and possible perceptual perspectives. Put abstractly, the deficiency of conceptualizations is not established by reference to something that is absolute but by reference to something that is itself already relative (WP 505).

If this is correct, then no self-defeating assumptions about the existence of absolute knowledge are required to sustain the simplification argument. Concepts are simplifications, they are necessarily simplifications, but they are not simplifications of something absolute, they are simplifications of something already relative. However, there are other claims to be considered. Nietzsche repeatedly claims that the world is one of "becoming," change, or flux, and that any view that suggests otherwise is wrong (WP 604). It is we who import a measure of stability into the flux with our perceptual systems and cognitive apparatus. But surely this presupposes that we know that the world is a world of becoming independently of any perspective—perceptual or conceptual. Certainly there are occasions on which he appears to be committed to the view that the claim that the world is in a perpetual state of flux is a perspective-independent and irrevocable claim (WP 616).

Even if we admit this point, however, it does not settle important issues. The important question is whether the arguments in favor of perspectivism demand premises that are stronger than those allowed for by perspectivism itself. Perhaps in this instance Nietzsche was making a claim that he was not entitled to make, but the important point is whether or not he *needed* the stronger claim. It is my view that he did not. If it is part of the currently best warranted perspective that the world is fundamentally in flux, then this can be used to criticize views that deny it. Its status as the currently most credible view warrants its deployment against less credible views. To be sure, the arguments can no longer be regarded as having the force they could have if the absolute theory of truth were operating. But diminished force does not mean no force, and it emphatically does not mean *not rationally compelling.*

Let me sum up. The critic of perspectivism, or indeed relativism in general, typically seeks to establish that the doctrine requires recourse to absolute truths either in the statement of the doctrine itself or in the premises of the arguments used to defend them. The defender of perspectivism must maintain that the doctrine of perspectivism and the arguments in its favor can be both stated and be rationally compelling, utilizing claims no stronger than those permitted by perspectivism. It is fair to conclude, as far as the arguments considered here are concerned, that the case against perspectivism has not been proved. However, what has been dealt with are only problems at the topmost layer. Immediately below there is a new set of intriguing problems worth mentioning.

Does the claim that one perspective gives greater control over the world and the realm of ideas than another perspective require recourse to absolute truth? Will perspectival truth suffice here? Suppose that there are two perspectives, A and B. Further, suppose that according to perspective A, A gives greater control over the world and the realm of ideas than perspective B, and according to perspective B, B gives greater control over the world and the realm of ideas than perspective A. Which is the better perspective? How can we decide? Would it help if there was a third perspective that sided with either A or B? Let me make three points concerning this issue. First, the matter may simply be irresoluble. Perspectivism carries no implication that every problem has a solution. As long as it is possible to pick between better and worse perspectives in general it is not fatal if there are cases where this cannot be done. Second, the resolution of the claims of superiority may not be entirely intellectual matters. It may largely be a matter of one perspective yielding to the inherently greater power of the other over time. Third, nonperspectival theories of truth also encounter serious problems of irresolubility, a point that will shortly be taken up in greater detail.

At this stage a general assessment of the revaluation of truth is in order. Nietzsche's arguments against the absolute theory of truth and for perspectivism constitute a strong initial case against the former and for the latter. Further, this case is not in any obvious way undermined by self-refutation. But it is not my main concern to defend a particular theory of truth on his behalf. My main concern is with how theories of truth can either be overthrown or established. At the core of Nietzsche's revaluation of truth is the claim that the prevailing theory of truth is incoherent. Should this be established, it would be rational to seek a replacement theory, and the process of revaluation in this instance would be rendered rationally intelligible. Nevertheless, it is natural for doubt to remain about whether some dependence on the prevailing theory of truth is required to mount the case against it. Indeed, there can be little doubt that the revaluation of truth constitutes the most problematic case for the whole enterprise of revaluation. In view of this, it is more than just appropriate to consider the broader context, it is highly desirable.

The Choice of a Theory of Truth

It is notable that the merits of particular theories of truth are repeatedly canvassed in the philosophical literature and that the epistemology of commonsense belief, scientific theories, and mathematical claims are matters of constant debate; a debate to which Nietzsche himself is a contributor. What is remarkable, however, is that it is rare to encounter discussions of the epistemology of theories of truth themselves, or the rational basis for accepting or rejecting theories of truth. Yet the questions, "How can we prove a theory of truth to be true?" or "How can we establish a theory of truth to be rationally acceptable?" or "What rational basis can be provided for a theory of truth itself?" are surely not merely important questions but are also independently intriguing. The very posing of the questions hints directly at the possibility of paradox and the threat of circularity. Naturally, these issues are central in considerations of the feasibility of replacing the absolute theory of truth with perspectivism.

Let me consider what coherent sense can be made of the epistemology or rational basis of theories of truth themselves. It is crucial to consider to what degree are the principles for rationally assessing theories of truth dependent upon a specific theory of truth? Consider some abstract possibilities. Suppose that the principles for rationally assessing the acceptability of theories of truth are entirely independent of any particular theory of truth. In such a case there would be no special problem; theories of truth would not be different from any other theories as far as choice between them was concerned. Competing theories of truth could be articulated and the neutral principles of rational assessment applied to determine which one warranted rational acceptance. If there were a prevailing theory of truth, it could be replaced by another theory for which a better rational case could be made, just as it is the case for theories in general. On the assumption that the principles of rational assessment are completely independent of theories of truth, there is no special problem for the epistemology of theories of truth, or for the reassessment and revaluation of a prevailing theory of truth.

On the other hand, if the principles of rational assessment are inextricably bound to a particular theory of truth, and it is the single prevailing theory of truth, then the situation is more problematic. The only possible path to revaluation here appears to be to show that the principles of rational assessment and their embodied theory of truth are either inconsistent or incoherent. The principles of rational assessment and the embodied theory of truth are then modified. Once this is done, the arguments that led to the conclusion that the old principles of rational assessment and their embodied theory of truth are inconsistent or incoherent need to be reconsidered in the light of the new principles of rational assessment and their embodied theory of truth to make sure that in the new framework these arguments have not lost all of their cogency. If they have lost all cogency in the new framework, we may conclude that both sets of principles of rational assessment and their embodied theories of truth are unacceptable or, at any rate, unwarranted, and we may be led to seek further alternatives. Nevertheless, there are genuine prospects for the revaluation of truth even if there is only one prevailing theory of truth and it is embedded in the prevailing principles of rational assessment. If the prevailing principles of rational assessment and the prevailing theory of truth embodied in them prove to be inconsistent or incoherent, then that does not, of course, establish that there are adequate replacements. Each candidate would have to be considered on its merits. But it is difficult to see how the possibility of an adequate replacement could be excluded.

Two general cases have been considered. First, the case in which the principles of rational assessment are entirely independent of any particular theory of truth. Second, the case in which there is a single prevailing set of principles of rational assessment that have a single prevailing theory of truth embedded in them. Neither furnishes an insuperable obstacle to revaluation. Yet there is a third possibility to be considered, namely, where we have a choice to make from among a number of theories of truth, each with its own truth-theory-dependent principles of rational assessment.

In considering this case I propose to take three traditionally discussed theories of truth and consider how rational choice between them might proceed. Before the central arguments can be presented some elaboration of the structure and elements of a theory of truth is required. I shall call candidates for truth or falsity *claims*. This term is used because its ontological neutrality is less likely to invite irrelevant disputes. A fundamental thesis central to the ensuing argument is that each of the traditionally discussed theories of truth, namely, the correspondence theory, the pragmatic theory, and the coherence theory implicitly contain a basic, schematic, optimal truth-establishing model. This will be called a *basic verification model* for a theory of truth. The basic verification model is at the core of the principles of rational assessment bound to a particular theory of truth.

Correspondence

The basic verification model for the correspondence theory[8] can be specified as follows:

  i. Select a *claim*.
 ii. Select an *appropriate segment of reality*.
iii. Establish whether the *relation of correspondence* obtains between the *claim* and the *appropriate segment of reality*.
 iv. Ascribe truth to the claim if the relation obtains, and falsity if the relation does not obtain.

Pragmatic

The basic verification model for the pragmatic theory can be specified as follows:

  i. Select a *claim*.
 ii. Select an *appropriate set of goals*.
iii. Establish whether *greater goal satisfaction* is a consequence of adopting this claim as opposed to its alternatives.
 iv. Ascribe truth to the claim if it gives rise to greater goal satisfaction than its alternatives, and falsity to it if some alternative to it gives rise to greater goal satisfaction.

Coherence

The basic verification model for the coherence theory can be specified as follows:

i. Select a *claim*.
ii. Select an *appropriate set of claims*.
iii. Establish whether the *relation of coherence* holds between the *claim* and the *appropriate set of claims*.
iv. Ascribe truth to the claim if the relation obtains and falsity if the relation does not obtain.

Whether ultimately satisfactory sense can be made of such fundamental notions utilized by these theories as "correspondence," "appropriate segment of reality," "coherence," "appropriate set of claims," "greater goal satisfaction," and "appropriate set of goals" is not an issue I propose to deal with. While the history of discussions on these matters does not inspire optimism, there is sufficient pre-theoretical intelligibility in these notions for the case to proceed.

In elaborating this simple framework, let me introduce the notion of a *nonbasic verification model* for a theory of truth. If, for a given theory of truth, the application of a verification model *other than* its own basic verification model yields judgments of truth and falsity identical with those yielded by its own basic verification model, in either all or a substantial majority of cases where both can be applied, and there actually exists a significant range of cases where both can be applied, then we can call that model a *nonbasic verification model* for the theory of truth. Clearly, an acceptable nonbasic verification model depends for its existence not only on the existence of a basic verification model for the theory in question but also on its successful application. Naturally, it is possible that there are several nonbasic verification models for a theory of truth, and they may even be ordered in accordance with the degree to which they yield results similar to those yielded by the basic verification model. To illustrate, we may find that the basic verification model for the pragmatic theory gives the same results in most cases as the basic verification model for the correspondence theory. In such circumstances, we could regard the basic verification model for the pragmatic theory as a nonbasic verification model for the correspondence theory and vice versa.

There has been a view, with significant adherents, that the *meaning* of truth is given by the correspondence theory, but that the *epistemology* of truth is given by the coherence theory.[9] Any such claim needs to be heavily qualified in view of the distinctions introduced. It may be possible that the meaning of truth is given by the correspondence theory and that a nonbasic verification model for it is the basic verification model for the coherence theory. But what appears not to be theoretically intelligible is to maintain both that the correspondence theory gives the meaning of truth and that the *basic* verification model for the correspondence theory is the basic verification model for the coherence theory. If we were to suppose otherwise, then we would, in principle, have no way of telling whether this basic verification model for the coherence theory gave us either correspondence theory results or any results that even approximated what the correspondence theory was after.

To be explicit, it is not argued that if the correspondence theory gives the meaning of truth then the only possible verification model for the theory is the basic verification model for the correspondence theory. The basic verification models for the coherence theory and the pragmatic theory may be nonbasic verification models for the correspondence theory. But for this to be the case it would have to be demonstrated that the results obtained by the use of the coherence model and the pragmatic model coincided with the results obtained from the application of the correspondence model. If "correspondence" furnishes the meaning of truth, it must also furnish its basic epistemology, and the same applies to the other theories.

One more preliminary consideration requires attention. What is the status of propositions that articulate a theory of truth? Are they analytic or synthetic? Of course if such a distinction cannot be adequately drawn the question lapses. But in any case some remarks are in order. For the purposes of the discussion it does not matter which of the two alternatives obtains. If theories of truth are analytic, then the evidence that will be relevant to choosing between them will be linguistic data and data about usage. The essential point is that choice will still depend on *evidence*. If theories of truth are synthetic, then it is even more directly clear that choosing between them will be dependent on evidence and it is precisely how the evidence is to be construed that is crucial.

Let me turn to the fundamental problem. Suppose that the correspondence theory, the pragmatic theory, and the coherence theory have been articulated and that they carry with them their own principles of rational assessment of which the basic verification model is a crucial component. On what rational basis can we choose between these competing theories? Which theory of truth do we use when we are seeking to determine which is the "true" theory of truth? Singling out any one would clearly be question-begging and unreasonable; we need to give each an equal chance to establish its rational superiority.

Imagine beginning as follows. We apply the basic verification model of the correspondence theory to the correspondence theory itself to find out if it is *correspondence-true*. We apply the basic verification model of the coherence theory to the coherence theory itself to find out if it is *coherence-true*. We apply the basic verification model for the pragmatic theory to the pragmatic theory itself to find out if it is *pragmatically true*. Suppose that we obtain the following result. The correspondence theory turns out to be correspondence-true, the coherence theory turns out to be coherence-true, and the pragmatic theory turns out to be pragmatically true. The problem of rational choice between the theories has not been advanced one iota, and this is so for two reasons. First, the support for each theory is circular, and second, whatever the support of one may be, it is canceled by an equal support for each of the other two. On the other hand, if in applying the theories of truth to themselves we obtain the following situation: the correspondence theory is correspondence-false, the coherence theory is coherence-false, and the pragmatic theory is pragmatically false, then rational choice between them may not be possible, but at least a rational move is possible, and that is to reject all of them. Self-refutation is possible even if self-validation is not.

These two pure cases naturally lead to a consideration of mixed cases. Suppose that in applying the theories to themselves we obtain the following result: the correspondence theory is correspondence-true, but the pragmatic theory is pragmatically false. We may reasonably contend that the pragmatic theory is self-defeating and rationally rejectable on that ground. However, the general problem of rational choice has not been resolved for there is still no ground for choosing between the correspondence theory and the coherence theory. Now suppose that in applying the theories to themselves, we obtain the following result: the correspondence theory is correspondence-true, the coherence theory is coherence-false, and the pragmatic theory is pragmatically false. Again we may reasonably contend that both the coherence and pragmatic theories are self-defeating and rationally rejectable on that ground. This would leave us with the correspondence theory. We could still argue that the *support* for it was merely circular, and hence no support at all, but since all the competing theories have canceled themselves out, it would be rational to accept it, however qualified our acceptance. In any event, the issue threatens to be irresoluble except in those special circumstances where all but one of the theories defeats itself.

Let me consider the bearing of these points on revaluation. Suppose that there is a prevailing theory of truth with its attendant principles of rational assessment; how can it be revalued? How can it be displaced from its pedestal? All that need be done is to articulate *another* theory of truth with its attendant principles of rational assessment, and provided that the new theory is *not* self-defeating, the old theory loses its unique status and becomes one of a number of theories between which a rational choice may be impossible. Each theory can be espoused, each can be circularly defended, but neither can be proved.

In summary, there are three basic ways a theory of truth can be revalued. First, if the principles of rational assessment can be articulated independently of any theory of truth then a prevailing theory of truth may simply be replaced by another theory that is deemed superior according to those principles. Second, even if the prevailing theory of truth is embedded in a set of principles of rational assessment it may still be displaced or replaced if it can be shown to lead to inconsistency or incoherence. Finally, even if the prevailing theory of truth is embedded in a set of principles of rational assessment and it is not shown to be inconsistent or incoherent, its *status* is altered if we can articulate an alternative theory of truth embedded in its own set of principles of rational assessment that is not self-defeating or incoherent. The mere articulation of a viable alternative weakens the previous theory. The alternative need not be better established to effect a weakening.

Nietzsche's revaluation of truth is pursued in the second of the three contexts identified. The absolute theory of truth is examined on its own terms and found to be incoherent: "The concept 'truth' is nonsensical" (WP 625). But it is instructive to note that as far as truth is concerned more than one strategy is available. Indeed, a prevailing theory of truth could only resist all attempts at revaluation if literally *all* of its competitors turned out to be either incoherent or self-defeating, and it itself did not. This does not seem at all likely, especially since prevailing concepts of truth have been riddled with paradox since antiquity,[10] a point that is conveniently forgotten by many who rush to find inconsistencies in relativism.

Of course Nietzsche also considers other factors in the revaluation of truth. These concern the genealogy of the absolute theory of truth, with whose interests it serves, what harm it does, and so on. But such considerations are peripheral in regard to truth in the abstract while being central in regard to other values, and hence will be dealt with later. To sum up, Nietzsche may or may not have produced a decisive case against the absolute theory of truth and in favor of perspectivism. But it is a challenging case, and his arguments have a relevance that has not been dimmed by contemporary discussions. The philosophically basic level of Nietzsche's arguments form an important complement to the more remote and technically sophisticated contemporary discussions.[11] The issues pursued so far have been abstract, but there is also the revaluation of truth on a more concrete level and it is to this that I now turn.

Truth and Life

Nietzsche's views on the value of truth did not remain static, but what I wish to focus on is the implications for the value of truth arising from perspectivism and from his higher-order values. Perspectivism and the nature of the arguments for it are hostile to the conception of truth as having intrinsic value (WP 423). There are only perspectives, and perspectives are framed to serve the interests of the perspective-framers (WP 584). The pursuit of truth for its own sake can be pointless, and at worst it is inimical to life (BGE 64).[12] The acquisition of knowledge must enhance life, and this enhancement must be something beyond the mere activity of acquiring knowledge. Knowledge must make a contribution to life beyond its mere possession. Since for the later Nietzsche all values had to contribute to the enhancement of life, it is a matter of note how knowledge differs from other values, and here comparisons with art are the most interesting.

To be sure, Nietzsche distinguishes different kinds of knowledge and different kinds of art, and among these kinds some are good, some are bad, and some are indifferent. It is not possible simply to take knowledge as a totality and art as a totality and sensibly ask how he ranks them. But there is a sensible issue to be dealt with if the problem is restated. Suppose we take art only at its best, namely, art that, for him, truly fulfils the potential of art, and take knowledge at its best, namely, knowledge that truly fulfils the potential of knowledge, and then raise the issue of how knowledge and art are to be ranked. Indeed, I take such a distinction to be implicit in many of his own discussions.

Accepting this distinction, Nietzsche's views on the relative merits of knowledge and art went through several phases.[13] For the later Nietzsche, the pursuit of art for its own sake is also problematic. Art also must enhance life beyond art itself. But even with these similarities, their value is not equal, art is typically ranked above knowledge. The ranking is not arbitrary, and follows directly from the application of his higher-order values. The capacity of knowledge and art to enhance life is not the same. The fundamental difference is that art has the greater potential to increase our enthusiasm for life; art can increase our bond to life more; the transforming visions of art can increase our sense of the enchantment of life to a greater degree. In short, art has the greater potential for invigoration, enrichment, and the cultivation of an affirmative attitude toward this world. "What is essential in art remains its perfection of existence, its production of perfection and plenitude; art is *essentially affirmation, blessing, deification of existence*" (WP 821). It is art that has the greater capacity to draw us more strongly to life. First, there is the power of artworks themselves to draw us to them, to enchant, to delight, to stimulate, to provoke, to compel admiration and reverence. One aspect of this greater drawing power is that artworks can engage the whole human being, the senses, the emotions, and the intellect, whereas knowledge once attained does not. By means of art we are more strongly drawn *to* life because we are more strongly drawn to art objects *in* life. Second, there is the limitless diversity of art with its great peaks and inexhaustible creative possibilities, ever furnishing new objects to be drawn to. The sheer vitality and creativity of the human spirit as evidenced in art constitutes an inspiration in its own right, and this fecundity cannot be matched by knowledge that seeks a single view. Finally, there is the capacity of art to transform the way we look at the world, to add a new luster, a new depth, and a new richness to our conceptions of it, thereby again drawing us more powerfully to the world.

In contrast, there is no reason to expect that knowledge understood as the best perspective—as what gives us the greatest power and control over the world and the greatest power and control over the cognitive realm—must also act to increase our bond to life. For Nietzsche, knowledge typically tends to blunt our enthusiasm for life, to loosen its bonds; it tends to dispel the enchantment (GM III:25). Indeed, truth is often hard to bear: "We possess *art* lest *we perish of the truth*" (WP 822). In short, art has the greater potential to enhance life.

THREE

Moral Values

The Place of Morality

Nietzsche is notorious as an enemy of morality, yet his relation to it is by no means simple. The place of morality is determined essentially by four factors. First, there is its relation to truth. The position relative to both the absolute theory of truth and to perspectivism needs consideration. Second, there is its relation to his higher-order values. Third, there is its relation to his specific values. Fourth, there is its relation to a range of considerations that, while not presupposing values themselves, bear directly on the tenability of particular moral values. For him there are no absolute truths; consequently, there are no absolute value judgments and no absolute moral truths. This is an important aspect of the revaluation of moral values, and indeed of the revaluation of all values. But the status of what he regarded as "moral judgments" needs to be addressed explicitly, especially their relation to the broader class of value judgments in general. Consider the following observation:

> One knows my demand of philosophers that they place themselves *beyond* good and evil—that they have the illusion of moral judgment *beneath* them. This demand follows from an insight first formulated by me: *that there are no moral facts whatever.* Moral judgment has this in common with religious judgment that it believes in realities that do not exist. Morality is only an interpretation of certain phenomena, more precisely a *mis*interpretation. Moral judgment belongs, as does religious judgment, to a level of ignorance at which even the concept of the real, the distinction between the real and the imaginary is lacking: so that at such a level "truth" denotes nothing but things that we today call "imaginings." To this extent moral judgment is never to be taken literally: as such it never contains anything but nonsense. (TI VI:1)

Nietzsche appears to be maintaining that moral evaluation is on a tier of subjectivity higher than perspectival truth. I accept he is maintaining what he appears to be maintaining, but this interpretation requires care. It does not mean he regarded value judgments in general as more subjective than perspectival truth. In the passage above, he is not dealing with the general category of value judgments, he is dealing directly with the narrower category he regards as "moral judgments." Essentially, these "moral judgments" are the articulation of the slave morality, the herd morality, and such other judgments as share some of their central features. It is specifically this narrower class he is condemning as nonsensical and to which he is attributing greater subjectivity and which he believes is in need of rejection and replacement. "Moral values as illusory values compared with physiological values" (WP 392).[1]

But the greater subjectivity of "moral judgments" does not remove them from the realm of rational assessment. The explicit link with religion in the quotation is instructive. For Nietzsche, religion can be subject to rational assessment and can be replaced by a rationally better based world view. The new world view may be the best currently available to us, it may pass our critical and evidential tests as nothing else does. Similarly, the moral mode of evaluation can be rationally assessed and can be replaced by a rationally better based mode of evaluation that can survive critical tests that the "moral" mode of evaluation cannot. It would be a misinterpretation of the above quotation to read it as proposing a radical subjectivity for all value judgments. The following quotations reinforce the point:

> War on all presuppositions on the basis of which one has invented the true world. Among these is the presupposition that moral values are the supreme values. The supremacy of moral valuation would be refuted if it could be shown to be the consequence of an immoral valuation—as a special case of actual immorality—it would thus reduce itself to appearance, and as such it would cease to have any right to condemn appearance. (WP 583 [B])

> We see how morality (a) poisons the entire conception of the world, (b) cuts off the road to knowledge, to science, (c) disintegrates and undermines all actual instincts (in that it teaches that their roots are immoral). We see at work before us a dreadful tool of decadence that props itself up by the holiest names and attitudes. (WP 584)

Clearly, Nietzsche regards it as a most serious issue of values that the "moral" system of evaluation be rejected. It is to be rejected on the basis of sounder values. There is no suggestion that value judgments in general warrant the condemnation meted out to "moral judgments." Indeed, the opposite is implied. The search for sound values is a major concern: "*All* the sciences have from now on to prepare the way for the future task of the philosophers: this task understood as the solution of the *problem of value*, the determination of the *order of rank among values*" (GM I:17). There is no inconsistency in maintaining that, while value judgments in general can be soundly based, "moral judgments" are without foundation. However, while there is no formal inconsistency, there is certainly a puzzle. Why should "moral values" be on a higher level of subjectivity? Persuasion is required that there is more here than mere prejudice.

The key lies in Nietzsche's conception of morality. For him morality is essentially a system of rules to regulate behavior, to change behavior, to alter the way things are. But this means that such rules cannot be directly grounded in how things are, since their whole point is *to change how things are.* When we have arrived at the best available perspective of *how things are*, it cannot contain moral rules, for such rules enjoin us to change the world, given our optimal view of it. This does not mean there cannot be warrant for rules that seek to change how things are, there can be such warrant, but how things are is not among them. "Every morality is, as opposed to *laisser aller*, a piece of tyranny against 'nature'" (BGE 188). His conception of morality as being on a higher level of subjectivity than perspectival truth has two core components. On the one hand, there is the point that morality cannot be directly grounded in reality. On the other hand, he also thinks it fails the other ways values might be warranted. He is quite prepared to accept that behavior-modifying rules may be justified in certain circumstances: "The essential thing 'in heaven and upon earth' seems, to say it again, to be a protracted obedience in one direction: from out of that there always emerges and has always emerged in the long run something for the sake of which it is worthwhile to live on earth, for example virtue, art, music, dance, reason, spirituality—something transfiguring, refined, mad and devine" (BGE 188).

For Nietzsche, value judgments in general can have the status of hard-won perspectival truths, and they do not necessarily involve a higher level of subjectivity, although they may in some cases such as the slave morality, the herd morality, and their like. But even the soundest value judgments will not be candidates for absolute truth. In the face of the claim that if value judgments are not candidates for absolute truth, then no rational assessment is possible; it can only be pointed out that the counter case has already been put in the discussion on truth. Perspectivism demands the application of reason, not its abandonment. His position is not that any view is as good as any other view either in regard to value judgments or to judgments about the world. In considering values, we cannot do better than perspectival *truth*, but we can certainly do worse. There are still better perspectives and worse perspectives, and these need to be sorted by subjecting them to rational scrutiny. Provided only that one desires to maximize value, the ground is set for an inquiry into how such a desire can be met. That such an inquiry cannot yield timeless and irrefutable valuational facts is no reason for not undertaking it.

The abandonment of the absolute theory of truth in favor of perspectivism implies that new methods of assessment come into play and that some methods of assessment drop out. There are three important issues here. First, what *means* does Nietzsche the perspectivist rely on in revaluing morality? Second, would *these means* retain any force if moral value claims were candidates for absolute truth? Finally, would *these means* retain any force if persons' moral claims were entirely subjective? Put generally, does Nietzsche's revaluation of morality depend essentially on his views of truth and the methods this brings with it, or are the means he employs in revaluing morality also effective if either absolutist positions or extreme relativist positions are adopted on the status of moral value claims? It will be argued that, while Nietzsche's view of truth furnishes new weapons for use in revaluation, there remain weapons whose force would not be diminished if moral value claims were candidates for absolute truth; and further, that there are weapons whose force would not be diminished even if extreme relativism obtained. The latter claim may appear surprising, but one of the views that will emerge is that rational consideration of values is possible even in the face of extreme subjectivism.[2]

Moralities

For Nietzsche, moralities are human products and no more than human products. If moral value claims were candidates for absolute truth, it would still be possible to maintain that they were human products, but then the overridingly important feature about them would be whether or not they were true. If moral value claims are candidates for absolute truth, it is not significant who thought them up, why they thought them up, who is advocating them, who is harmed by them, who derives benefit from their espousal, and so on. If a moral value claim is absolutely true, the question of value is settled; if it is absolutely false, the question of value is settled. On the other hand, if moral values are human products and no more than human products, then considerations that are relevant to an assessment of human products come into force.

In assessing human products, five considerations are important, although their relative importance varies according to context. First, who brought the product into existence? Second, what conditions was it produced in? Third, what function is it intended to serve? Fourth, what is its general nature? Finally, what function does it actually serve? Let me designate these five elements as the *producers*, the *conditions of production*, the *intended function*, the *general nature*, and the *actual function*. Nietzsche regards each of these elements as important in the evaluation of moral values, and they play a key role in his genealogical method: "under what conditions did man devise these value judgments good and evil? and what value do they themselves possess? Have they hitherto hindered or furthered human prosperity? Are they signs of distress, of impoverishment, of the degeneration of life? Or is there revealed in them, on the contrary, the plenitude, force, and will of life, its courage, certainty, future?" (GM Preface, 3). Nietzsche accepts that there are many moralities and that a developed "science of morality" needs to deal with all of them, but his own thinking is dominated by three types—the master morality, the slave morality, and the herd morality.[3] His articulation of the three viewpoints takes for granted two basic human propensities. On the one hand, a propensity for hierarchical ordering is natural to human beings, and would obtain unless interfered with (BGE 199), and on the other hand, human beings have a propensity to form groups with their similars. He conceived of the moral viewpoints represented by master morality and the slave morality as being generated in a hierarchically ordered group. Put simply, being at the top generates one moral viewpoint, being at the bottom generates another.

The Master Morality

This is generated by those at the top of the hierarchical ordering. Nietzsche assumes those at the top are there because of such characteristics as being more powerful, more dynamic, more daring, more confident, more courageous, more spontaneous, healthier, sterner, harder, and so on. The master morality is *produced* by those who are strong, vital, fearless, and life-affirming (GM I:10). The morality is produced in the *conditions* of autonomy, abundance, power, and unfettered capacity felt by those at the top. The *intended function* is to enhance the life of the masters and promote the characteristics that they possess: fearlessness, vitality, dynamism, power, and so on. In short, it seeks to add to life, to enrich it. The *general nature* of the morality centers on self-fulfillment; it is not universal; it is not prescriptivist; it does not seek to change all persons to fit one mold; it is not punitive. In short, it is essentially nonreforming and noncoercive. It is directed to the enhancement of life for the masters rather than the control of others. As far as the *actual function* is concerned, in favorable circumstances it will coincide with the intended function and enhance life for the masters. In unfavorable circumstances the intended function will be defeated:

> The noble type of man feels *himself* to be the determiner of values, he does not need to be approved of, he judges "what harms me is harmful in itself," he knows himself to be that which in general first accords honor to things, he *creates values*. Everything he knows to be part of himself, he honors: such a morality is self-glorification. In the foreground stands the feeling of plenitude, of power that seeks to overflow, the happiness of high tension, the consciousness of a wealth that would like to give away and bestow—the noble human being too aids the unfortunate but not, or almost not, from pity, but more from an urge begotten by superfluity of power. (BGE 260)

The Slave Morality

This is generated by those at the bottom of the hierarchical ordering. Nietzsche assumes those at the bottom are there because of such characteristics as being weaker, lacking vitality, being fearful, lacking confidence, being constrained, being sicklier, ease-seeking, and so on. The morality is produced in *conditions* of resentment, fear, powerlessness, and hatred, that is, it is produced nonautonomously. The morality is produced as a reaction to the unfavorable position the slaves find themselves in (GM I:10). The principal *intended* function, though not necessarily the *announced function*, of the morality is to advance the interests of the slaves. This requires that anybody whose power or exceptional nature constitutes a threat to the slaves be cut down to a suitable level of harmlessness. The morality is essentially reactive, defensive, and negative.

> Suppose the abused, oppressed, suffering, unfree, those uncertain of themselves and weary should moralize: what would their moral evaluations have in common? Probably a pessimistic mistrust of the entire situation of man will find expression, perhaps a condemnation of man together with his situation. The slave is suspicious of the virtues of the powerful: he is skeptical and mistrustful, *keenly* mistrustful, of everything "good" that is honored among them—he would like to convince himself that happiness itself is not genuine among them. On the other hand, those qualities that serve to make easier the existence of the suffering will be brought into prominence and flooded with light: here it is that pity, the kind and helping hand, the warm heart, patience, industriousness, humility, friendliness come into honor—for here these are the most useful qualities and virtually the only means of enduring the burden of existence. (BGE 260)

The *general nature* of the morality centers on reform. Specifically, it seeks to cut down those whose power and abilities exceed those of the slaves. It is universalist and prescriptivist;[4] it seeks to enforce behavior that is beneficial to the slaves. It is both punitive and coercive. However, it is not coercive out of free choice but from necessity, arising from the inferior position of the slaves. It is directed toward the control of others rather than toward self-fulfillment. As for its *actual function*, this depends on circumstances. In circumstances favorable to it, the interests of the "slaves" will be promoted at the expense of the masters. The exceptional and the powerful will be declawed and cut down to size.

Herd Morality

This is generated by the inherent dynamics of groups independently of hierarchical ordering or external pressures. "All community makes somehow, somewhere, sometime—'common'" (BGE 284). Typically, the majority of members of a group will cluster around the average for that group. Most group members will be of average strength, average vitality, average courage, average confidence, average health, and so on. Unlike the slave morality, the herd morality is not essentially reactive. The herd morality is produced in *conditions* of contentment. The principal *intended* function of the morality is to maintain the life of the herd. This requires as a major objective that herd animals be produced as close to the herd average as possible (BGE 268). The greater an individual's deviation from the herd average the greater the individual's potential to disrupt the life of the herd (BGE 201). Whereas the slaves want to *change* their situation, the herd animals want to *preserve* theirs. The morality is essentially the positive embrace of mediocrity: "The instinct of the herd considers the middle and the mean as the highest and most valuable: the place where the majority finds itself; the mode and manner in which it finds itself. It is therefore an opponent of all orders of rank, it sees an ascent from beneath to above as a descent from majority to minority. The herd feels the exception whether it is above it or below it, as something opposed and harmful to it" (WP 280). The *general nature* of the morality centers on the reproduction of a type as close as possible to the herd average. It is also universalist and prescriptivist; it seeks to control behavior that disturbs herd life. It is directed toward maintaining whatever fulfillment is available in subordinating oneself to the herd. Its dominating ideal is mediocrity, but it is not as strongly oriented toward altruism as the slave morality. As for its *actual function,* this is not so clear. Nietzsche suggests that the conditions most conducive to the production of the herd animal are also conditions conducive to the production of exceptional types (BGE 242). One fundamental difference between the slave morality and the herd morality is this: the slave morality is a morality of discontent, the slaves want their situation to change. On the other hand, the herd morality is a morality of contentment, the herd wants its situation to be preserved. In short, the herd has a positive orientation to its situation, the slaves have a negative orientation to theirs.

This is a schematic presentation of the master morality, the slave morality, and the herd morality. More concrete aspects, particularly of the slave morality, will be dealt with; nevertheless, this outline yields points concerning revaluation. For Nietzsche, values are human products, and one element in the evaluation of moral values is determining the characteristics of their *producers.* The system of moral values produced by the strong and healthy is better than the value system produced by the weak and ailing. Being produced by the weak and ailing is seen as constituting a ground for regarding it as worse. It may not be a decisive ground, but it counts. The underlying rationale is that the product can neither escape an inheritance from its producers nor can it be fully understood in isolation from its producers. Further, if the *intended function* of a system of moral values is to produce stronger and healthier types than another system of moral values, then this is a ground for preferring it. If the *actual function* of a system of moral values is to produce stronger and healthier types than another system of moral values, then this is a ground for preferring it. Systems of value generated in conditions of autonomy are preferable to systems of value generated in conditions of constraint. Each of these elements plays a role in assessment, and each is a consequence of the application of his higher-order values.

As for the status of the master morality, there is no doubt he regards it as superior to both the slave morality and the herd morality, but it is not correct to see the matter as one in which the master morality is espoused and every other morality criticized from its standpoint. Rather, the superiority of the master morality follows from the application of his higher-order values. On this, two points need to be noted. First, Nietzsche nowhere suggests that the value crisis Western civilization finds itself in can be resolved by returning to a preexisting master morality. Second, he repeatedly maintains that it is vital that there be a "new table of values," that there is a desperate need for creators of new values. Indeed, philosophers are needed to take such a role: "But these are only preconditions of his task: this task itself demands something different— it demands that he *create values*" (BGE 211). Of course, the adequacy of any newly created values will itself have to be assessed in terms of his higher-order values. However, the demand for new values does not square with the supposition that the already identified values of the master morality can solve the problem.

On the other hand, Nietzsche's attitude toward the slave morality is not infected with comparable ambiguities. He regards it as having had, and as still having an unhealthy grip on Western civilization, even though its metaphysical underpinnings have collapsed. One aim of revaluation is to loosen its grip. The slave morality has dominated Western civilization coextensively with, and as part of, the domination of Christianity. There is the danger that the slave morality will continue its dominance in spite of the collapse of its metaphysical underpinnings. In his view, it is not a trivial activity to expose the weaknesses of the slave morality, and his moral revaluations are largely directed to this end. His attitude toward the herd morality is more ambiguous. Its effects are disastrous if permitted total sway. "'The masters' have been disposed of; the morality of the common man has won" (GM I:9). But if it is not accorded total sway, the herd morality may have a positive role to play.

Crucial Targets

Let me take specific revaluations to uncover their underlying strategies. The targets are all important features of the slave morality and the herd morality. However, Nietzsche had an antipathy for the slave morality in particular that it would be difficult to rival.

Altruism

There is a range of self-interest suspending or self-denying value orientations ranging from unselfishness to self-sacrifice.

Altruism falls in the middle of this range; it contains more of the idea of actively helping others than unselfishness, but it is not as extreme as self-sacrifice. Nietzsche is opposed to these value orientations, and the opposition increases as the element of self-denial increases. He was a persistent critic of altruism,[5] and a consideration of altruism is a good way to advance understanding of his revaluation of self-denying values. For the sake of simplicity, I begin by considering the issue in terms of altruistic acts. This is an instructive way to start, but he has other ways of looking at the matter, and indeed, looking at issues of value in terms of *single acts* does not constitute his preferred way. This point will be taken up later.

An altruistic act is essentially one done for the benefit of another person who is some way in need. There is more to altruism than merely benefiting another person. A million dollars given to a person who already has millions may be of benefit to him or her, but it is not altruism because the element of need is missing. Nor does altruism necessarily impose serious costs on the altruist. If a multi-millionaire wins a lottery and gives the proceeds to the needy, the act is altruistic, but it does not involve personal cost in any serious way. When the act to benefit another is of considerable personal cost to the doer, it is more appropriate to speak of self-sacrifice. There is a tendency in Nietzsche to take things in their extreme form and, in this instance, to conflate altruism and self-sacrifice. Such a conflation is not harmless, for there are good points against self-sacrifice that are ineffectual against altruism in general.

Nietzsche takes altruism to be one of the highest values advocated by the slave morality, and, in any event, it is clearly ranked above self-interested values in that morality. It is important to understand why altruism is a significant feature of the slave morality. One way of viewing altruism is as a transfer of resources from the *haves* to the *have-nots*. It is precisely the have-nots who are the generators of the slave morality. If the slaves can get altruism espoused by the whole community, it is they who will be the beneficiaries. The calculated self-interest of the slaves lies behind the advocacy of altruism. This claim about the advocacy of altruism is relevant to an evaluation of its value, and will be dealt with separately later. For the moment, my concern is the direct difficulties associated with altruism.

There is ground for supposing Nietzsche thought of altruism not only as the highest value in slave morality, but even as the value that completely dominates it: "Loss of center of gravity, resistance to natural instincts, in a word 'selflessness'—that has hitherto been called *morality*. . . . With 'Daybreak' I first took up the struggle against the morality of unselfing" (EH VII:2). As a lead-in to his arguments against altruism, it is illuminating to consider whether altruism could in principle be the highest value in a value system. Here, a case can be developed that it is conceptually incoherent to have altruism as the highest value in a value system. The argument is as follows. To act altruistically is to act for the benefit of another person. The *point* of the act is that it *produces* a benefit for the *other* person. If no benefit to another person is intended or results, the act cannot be altruistic. Take a case. If food is given to a starving man whose life is saved and whose health is improved, then clearly a benefit has accrued to him. On the other hand, if the very same food is given to a person who is already overfed, no benefit is produced and the act is not altruistic. Altruism presupposes that there are states of persons—in this case, states of the recipient—that are valuable in their own right. An altruistic act is a *means* to producing one of these states. Take away states of persons that are valuable in their own right, and altruism loses all of its point. One can only do something of value *for* a person if there is something of value *to* that person. Unless some *self* is benefited, altruism is pointless. In other words, altruism presupposes self-centered interests or needs in the beneficiary.

If the concept of an altruistic act is essentially the concept of an act that is the *means* to a good, then it cannot be the highest value in any hierarchy of values. As a means its value is entirely dependent upon the values it seeks to attain. The point can be graphically illustrated if we consider the more extreme case of self-sacrifice. Suppose that a person sacrifices his or her life to save the life of another, who immediately sacrifices his or her life to save the life of another, who immediately sacrifices his or her life to save the life of another, and this process is repeated without end. We do not stand back, agape with admiration at the magnificence of this chain of self-sacrifice. The whole process is absurd and pointless. Self-sacrifice has no value as an act in its own right, it only has value if it attains its end, and it is from this end that value accrues to it. From time to time Nietzsche uses the term "altruistic morality," which indicates a morality entirely dominated by altruism, and it is difficult to identify this "altruistic morality" with anything other than the slave morality. If altruism is the highest value in slave morality, as Nietzsche appears to think, then the slave morality is guilty of the valuational absurdity pointed out.

Not only can altruism not be the highest value, it is also important to note that altruism is not a value capable of standing on its own; it cannot be an independent self-contained value. A value system containing only altruism as a value would contain no value at all. The underlying absurdities are brought out in the following quotation:

> The phenomena of morality have occupied me like riddles. Today I would know how to answer the question: What does it mean that the welfare of my neighbor *ought* to possess for me a higher value than my own? but that my neighbor himself *ought* to assess the value of his welfare differently than I, that is, that he should subordinate it to *my* welfare? What is the meaning of that "Thou shalt," which even philosophers regard as "given"? The apparently crazy idea that a man should esteem the actions he performs for another more highly than those he performs for himself, and that this other should likewise, etc. (that one should call good only those actions that a man performs with an eye, not to himself, but to the welfare of another) has a meaning: namely, as the social instinct resting on the valuation that the single individual is of little account, but all individuals together are of very great account provided that they constitute a community with a common feeling and a common conscience. Therefore a kind of training in looking in a certain direction, the will to a perspective that seeks to make it impossible to see oneself. My idea: goals are lacking and these must be *individuals'*! We observe how things are everywhere: every individual is sacrificed and serves as a tool. Go into the street and you encounter lots of "slaves." Whither? For what? (WP 269)

Allowing that altruism and self-sacrifice require other values to have point, what can be made of this? Nietzsche does not generally maintain that altruism is the only value espoused by the slave morality. But taking his arguments as a suggestive beginning, there are independent points of interest to be extracted. It would certainly be conceptually incoherent to have altruism as the only value espoused. What needs emphasis is that this conceptual incoherence persists irrespective of whether the person espousing this supposed value is an adherent of the absolute theory of truth, or perspectivism, or extreme relativism. If it is proposed as the only value, then there is no value to embrace. It is not open even to the extreme relativist to say that he or she values altruism and only altruism, for in this instance there is literally nothing to value.

While Nietzsche does not always claim that altruism is the only value espoused by the slave morality, his settled view is that it is at least one of the highest values in it and that it clearly ranks altruism above self-regarding values. Suppose we accept this assumption, what problem remains? Certainly, there is still a real problem, but not a problem as acute as conceptual incoherence. Let me consider altruism as a high value among a set of values some of which can give altruistic acts their point. Suppose health is one such value, but that it is ranked below altruism in the hierarchy of values; then an altruistic act can have the point of promoting the health of a person. But according to the envisaged value hierarchy, the act of seeking to promote the health of a person—the altruistic act—would be more highly valued than the actual health of the person. This is surely a valuational absurdity. It is the absurdity of valuing the means more highly than the end, when the only feature about the means that could give it value is the end it produces. Practical examples of such absurd valuation abound. There are those who value money more than the goods that can be purchased with it; there are those who value training for a sport more than playing it, and so on. Now provided that there is no additional feature of the means to confer value on it besides its capacity to produce the end, it is irrational to value the means more than the end.

The latter qualification is important. Take the case of valuing the playing of piano exercises more than playing genuine pieces of music. Consider a person who can play his or her exercises with fluency, ease, and satisfaction due to their simplicity, but finds the same fluency, ease, and satisfaction evading him or her in playing genuine pieces of music. If the person is incapable of developing to the point of deriving greater or even equal satisfaction from playing genuine pieces of music, then there is no manifest absurdity in this person valuing the playing of exercises more than playing genuine pieces of music, even though the person still conceives of the playing of exercises as a means. The means themselves are capable of furnishing independent satisfactions without attaining their ends.

Let me relate these considerations to Nietzsche. If altruism is essentially a means and altruism is held to be one of the highest values in a value hierarchy, then we have a valuational absurdity, if the only values that can give altruism its point are either ranked lower than altruism, or even worse, regarded as positive disvalues. This is an important part of the point he is making. The value of altruism rests squarely on the self-centered interests of the recipient. Furthermore, this point is surely a good point. To strengthen the case, however, it would have to be established that altruistic acts have no additional value-conferring features above those that accrue to them in virtue of attaining the relevant, other-person-benefiting, ends. In my view this is not done, but while that reflects on the conclusiveness of the case, it does not reflect on its importance. In any event, one is genuinely at a loss to imagine what the additional, end-independent, value-conferring features of altruism could be.

From a bird's-eye point of view, there is a lesson to be extracted for the enterprise of revaluation. A valuation may be absurd through a means being valued more highly than the end it is intended to bring about when there are no additional value-conferring characteristics belonging to the means other than its capacity to produce the end. There is a natural hesitancy in calling this a conceptual incoherency, since people do on occasion value in this way, but it seems appropriate to call it a valuational absurdity. It constitutes a legitimate critical move against a value hierarchy, but it is not simply counterpoising one substantive moral value against another. This is a point that can be applied to cognitive values, moral values, aesthetic values, and so on. Here is a way of evaluating, for example moral values, that consists of something other than merely embracing alternative moral values. The reliance is on a quasi-formal valuational principle that where the means has no independent value beyond its end, there the means cannot have a value greater than that end, or indeed, distinct from that end.

Let me consider another aspect of Nietzsche's case. He maintains that altruism is at least one of the highest values advocated by the slave morality, and the difficulties are then developed within the framework of this assumption. But the question of whether anybody actually espouses the value cluster he calls the slave morality, and whether those who do so also typically regard altruism as one of the highest values in that cluster has not been addressed. To my mind, the best that can be said is that many people certainly appear to espouse such a value system. In any event, the points are important points for such value systems. In addition, coming to the self-conscious realization that altruism is a means and positively requires the beneficiary to have self-centered values to give it point is hardly likely to leave the valuation of altruism untouched for someone who had not recognized the point previously.

In the case Nietzsche mounts, the *actual* valuational absurdity of altruism depends on assumptions about persons and their value hierarchies in the real world, assumptions that it may be legitimate to doubt. But the abstract point remains undiminished; here is a tool for criticizing value hierarchies that consists of something other than merely espousing a rival value hierarchy. There is, of course, the additional issue of who is entitled to use this tool. There is no problem about its deployment by adherents to the absolute theory of truth or by perspectivists. The issue is more problematic in regard to the extreme relativist, since he or she may have no objection to absurd valuation. But there is no reason why the extreme relativist ought not to espouse the principle that in his or her own subjective value hierarchy a means will not be subjectively valued more highly than the end it is meant to produce unless the means independently has additional subjective value. No doubt, extreme relativists are not obliged to espouse this principle, but if they wish to maximize subjective value, they have every reason to embrace it and modify their subjective value hierarchies in the light of it. If maximizing value is the aim, then irrespective of whether value is objective or subjective, it is not the case that anything goes. It is not the case that extreme subjectivism rules out the possibility of bringing rational considerations to bear on values.

There are other important objections Nietzsche has to altruism. By an altruistic act one secures for another a benefit that could have been secured for oneself or whose equivalent could have been secured for oneself. According to him this reveals that one is valuing the other person more highly than one is valuing oneself. The claim is most plausible in the case of ultimate self-sacrifice. If one is prepared to give up one's life for the life of another, seemingly, the only way to make sense of such an act is to suppose that the sacrificer believes his or her life to be of less value and less deserving of being continued than the life being saved. For such a person, that can only arise where the self-sacrificer has an impoverished self-conception. This impoverished self-conception itself can only arise in degenerate, devitalized, and declining forms of life. "The preponderance of an altruistic mode of valuation is the consequence of an instinct that one is ill-constituted. The value judgment here is at bottom: 'I am not worth much': a merely physiological value judgment; even more clearly: the feeling of impotence, the absence of the great affirmative feelings of power (in muscles, nerves, ganglia)" (WP 373). Healthy, dynamic, ascending forms of life have a robust self-conception, they take their own worth for granted. Ascending life forms simply expropriate; they insist on the right to endure, to expand, and to increase. Only declining life forms voluntarily surrender what they have and diminish both themselves and their resources.

While the claim has greatest impact where a life is sacrificed to save another life, it is not without impact in cases where the benefactor undergoes a genuine cost for the sake of the beneficiary. Of course not all cases of altruism are like that; there are cases of altruism where what is given to the person in need does not, in any nontrivial way, cost the giver anything; and cases are conceivable where both may benefit. But in these cases Nietzsche really has no point, nor would he be interested in them. Thus we can restrict our consideration to cases where there is a significant cost to the benefactor. His case is this. In performing an altruistic act, the benefactor must be setting his or her own worth lower than that of the beneficiary. To set one's own worth lower than that of another is an expression of declining life and adds to its decline. Altruism is ruinous because it not only expresses declining life, but also contributes to its further decline. Of course these judgments need to be understood in terms of Nietzsche's higher-order values. Declining life represents a reduction in vigor and capacity to enrich life, and contributes to their further decrease. Ascending life represents an increment in vigor and capacity to enrich life, and contributes to its further enhancement.

There are two main issues in this approach to altruism. First, does an altruistic act containing a significant element of self-sacrifice presuppose that the benefactor is placing a lower value on himself or herself than on the beneficiary? Second, were a benefactor to place a lower value on himself or herself than on the beneficiary would this constitute an expression of declining life and contribute to its further decline? Consider the assumption that an altruistic act containing a significant element of self-sacrifice presupposes that the benefactor is placing a lower value on himself or herself than on the beneficiary. If we conceive of the situation as a *two person zero-sum game*, then the assumption will no doubt appear plausible. But not all cases are like this. Imagine the following wartime situation. A grenade is lobbed into the trenches; one man, by smothering the grenade with his body, can save his five companions, or he can save himself and let the others die. Suppose he sacrifices himself, what does this imply about his valuing of himself? Certainly he must be valuing his single life less than that of the five he saves. But this is not saying much; it is compatible with this person regarding his *single* life of more value than the single life of any other human being in the world, and of not being prepared to sacrifice himself in any circumstances to save only one other human being.

Sacrificing oneself to save five is compatible with one of the most robust self-conceptions imaginable. It is difficult to square this self-conception with declining life. In fact, if the person who could save the others by smothering the grenade with his body failed to do so, and the other five died, then, insofar as we have any intuitive mastery of the notions of "declining life" and "ascending life," we would be inclined to regard *this* as the expression of a declining form of life. We would be inclined to regard the self-sacrifice as the expression of ascending life, assuming, of course, that the differences between these trench occupants were not exceptional. With the self-sacrifice there are more lives left with the potential for thriving than without the self-sacrifice. Self-sacrifice does not require an impoverished self-conception, nor need it be an expression of life in decline, for it is clearly capable of promoting the thriving of life.

One could reply that whatever the case may be where one person self-sacrifices to save many, Nietzsche is surely right when it comes to one person sacrificing him- or herself for just one other person. However, even this is dubious. Take a case. Suppose a middle-aged parent can save the life of her child, but only at the cost of losing her own life. If the parent gives up her own life for the child, does this entail that the parent regards her own life of lesser value than that of the child? Such a valuation could occur, but it need not occur. One way the parent might conceive the situation is this. While the child's life and the parent's life are equally valuable, what needs to be considered is the temporal dimension; there is a greater potential for extended life in the child than in the adult. It could be put in numerical terms as follows. Suppose that the child has the potential to live for another sixty years and the adult has the potential to live for another thirty years. The parent may maintain that an additional sixty years for the child is more valuable than an additional thirty years for herself. What the case shows is that even where one person gives up her life for only one other person, it does not entail that she has a lower conception of her own worth than that of the person for whom she is sacrificing. Indeed, the parent might even regard her own life as slightly more valuable, but that thirty more years of her slightly more valuable life is outweighed by sixty more years for the life of her child. The parent may reason that the new life the child represents deserves some of the same opportunities the parent has already savored.

Even where one person sacrifices his or her life for just one other person, it does not follow that the sacrificer must have a lower conception of his or her own value than that of the beneficiary. If we relate this to life in general, it would be natural to regard a parent who refused to sacrifice him- or herself in this case as an expression of life in decline, and to regard a parent who sacrifices him- or herself as an expression of life in ascent. After all, there is a net gain of thirty years of life, and hence of additional productive potential, from the act of self-sacrifice. How can one fail to regard it as more life promoting? As the example makes clear, self-sacrifice does not imply a deficient self-conception on the part of the sacrificer even where one life is sacrificed to save just one other life; nor does it imply that life in decline is expressed or abetted.

In less extreme cases of altruism, those not requiring a significant element of self-sacrifice, Nietzsche's case is even weaker. In general, the case that altruism is an expression of declining life and hastens its decline, that it acts against the enhancement of life does not appear to be strong if we conceive of the matter in terms of *single acts of altruism*. Indeed, it is possible to argue within *this framework* that Nietzsche has reversed the actual state of affairs. To be altruistic, to be prepared to benefit other persons besides oneself suggests that the benefactor's self-conception is that he or she has enough health, strength, vitality and resources not just for him- or herself, but also enough for others. It suggests the opposite of an impoverished self-conception or of declining life. Surely, persons who believe that they have only enough health, strength, vitality, and resources to get by themselves, who believe that giving anything to another person constitutes a threat to oneself and an unacceptable loss to oneself have impoverished self-conceptions and are more likely to strike us as an expression of life in decline.

Nietzsche thinks that acting altruistically is both an expression of life in decline and contributes to its decline. But the altruist looks after both him- or herself and others. One can argue that to encourage altruists is to encourage strong types who have strength not only for themselves, but who can also carry others. To discourage altruists is to encourage weaker types who have strength only for themselves and who can carry no others. Of course there are cases where the giver is in greater need than the recipient, where the giver is destroyed by the giving, where the giver lacks the resources to give. But this is hardly typical. It is possible to accept his premise that what is an expression of ascending life and contributes to its ascent is good, and that what is an expression of declining life and contributes to its decline is bad, without accepting that altruism is an expression of declining life and contributes to its decline. At any rate, this is how it looks if we think of altruism in terms of isolated actions. But this way of regarding the matter misses something important in his thought about the issue, and this needs to be dealt with.

Nietzsche's thinking is not mainly directed at particular actions, nor is it specifically directed at altruists as concrete individuals. His thinking is directed mainly toward types. The type is an abstraction, a simplification and an intensification of the ordinary altruist. *"The ideal slave* (the 'good man').—He who cannot posit *himself* as a goal, not posit any goals for himself whatever, bestows honor upon *selflessness*—instinctively" (WP 358). The altruist, as a pure type, is a being oriented exclusively toward *the interests of others.* This is Nietzsche's conceptual model of the altruist;[6] it is not the conception of a person who merely occasionally or even frequently performs altruistic acts; it is the conception of a person whose orientation toward the interests of others is total. Nietzsche's reflections are often centered around such "ideal types,"[7] where characteristics are taken to extremes and irrelevant characteristics deleted. Indeed, he prefers to consider altruism in terms of the type of the altruist, that is the type who is oriented exclusively toward *the interests of others,* and this casts the issue in a new light.

Analytically, the type of the altruist is a type with no independent projects, goals, or interests of his or her own. There is no independent urge to produce, to create, to construct in one's own right and for oneself, to make one's own mark. Resources are spent on furthering the projects, goals, and interests of others. Of course the whole situation presupposes that having projects, goals, and interests is a good thing, otherwise the altruists furthering these in others would not be doing good. But the altruist lacks the very characteristics that warrant his or her aid to others. So conceived, the altruist is simply making a slave of him- or herself to others, a willing slave no doubt, but a slave nevertheless. The altruist has no independent vision or independent vital concerns of his or her own. However active the altruist may be in the aid of others, it is essentially the activity of a servant or a slave. Unavoidably, such an *exclusive* orientation toward the interests of others presupposes a lower valuation of oneself, and is quite plausibly connected with declining life.

But even this focus on the type does not fully bring out Nietzsche's underlying concerns. He is not worried by the decayed, the anaemic, and the declining spending their meager resources on others, just as he is not concerned about the superabundantly endowed directing some of their resources to others. The basic fear is that the advocacy of this ideal will induce the capable to sacrifice themselves for the incapable. "The sick represent the greatest danger for the healthy; it is *not* the strongest but the weakest who spell disaster for the strong. Is this known?" (GM III:14). There is no problem about a "nobody" sacrificing himself to save a threatened Mozart. There is everything wrong with a Mozart sacrificing himself for a threatened "nobody." "But no worse misunderstanding and denial of *their* task can be imagined: the higher *ought* not to degrade itself to the status of an instrument of the lower, the pathos of distance *ought* to keep their tasks eternally separate!" (ibid.). To develop the point, suppose that the hundred greatest composers, the hundred greatest scientists, the hundred greatest writers, the hundred greatest artists, and the hundred greatest scholars had devoted all of their creative energies directly to caring for the poor, the sick, the depressed, the starving, and the dying; would the world have been a better place? One can plausibly conjecture that overall there would, in any event, have been more suffering from poverty, disease, and starvation had this occurred, due to the retardation of knowledge, but that is not Nietzsche's point. The loss to humanity of their creations would be catastrophic. Human life as a whole would be enormously impoverished and diminished.

What is uppermost in Nietzsche's mind is not the single altruistic act, nor even the occasional individual altruist; what concerns him most about the embrace of the altruistic ideal is the deleterious influence on life as a whole.

> *A criticism of décadence morality.*—An "altruistic" morality, a morality un-der which egoism *languishes*—is under all circumstances a bad sign. This applies to individuals, it applies especially to peoples. The best are lack-ing when egoism begins to be lacking. To choose what is harmful to *oneself*, to be *attracted* by "disinterested" motives, almost constitutes the formula for *décadence*. "Not to seek *one's own* advantage"—that is a mor-al fig leaf for a quite different, namely physiological fact: "I no longer know how to *find* my advantage." . . . Disintegration of the instincts!— Man is finished when he becomes altruistic.—Instead of saying simply "*I* am no longer worth anything," the moral lie in the mouth of the *déca-dent* says: "Nothing is worth anything—*life* is not worth anything." . . . Such a judgment represents, after all, a grave danger, it is contagious— on the utterly morbid soil of society it soon grows up luxuriously, now in the form of religion (Christianity), now in that of philosophy (Schopenhauerism). In some circumstances the vapors of such a poison-tree jungle sprung out of putrefaction can poison *life* for years ahead, for thousands of years ahead. (TI IX:35)

Let me sum up the case regarding altruism. It is conceptually incoherent to suppose that altruism could be the only value, and it is valuationally irrational to regard altruism as the highest value. Even where altruism is not *the* highest value, it is valuationally irrational to value altruism more highly than the values that serve to give it its point. However, that altruism, construed as the performing of individual al-truistic acts, cannot be an important value has not been proved. In-deed, on occasion, individual acts of altruism can clearly contribute to the enhancement of life. That altruism, conceived of as a whole life orientation for individuals, is of dubious value is persuasively put. But the real objection arises from considering altruism as a universal ide-al. The greater the proportion of persons who approximate to the al-truist type, the worse things are for the society and life in general. A few may be harmless, but many are fatal. There is a case of substance here that may be able to be met, but which it is difficult to see as not shaking altruism to some degree.

However, these considerations do not exhaust the case against altruism. Nietzsche also maintains that the advocacy of altruism has been self-undermining. With altruism and self-sacrifice explicitly in mind he writes as follows:

> This indicates the fundamental contradiction in the morality that is very prestigious nowadays: the *motives* of this morality stand opposed to its *principle*. What this morality considers its proof is refuted by its criterion of what is moral. In order not to contravene its own morality, the demand "You shall renounce yourself and sacrifice yourself" could be laid down only by those who thus renounced their own advantage and perhaps brought about their own destruction through the demanded sacrifice of individuals. But as soon as the neighbor (or society) recommends altruism *for the sake of its utility,* it applies the contradictory principle. "You shall seek your advantage even at the expense of everything else"—and thus one preaches, in the same breath, a "Thou shalt" and "Thou shalt not." (GS 21)

The core of the case is that the selfish advocacy of altruism undermines altruism as a value. Of course the underlying factual claim that altruism has basically been advocated for selfish reasons is difficult to establish; but even if the factual assumption is granted, the argument remains intriguing. It has an undeniable intuitive plausibility, but the mechanisms of the argument are not transparent. The nature and strength of this argument is assessed at greater length in chapter 7. However, it is useful to mention the argument here to illustrate the variety of Nietzsche's weapons against altruism, and his level of preoccupation with it.

If we consider developments since Nietzsche's time, we are faced with something of an ironic twist. He thought of himself as taking a biologically realistic stance against the "unrealistic" moral and religious advocacy of altruism, yet the most serious problems for his views have arisen from within biology itself. The way the issues have been conceptualized and the plausible mechanisms that have been proposed for the evolution of practices such as "reciprocal altruism"[8] in particular, would at the very least require him to restate his position in a more circumspect way.

Let me illustrate the point with an example of "reciprocal altruism."[9] Suppose that on a fishing expedition my friend is bitten by a snake whose bite will kill him unless I drive him to a hospital ten miles away. I drive him there and save his life. The cost to me is trivial, but the gain to him is enormous. Suppose that several years later I am with the same friend and I am bitten by the same kind of snake and I will die unless driven to a hospital. He drives me the ten miles to the hospital and I am saved. The cost to him is trivial, but the gain to me is enormous. From my standpoint, I have bought my own life for the mere cost of a ten mile car trip. The return on my "altruistic" investment is prodigious. Of course, the same obtains for my friend; we both recoup far more than we invest.[10] "Reciprocal altruism" has a great capacity to promote the thriving of life. The challenge for Nietzsche is that this altruism not only pays—it can pay handsomely, and it is perfectly compatible with both a robust self-regard and with a furtherance of the thriving of life.

Naturally, Nietzsche could reply that it is not *this kind* of altruism he has in mind when attacking altruism, that what he has in mind is altruism that costs the benefactor dear and returns nothing. But such a reply is not the simple solution it appears to be, for if the vast bulk of what is taken to be human altruism should turn out to be "reciprocal altruism," then it is difficult to see how the small remainder could be a significant threat to the thriving of life, or that there is much point in railing against it. Indeed, analysis of evolutionary possibilities suggests that there is no way that "extreme" altruism could ever come to predominate, and hence, no way it could ever pose the threat he feared. However, while his relation to these new developments calls for more extensive study, I have thought it preferable to touch on the matter rather than ignoring it entirely.

Let me turn to a more formal characteristic of the slave morality, but one that is also of considerable wider relevance.

Universality

First, let me introduce a distinction. In one sense perspectivism entails that nothing can be universally true; for any perspective, there is in principle always an alternative perspective. Now what belongs to all perspectives can be called globally universal. Apart from metatheoretical claims about perspectives themselves, perspectivism rules out global universality. However, there is nothing to prevent the making of universal statements within a perspective; typically many will be made. We can call this local universality. Naturally, it follows from perspectivism that moral claims cannot be globally universal, and if this was all that was meant by Nietzsche's denial of universality then the argument would not have to proceed beyond perspectivism. But the attack on universality in the slave morality is more than that; it is also an attack on the local universality of moral claims. Put another way, he thinks that our currently best perspective bars locally universal moral claims. Hence, the arguments against universality here are necessarily more specific than in the case of perspectivism as a general doctrine.

While Nietzsche sees the demand for universality in moral rules as arising principally from the slave desire to cut down the masters to their own size, to tame and render harmless the strong, the exceptional, and the powerful, and of the herd to compel what it feels comfortable with, the importance of the issue is not contingent upon accepting the slave morality and herd morality as soundly based ideas. For it has been widely accepted that universality is an essential feature of morality.[11] A successful attack on universality would be of major significance even if the slave morality, herd morality, and master morality conceptions were found to be entirely untenable. Two of his objections to universality will be considered.

The main argument is that universality is anti-nature. Nature contains such a rich diversity of types it is absurd that this rich diversity should be required to conform to one set of rules. "Let me consider finally what naîvety it is to say 'man *ought* to be thus and thus!' Reality shows us such an enchanting wealth of types, the luxuriance of a prodigal play and change of forms: and does some pitiful journeyman moralist say at the sight of it: 'No! man ought to be *different?*' . . . He even knows *how* man ought to be, this bigoted wretch" (TI V:6). Take a nonmoral example. It would be absurd to require human beings to live underwater without artificial assistance or fish to live out of it. Their respective natures do not fit them for the change. Any general rule, of the form all shall live on land or all shall live under the sea, would by common consent be absurd. If we required dogs always to walk on their hind legs as their masters do, we would be making a proposal only marginally less absurd. If these are apt cases, then the requirement of universality is both pointless and pernicious in a world as diverse as ours. The insistence on universality must diminish overall value.

The natural reply is that we are not dealing with different species such as human beings and fish, or human beings and dogs, but with one species. Specifically, we are addressing the moral rules to beings at least sufficiently alike in nature to be able to grasp the moral rules. Whatever the diversity is in nature as a whole, and whatever the absurdity there may be in rules applied to nature as a whole, there is in no way a comparable diversity in the human species alone, and hence, there is in no way a comparable absurdity in universal rules for human beings. One can argue that although the differences between human beings are indeed striking, so are the similarities. Of course Nietzsche held that there were differences among human beings as great as the differences between species. While steering clear of moral cases, it is true that persuasive examples can be presented. It would be absurd to have a general rule that everybody should compose operas in the style of, and of comparable quality to, Mozart's operas. The proportion of the population capable of composing any opera is tiny, and the proportion of those capable of composing operas of a quality comparable to Mozart's is either infinitely small or entirely nonexistent.

Citing what some people can do but others cannot is certainly relevant, but it is not decisive. A more direct focus is required. If it is conceded that the differences among human beings are as great as the differences between human beings and other species, then the case against the universality of moral rules would have a strong basis. But the claim that there are differences as great among human beings as between human beings and other species borders on conceptual falsehood. For if the differences were that great we would not have a human species but simply a plethora of different species. It would still be possible to maintain that the differences between human beings, while not as great as the differences between species, are nevertheless so large as to make any requirement of universal conformity to any rules absurd.

At this stage a counterexample can usefully be considered. Language consists of a system of rules that, to all intents and purposes, all human beings can learn to conform to. Even if one takes human beings as diverse as one likes, they can all learn to conform to linguistic rules without this in any obvious way harming them. Indeed, language is a particularly unwelcome example for Nietzsche, since language can plausibly be regarded as the foundation of all human cultural development. Hence, if language requires universal conformity to rules, then all human cultural development is based ultimately on universal conformity to rules.[12] It simply does not follow that if human beings are diverse they cannot conform to universal rules, or that conformity to universal rules is inherently damaging. An argument against the universality of moral rules based on the diversity of types among human beings must establish either that the diversity of types simply makes conformity to the rules impossible or else that universal conformity is substantially harmful. Given that language gives us an instance where within the recognized diversity of human types we know conformity to universal rules to be possible and, putting it conservatively, for such a conformity not to be substantially harmful, then there would have to be additional considerations required to show that the moral rules are in some special category.[13]

To be fair, Nietzsche has further considerations to bolster the claim that morality is anti-nature. For example, there is the attack on morality's propensity to take a repressive attitude toward the passions (TI V:1). But my concern is to focus on the claim that universality is inimical to nature in its own right and is to be rejected on this account. Nietzsche's case is not convincing; but, what requires note is the revaluation strategy. If it could be shown that the diversity of human types precluded substantial conformity to moral rules or that substantial conformity to moral rules had harmful consequences—that it acts against the invigoration and enrichment of life, then surely this would force a revaluation.

There is another argument deployed against universality. A morality is required to articulate what is *good* or what is *valuable*. Yet, a universalizing morality advocates as good or valuable what it is expected everybody can attain. If we suppose that acts in conformity with the moral rules are good, and that conformity to the moral rules is possible for every moral agent as is required by a universalizing morality, then the good is in principle attainable by all moral agents. Nietzsche's difficulty with this is of how anything that is attainable by all, anything that is so common, could possibly be valuable. "One has to get rid of the bad taste of wanting to be in agreement with many. 'Good' is no longer good when your neighbour takes it in his mouth. And how could there be a 'common good'! The expression is a self-contradiction: what can be common has ever but little value. In the end it must be as it has always been: great things for the great, abysses for the profound, shudders and delicacies for the refined, and, in sum, all rare things for the rare" (BGE 43). To gain a sympathetic insight into this point, let me start with some nonmoral cases. Just about anybody can run the mile in forty minutes; this is not regarded as a particularly valuable achievement. Few can run the mile in four minutes, and we regard this as a more valuable achievement. Just about anybody can bang garbage can lids; this is not regarded as a particularly valuable achievement. Few can play the piano like Cyprien Katsaris, and we regard this as a far more valuable achievement. An important reason why the greats, Shakespeare, Raphael, Mozart, for example, are what they are, is that either only a few can do what they did, or that nobody else can do what they did.

In these cases a crucial component of the value, although certainly not the only component, is its rarity and the sheer difficulty of producing a matching performance. This is characteristic of aesthetic evaluation. In the arts, it is precisely the *exception*, the *unique* achievement, the *unrepeatable* performance, the attainment of standards not attainable by others that is valued most. In the case of morals, this does not obtain. Everybody is expected to refrain from causing needless suffering, from lying, robbing, raping, and killing. In brief, in morals everybody is expected to do the *same* and to continue doing the *same*. In art, everybody is, by and large, expected to do something *different* and to keep doing something *different*. If time after time I save children from drowning in exactly the same circumstances, then I am morally advanced. If time after time I paint exactly the same picture, then I am aesthetically backward.

The difference is sufficiently striking to speak of an *aesthetic value-model* and a *moral value-model*. Nietzsche maintains we ought to assess persons, actions, and lives on an aesthetic value-model rather than a moral value-model.

> As he loves a fine work of art but does not praise it since it can do nothing for itself, as he stands before the plants, so must he stand before the actions of men and before his own. (HAH I:107)

> *The realm of beauty is bigger*—As we go about in nature, with joy and cunning, bent on discovering and as it were catching in the act the beauty proper to everything; as we try to see how that piece of coastline, with its rocks, inlets, olive trees and pines, attains to its perfection and mastery whether in the sunshine, or when the sky is stormy, or when the twilight is almost gone: so we ought to go about men, viewing and discovering them, showing them their good and evil, so that they shall behold their own proper beauty which unfolds itself in one case in the sunlight, in another amid storms, and in a third only when night is falling and the sky is full of rain. Is it then forbidden to *enjoy* the *evil* man as a wild landscape possessing its own bold lineaments and effects of light,

if the same man appears to us as a sketch and caricature and, as a blot in nature, causes us pain, when he poses as good and law-abiding?—As surely as the wicked enjoy a hundred kinds of happiness of which the virtuous have no inkling, so too they possess a hundred kinds of beauty: and many of them have not yet been discovered. (D 468)

His proposal to replace a moral valuation model by an aesthetic valuation model has been noted before, but a rationally unmotivated recommendation to replace one value-model by another would have little capacity to warrant actual replacement. But in reality the position is better grounded than that. There is an important case against the moral value-model and in favor of the aesthetic value-model, at any rate, insofar as constituting an adequate model for the highest values is concerned.

Nietzsche makes the point that the moral values have hitherto been taken to be the *highest values* (WP 401). Now, the highest values have a role to fulfil in the context of human life. The issue is whether moral values can fulfil the required role. To begin, the issue of one's life having a point or meaning is clearly an important one for him: "If we possess our *why* of life we can put up with any *how*" (TI I:12). Further, it appears incontestable that it is the highest values that must give value, meaning, or point to one's life. If the highest values cannot give value, meaning, or point to one's life, it is hard to see how anything else could possibly fulfil this role. The point appears almost too obvious to state. The ensuing puzzle is how universal moral rules could fulfil the role of giving point or meaning to an individual's life. The actual set of rules we adopt is unimportant, since it is the universality of the rules that is the key point, so let me accept that the universal moral rules are not to lie, not to kill, not to steal, and to help persons in distress.

Suppose I have adhered to these rules all of my life; I never lie, never kill, never steal, and I always help persons in distress when able. Of what value is my life to *me?* What point is there to *my life?* Where is the meaning for *me?* To begin, there is no more point, meaning, or value to *my life for me* than there is point, meaning, or value to *another person's life for me* who has adhered to the moral rules in exactly the same way I have. For all who adhere to the moral rules, given that moral rules constitute the highest values, there are no further value considerations that can lend special value to their individual lives. I must regard my own life as no more valuable, no more meaningful, and as having no more point than the life of any other person who has conformed equally to the moral rules. This implies that I ought to have no qualms about being replaced by another person, as long as there is an equivalent adherence to the moral rules by that person: "A virtuous man is a lower species because he is not a 'person' but acquires his value by conforming to a pattern of man that is fixed once and for all. He does not possess his value apart: he can be compared, he has his equals, he *must* not be an individual" (WP 319). The point can be strengthened as follows. Suppose that I had, for all of my life, been replaced by an automaton[14] that behaved in exactly the way I had, and had been taken to conform to the moral rules just as I did. The automaton refrains from killing, stealing, lying, cheating, and so on. If conformity to moral rules lends value, point, or meaning to life, then the automaton's life is as valuable and as meaningful as my own. Or, to put it in its proper perspective, my life has no more value than the automaton's. But surely, literally to believe that one is of no more value than an automaton is to believe that there is either little or no value, meaning, or point to one's life.

Whatever it may be that others judge us by, what *we* require to give special point or meaning or value to our *own lives* is something special, something unique, something individual, something that cannot be readily replaced or readily reproduced (WP 349). If one asks what life should mean to human beings in general, then a general answer is appropriate; but if one asks what life should mean to *me specifically*, then a merely general answer, applying equally to everybody, is insufficient. An answer to the question concerning the specific point, meaning, or value of *my life* that implies that the value situation is not in the slightest degree affected if my life is replaced by any other human life, by a clone perhaps, is simply not the answer I am seeking. Should this answer be the only one available, then there is no special point, value, or meaning to one's life, one is superfluous, and certainly one is unproblematically replaceable.

Put another way, what I want to know is what is *different* about my life, what is *special* about my life, what is my life or can my life be that *no other* life is or can be? It appears that *uniqueness* is an essential element of this personal or individual sense of worth. If the personal or individual sense of the meaning or value or point of one's life is essentially something unique, something that differentiates one from others, then of necessity this cannot be supplied by mere conformity to universal rules.

My brother, if you have a virtue and it is your own virtue, you have it in common with no one.

To be sure, you will want to call it by a name and caress it; you will want to pull its ears and amuse yourself with it.

And behold! Now you have its name in common with people and have become of the people and the herd with your virtue!

You would do better to say: "Unutterable and nameless is that which torments and delights my soul and is also the hunger of my belly."

Let your virtue be too exalted for the familiarity of names: and if you have to speak of it, do not be ashamed to stammer.

Thus say and stammer: "This is *my* good, this I love, just thus do I like it, only thus do *I* wish the good.

"I do not want it as a law of God, I do not want it as a human statute: let it be no sign-post to superearths and paradises." (Z I:5)

To sum up, individual value requires uniqueness, and uniqueness cannot arise from universal rules. The moral rules are supposed to embody the highest values, and as the highest values they must ultimately lend value to life, but it is specifically their universality that precludes them from giving individuals any unique sense of their worth or their own way. "'This—is now *my* way: where is yours?' Thus I answered those who asked me 'the way.' For *the* way—does not exist!" (Z III:11).

We have available the aesthetic value-model and the moral value-model. Essential to the former is uniqueness, and essential to the latter is universality. Nietzsche is not arbitrarily recommending the aesthetic value-model replace the moral value-model. The moral value-model simply cannot fulfil one of the key roles required of the highest values, and this role can only be fulfilled by adopting the aesthetic value-model. Do we have a successful revaluation here? Has it been shown that any morality that has universality as an essential component is necessarily deficient? If it is a requirement of the highest values that they provide meaning for an individual's life, then the case is sound that no morality of universal rules can fulfil this role.[15] But care is needed about what this amounts to. It means that a system of universal moral rules cannot constitute the highest values, but it does not mean that they are of no value or that they need *complete* replacement by a different mode of valuation.

Given that a negative attitude toward universal moral rules is so prominent in Nietzsche's thought, it is useful to look at the issue from another point of view. There have been two fundamental questions underlying ethical theorizing. On the one hand, what must I do with myself to live the most valuable life possible for me? And on the other, what is the proper way for me to deal with other human beings? The direct answers to these questions lead to the morality of self-realization in the first case and to the morality of duty in the second. What tends to blur matters is that there are some theories, such as utilitarianism, that answer both questions at once and hence tend to veil the fact that there are two distinct questions here. But there is no reason to expect that what constitutes a good answer to one of the questions is also going to constitute a good answer to the other question.

If it is the very function of moral rules—morality of duty—to provide a stable framework in which human beings can pursue the values that they regard as *really* important—morality of self-realization—then it cannot reasonably be objected against the moral rules that they do not give ultimate meaning, point, or value to life, for this is not their intent. Nietzsche may be right to argue that moral values conceived as universal rules cannot embody the highest values, but it does not follow from this that they are of no value. Adherence to the moral rules may constitute necessary conditions for the attainment of the highest personal values.[16] Occasionally it is possible to detect in Nietzsche a tendency to drift into accepting that because something is not the highest value it is of little or no value. The inference is, of course, unsound, but it may explain his sometimes harsh way with morality. In any event, it is possible to acknowledge the case against moral values, conceived of as universal rules, being the highest values, without at the same time having to accept that morality is of little or no value.

In any event, Nietzsche's more settled view is not merely that some system of rules *may* be justified, but that, depending on circumstances, some system of rules *will be* justified by appeal to his higher-order values (BGE 188). Nietzsche's principal attack is against certain kinds of morality, and against the placement of morality at the peak of a value system; it is not principally an attack against morality conceived in the broadest sense. Indeed, for him the enhancement of life is inconceivable without protracted constraint at both a group and individual level.

Mediocrity

Mediocrity is the main value fostered by the herd morality. It is not fostered as an accidental by-product of a more lofty enterprise, but as its essential aim. The herd wants herd animals it feels comfortable with. The herd morality is not principally concerned with the regulation of behavior, it is principally concerned with the production of an average type of human being. Of course this is still closely related to universality and some of the objections to universality immediately carry over. The enforcement of mediocrity is harmful to the exception, and making the herd animals the same rules out any capacity to furnish special meaning to an individual's life.

But typically Nietzsche's attack on mediocrity is not mediated by subtle strategies; rather, there is a direct confrontation between mediocrity and his higher-order values. The mediocrity promoted by the herd is in direct conflict with the enhancement of life. The herd likes the level that it is at and does not want to change; the herd average is the herd's standard of good, and it cannot see change as improvement. Thus the herd not merely does not seek invigoration, it positively opposes it. It will tolerate enrichment provided that it is suitable for all herd animals; what is not is anathema. The mediocrity so promoted keeps the herd at about the level of survival and not much above it, with no inherent drive to increase the distance. The stance is against intensity, it is against fecundity, and it is especially against coherent multiplicity—it wants a comfortable uniformity.

It is useful to recall the point of Nietzsche's higher-order values, and that is to optimize value as understood in his theory of value. In this context, the policy of pursuing mediocrity is a policy of diminishing overall value, not diminishing value for Nietzsche the spectator, but diminishing value for those in pursuit of such a policy. It is one thing to pursue policies that accidentally prevent us from garnering all the potential value available; it is quite another to pursue policies that deliberately prevent us from garnering all the potential value available, yet this is precisely what the pursuit of mediocrity does.

Utilitarianism

Nietzsche was a fierce critic of utilitarianism. As is well known, utilitarianism has more than one version and can be understood in more than one way. At one extreme it can designate consequentialism in general; at the other extreme it can take a narrow hedonistic form. There is, however, a characteristic that is common to this broad spread. The utilitarian, of whatever variety, is committed to performing a cost/benefit analysis before he or she acts. What is counted as cost and what is counted as benefit will depend on the particular version of utilitarianism, but a cost/benefit analysis must be made, and the benefit must outweigh the cost before the action is undertaken.

Nietzsche regards the utilitarian way of thinking as part of slave morality in particular but also as part of the herd morality: "Slave morality is essentially the morality of utility" (BGE 260). The underlying idea is this: the slaves or the herd are by their very nature of limited resource, be the resource mental, physical, material, or whatever. Those of limited resources must calculate the expenditure of their resources carefully. If they do not, they may not have enough to survive. On the other hand, for those whose resources are boundless, it is pointless to count the cost. Utilitarianism belongs to the herd because it favors the preservation of the herd; it enjoins a course of conduct that is a requirement for the underendowed while it is at best a hindrance to the masters. Two considerations relating to utilitarianism will be dealt with. One concerns the relation between utilitarianism and autonomy and the other concerns the functional status of the states deemed to be ultimately desirable and ultimately undesirable in utilitarianism.

In considering the relation between autonomy and utilitarianism, I propose to take utilitarianism in its hedonistic rather than ideal form, since this is what Nietzsche usually has in mind. Clearly, as far as hedonistic utilitarianism is concerned, the autonomy of an individual does not, and cannot, constitute an independent value. Thus hedonistic utilitarianism is committed to the following valuation. If capturing a person, entirely depriving him or her of freedom, and continually administering a drug that induces in him or her a state of perpetual euphoria of a high hedonic value outweighs the hedonic value accruing to the person if he or she were permitted to freely pursue his or her own ends, then the hedonistic utilitarian is morally obligated to deprive that person of his or her freedom and administer the drug. To the extent that this is repulsive to our pre-theoretical moral intuitions, and to the extent that pre-theoretical moral intuitions have to be either accommodated in an acceptable moral theory or satisfactorily rebutted by it, this constitutes a serious difficulty for hedonistic utilitarianism.

Let me make the point in general terms. Suppose that we can compare lives with respect to autonomy and hedonic value—let it be called happiness. Consider the following four cases of lives:

a. autonomous and happy;
b. autonomous and unhappy;

c. nonautonomous and happy, and
d. nonautonomous and unhappy.

Suppose that (a) and (b) are equal in respect of autonomy, (c) and (d) are equal in respect of nonautonomy, (a) and (c) are equal in respect of happiness, and (b) and (d) are equal in respect of unhappiness. I take it that if there is a choice, (d) would not be the preferred option of anybody. Nietzsche has no objection to (a). But the significant point is that the hedonistic utilitarian can in principle have no reason for preferring (a) to (c), since by hypothesis the hedonic value is equal. For example, suppose that there is a master and a slave, and the life of each contains the same amount of hedonic value. For the hedonistic utilitarian there is no basis for choosing between them; it is a matter of complete valuational indifference whether one is the master or the slave, provided that the level of happiness is the same.

Nietzsche is totally opposed to such a valuation. For him, self-directed, self-initiated, self-controlled activity is the essence of healthy life forms. To either permit or not be able to prevent one's life from being controlled and directed by others is a manifestation of diminished life capacity, and hence of diminished value. Indeed, if the choice were between (b) autonomous and unhappy, and (c) nonautonomous and happy, alone, then Nietzsche's preference would be for (b) rather than (c). That is to say, for him not only is autonomy an independent value, it is an independent value higher than happiness.[17] It is better to be in charge of one's life and unhappy than to have one's life controlled by others and be happy.

> *The impossible class*—Poor, happy and independent!—these things can go together; poor happy and a slave!—these things can also go together—and I could give no better news to our factory slaves: provided, that is, they do not feel it to be in general a *disgrace* to be thus used, and *used up*, as parts of a machine and as it were a stopgap to fill a hole in human inventiveness! To the devil with the belief that higher payment could lift from them the *essence* of their miserable condition—I mean their personal enslavement! . . . What we ought to do, rather, is to hold up to them the counter-reckoning: how great a sum of *inner* value is thrown away in pursuit of this external goal! But where is your inner value if you no longer know what it is to breathe freely? if you no longer possess the slightest power over yourselves? (D 206)

There are two main models of nonautonomy. There is the prisoner model already referred to, but there is also the model of the parasite. The parasite is the person who permits everything to be done for him or her; every whim, need, or desire is satisfied by others. The parasite is not self-action initiating, self-action controlling; the model is of the passive consumer of the products of other peoples' labor. On the utilitarian view, there is absolutely nothing wrong with such a situation provided that the parasite is happy and does not increase the misery of others. Nietzsche, on the other hand, finds both the happy prisoner and happy parasite models repulsive. "Freedom means that the manly instincts that delight in war and victory have gained mastery over the other instincts—for example, over the instinct for 'happiness.' *The man who has become free*—and how much more the *mind* that has become free—spurns the contemptible sort of well-being dreamed of by shopkeepers, Christians, cows, women, Englishmen and other democrats. The free man is a *warrior*" (TI IX:38). But the high value placed on autonomy does not mean that autonomy is possible for everyone (BGE 29).

How does this case relate to revaluation? Can the mere advocacy of an alternative set of values, which is what appears to be taking place here, be considered a significant technique for revaluing values? There are two points to be made. First, the discovery or invention or reminder of cases that elicit strong pre-theoretical intuitions that run counter to a moral theory are important challenges to a theory that need to be met. These examples do not have the compelling force of mathematical argument, but that does not leave them without effect. For the hedonistic utilitarian it does not matter whether you secure your own happiness or whether some other person secures it for you, whether you control your own life or whether some other person controls it for you, provided that the amount of happiness is the same. To point out that these are matters of indifference to a hedonistic utilitarian is to point to factors that significantly affect the acceptability of the theory. Or, to put the point in a more modest form, if such points are without force in the assessment of utilitarianism, it is difficult to imagine what points could have force.

This brings me to the second consideration. The mere articulation of values that conflict with hedonistic utilitarianism and are not independently refutable weakens hedonistic utilitarianism, provided that hedonistic utilitarianism has not already been proved to be true. Put another way, the articulation of alternatives that cannot be rationally dismissed must of necessity weaken the rational grip of that to which they are alternatives. It is not required that the alternatives refute; it is sufficient that they in turn are not refuted for them to have an undermining effect. Thus, the case against utilitarianism, arising from considerations concerning autonomy, can be seen in two ways. Either they constitute directly unfavorable cases or they constitute valuations whose rational warrant is no worse than that to which they are alternatives. In either case, a revaluation of utilitarianism is warranted.

For Nietzsche, an additional difficulty arises for hedonistic utilitarianism from considering the role of pleasure and pain in animals and human beings. There is no doubt that pain is a functional state, the express purpose of which is to limit or avoid organic damage. Similarly, though allowably not as obviously, pleasure is a functional state, the express purpose of which is to maintain conditions favoring organic well-being. From the standpoint of the body, pain is only a means to avoiding a more important *disvalue* than the pain itself, namely organic damage. Similarly, from the standpoint of the body, pleasure is only a means to a more important value than the pleasure itself, namely organic well-being. "To measure whether existence has value according to the pleasant or unpleasant feelings aroused in this consciousness: can one think of a madder extravagance of vanity? For it is only a means—and pleasant or unpleasant feelings are also only means!" (WP 674).

From a biological standpoint, to judge pain as a greater disvalue than bodily damage, and pleasure a greater value than bodily health is an absurd valuation. Perhaps there are aspects of pain that contribute to its disvalue in its own right and independently of its being a means, and there are aspects of pleasure that contribute to its value in its own right and independently of its being a means. But even if one concedes this, it does not follow, and it is difficult to see what could make it follow, that pleasure and pain are of greater value and disvalue than those bodily states that they are a means to producing or preventing. "*Wisdom in pain.*—There is as much wisdom in pain as there is in pleasure: both belong among the factors that contribute the most to the preservation of the species. If pain did not, it would have perished long ago; that it hurts is no argument against it but its essence" (GS 318). No utilitarian has yet provided an account of what warrants the transformation of pleasure and pain from mere means for the organism to ultimate values for the person.[18] The problem is particularly acute for those for whom these are the only ultimate values and disvalues.

For Nietzsche, the health and vitality of the body take precedence over feelings of pleasure and pain. Furthermore, once their nature as a mere means is understood, then other important goals can come into play and override both pleasure and pain. "Brave and creative men *never* consider pleasure and pain as ultimate values—they are epiphenomena: one must *desire* both if one is to achieve anything" (WP 579).[19]

This is, of course, flatly counter to hedonistic utilitarianism. Again, this may not constitute an outright refutation of that doctrine, but if the hedonistic utilitarian cannot furnish a rational basis for the transformation of means for the organism into ends for the person, then it reveals a damaging weakness in the position. If we can point to cases where naturally occurring means are transformed into ends, we are entitled to ask what the warrant for this is, and if such a warrant is not forthcoming we can correspondingly downgrade our endorsement of the transformation. This constitutes a significant technique of revaluation. Of course, Nietzsche also takes the disregard for autonomy and the elevation of pleasure and pain to ultimate values as signs that utilitarianism springs from decadent and declining life, and represents decreased vitality. Thus, his higher-order values also come into play in the revaluation of autonomy, pleasure, and pain.

Naturally, I have not exhausted all the points Nietzsche deals with in his revaluation of morality. I have not even exhausted all the points he makes against altruism, universality, and utilitarianism. Nor have I touched on such topics as his thesis about the origin of the terms "good and evil," and "good and bad" (GM I), his critique of the ascetic ideal (GM III), or his denial of free will (TI VI:7; BGE 21). However, I hope to have shown in this selection from his revaluation of moral values that he displays a number of weapons worth noting. The matter will be taken up again explicitly in chapter 7. Whether he conclusively demolishes his targets is arguable, but that he damages them is undeniable.

FOUR

Religious Values

The Place of Religion

Nietzsche's proclamation that *God is dead* is undoubtedly his best known saying. Yet assessing his views on religion is no easy matter; the extremity and vehemence of some of his language can easily raise doubts whether there is any rational case to assess. To fuel such thoughts, explicit arguments for the nonexistence of God are difficult to find, and he has little interest in the traditional arguments.[1] Despite this, religion and its values is unquestionably a major philosophical preoccupation, and there are important views to consider. The claim that his works contain a strong rational case for the nonexistence of God has been persuasively put by Schacht,[2] and I do not wish to recanvass the whole issue. But there remains a genuine puzzle worth addressing.

Why was Nietzsche so little interested in the traditional arguments for the existence of God? Why is there so little direct discussion of the existence of God? In the circumstances, some have simply accepted that there just are no serious arguments for the nonexistence of God in his works.[3] According to these interpretations, the nonexistence of God is an *assumption* for him and not a *conclusion*. Nor need one look far for support. "I have absolutely no knowledge of atheism as an outcome of reasoning, still less as an event: with me it is obvious by instinct" (EH II:1). No doubt this is how he liked to think of the matter at the time, but he was a believer as a boy, and even commenced theological studies. It is stretching credulity to suppose argument played no role in the loss of belief that led to abandoning his theological studies. However, there is another explanation why direct arguments for the nonexistence of God are difficult to find in his works, and furthermore, an important explanation from the standpoint of revaluation. The basic issue concerns the crucial question: What is the function of a religious belief system?

Function

There are two important answers. According to the first view, the function of a religious belief system is to articulate an ontological thesis, to state truths about the nature of being. It is essentially concerned with existence and only secondarily with value. The "will to truth" dominates the enterprise; a religious belief system is the direct consequence of a quest for the truth about the constitution of the universe. According to the second view, the function of a religious belief system is to express and reinforce a value system. It is essentially concerned with value and only secondarily with existence and claims about the nature of being. The "will to truth" has at best only a minor role; a religious belief system is not the direct consequence of a quest for the truth. Nietzsche clearly takes the second view. "Christianity is a *way of life*, not a system of beliefs. It tells us how to act, not what we ought to believe" (WP 212). This would itself, of course, explain his seeming lack of interest in arguments about the existence of God. But there is something even more important here.

We need to ask what the function of the ontological component of a religious belief system is. According to Nietzsche, the principal function of the ontological component is to promote the entrenchment of the value system. The "beyond" is absolutely necessary if faith in morality is to be maintained (WP 253). The ontological component is merely a *means* and not an *end*. God is invented, perhaps unselfconsciously by the original believers, but deliberately invoked by Kant,[4] to bolster morality and defend a value system. The ontological component is not there because it antecedently recommends itself as worthy of belief to the impartial seeker after truth. Nietzsche makes the following observation: "on the other hand, we have recognized in instinctive hatred *for* actuality the driving element, the only driving element in the roots of Christianity" (A 39). The primary function of the ontological component is not to reflect reality, not to report disinterestedly on the constitution of the universe, but to cement in place a value system. As a matter of abstract possibility, the ontological component is capable of reflecting reality, and the matter can come under rational scrutiny, but this is not what is important about it.

According to Nietzsche, the advocates of religion have hidden the true nature of a religious belief system by misrepresenting it as essentially making an ontological claim.

Certainly, one can gain very much towards an understanding of Christianity and other religions from Schopenhauer's religio-moral interpretation of the world; but it is just as certain that he blundered over the value of religion with respect to knowledge. In this he himself was an all too docile pupil of the scientific teachers of his time, who one and all paid homage to romanticism and had renounced the spirit of Enlightenment; born into our own time, he could not possibly have spoken of the sensus allegoricus of religion; he would, rather, have done honor to the truth after his usual fashion with the words: a religion has never yet, either directly or indirectly, either as dogma or as parable, contained a truth. For every religion was born out of fear and need, it has crept into existence along paths of aberrations of reason; once, perhaps, when imperilled by science, it lyingly introduced some philosophical teaching or other into its system, so that later it could be discovered there: but this is a theologian's artifice from the time when religion is already doubting itself. (HAH I:110)

This comes from a section titled "Truth in Religion," and deserves reading in full. Plainly, Nietzsche not only thinks that religion does not contain truth, but that it has never been the function of religion to contain truth. He has Christianity principally in mind, but the observation is clearly general. While the intellect is preoccupied with the question of existence, defended by theological and philosophical artifice, the more crucial issue of value is untouched. A deliberate functional miscategorization of a religious belief system has been effected to preserve from critical scrutiny what is genuinely important to it. The reason why there is so little direct discussion of the existence of God is that he refuses to be taken in by what he perceives as a subterfuge for avoiding the really important issues concerning values. "Christianity has a number of subtleties in its foundations that belong to the Orient. Above all, it knows that it is a matter of absolute indifference whether a thing be true, but a matter of the highest importance *to what extent* it is believed to be true" (A 23). His procedure is the logical consequence of his conception of the essential function of a religious belief system. It would be pointless to make the rational case for the existence of God one of his main preoccupations, having come to the view that insistence on the centrality of the issue was a deliberate smoke screen. In any event, if the function of the ontological component is principally to reinforce the value system, then if the value system is shown to be untenable the need to endorse the ontological claim will disappear. Nor are these the only reasons for not dealing with the issue directly in a traditional way. *"Historical refutation as the definitive refutation.*—In former times, one sought to prove that there is no God— today one indicates how the belief that there is a God could *arise* and how this belief acquired its weight and importance: a counter-proof that there is no God thereby becomes superfluous.—When in former times one had refuted the 'proofs of the existence of God' put forward, there always remained the doubt whether better proofs might not be adduced than those just refuted: in those days atheists did not know how to make a clean sweep" (D 95).

Religion is not alone in undergoing a reassessment of function. Philosophy evokes a similar treatment, and this can fairly be taken as additional, although indirect, support for my interpretation of his view of religion.

> It has gradually become clear to me what every great philosophy has hitherto been: a confession on the part of its author and a kind of un- conscious memoir; moreover, that the moral (or immoral) intentions in every philosophy have every time constituted the real germ of life out of which the entire plant has grown. To explain how a philosopher's most remote metaphysical assertions have actually been arrived at, it is always well (and wise) to ask oneself first: what morality does this (does *he*—) aim at? I accordingly do not believe a "drive to knowledge" to be the father of philosophy, but that another drive has, here as elsewhere, only employed knowledge (and false knowledge!) as a tool. (BGE 6)

If the "drive to knowledge" is not the father of philosophy, then the "drive to knowledge" is certainly not the father of religion.

Even granted the soundness of this interpretation, one could not resolve the substance of the matter concerning the function of religion even if one devoted a whole treatise to it; but Nietzsche's view is chal- lenging. Looking around the world one cannot help being impressed by how the most diverse cultures are converging on their conception of how the natural world works. The knowledge required to build or run television, computers, power stations, communications, shipping, aviation, armament manufacture, sophisticated medical procedures, and so on, appears to be readily agreed upon and easily absorbed. Hin- dus, Moslems, Buddhists, Jews, Shintoists, Christians, and others ap- pear to encounter no problem in achieving a consensus on the knowl- edge required to build an electric power plant, irrespective of their previous views of the natural world. In stark contrast, no such convergence is taking place in regard to religious views. It is hard to maintain that the same "will to truth" that leads to consensus on the knowledge required to build an electric power plant is equally in operation in the formation of religious views. Of course, even an equal "will to truth" would not require an equal convergence, but why is there hardly any convergence at all? His view furnishes an explanation that deserves to be taken seriously.

Let me consider the issue from the standpoint of revaluation strategy. To begin, if the function of a belief system is principally to make an ontological claim, it falls under certain assessment criteria. If the function of a belief system is principally to reinforce a value system, then it falls under different assessment criteria. Explicitly, let me call the mistaken attribution of a function to a belief system a functional miscategorization. Such a miscategorization can have more and less extreme forms. It can be the outright attribution of a function that the belief system does not have at all, or it may involve a claim that a peripheral function is central, or that a central function is peripheral. In either case, functional miscategorization leads to the application of inappropriate assessment criteria.

It was argued previously that Nietzsche is proposing the current moral value-model be replaced by an aesthetic value-model. Put simply, what is argued is that the traditional criteria for assessing people and actions are wrong and need to be replaced by new criteria. An analogous claim is made about religion, but, in the first instance, it is not as extreme, although extreme consequences follow. Whereas what he regards as the moral mode of valuation needs to be directly rejected, in the case of religion we need first to move from assessing it primarily as a system of value-neutral truth-claims about the universe to assessing it primarily as a value system, with its ultimate fate depending on such an assessment.

If a charge of functional miscategorization can be sustained, the belief system will have to be reassessed according to the appropriate new criteria, and not according to the inappropriate old criteria. This is a meta-revaluation; if it is successful it establishes that a revaluation must take place with different criteria, without yet having conducted such a revaluation. This meta-revaluation will be regarded as radical in its own right by some, at any rate, as far as their own religion is concerned, but it does not necessarily have negative connotations for a belief system. It is in principle possible for such a revaluation to be positive.

Nietzsche's revaluation of religion, then, has a two tier structure. First, there is the meta-revaluation that the function of a religious belief system is principally the reinforcement of a value system; it is not principally the articulation of an ontological thesis. It is not driven by the "will to truth." The function of the ontological component is simply to bolster the value system. Second, there is the revaluation of religion based on more appropriate criteria. "The only way to refute priests and religions is this: to show that their errors have ceased to be beneficial— that they rather do harm; in short, that their own 'proof of power' no longer holds good" (WP 157). The scope and intensity of his interest in religion is such that there is no short way of doing it justice; selection is inevitable. I propose to concentrate on strategies in his negative valuation of monotheism and Christianity.

Monotheism and Christianity

Initially it appears that the main questions for Nietzsche concern the origins, nature, and effects of these beliefs, and that the inquiry is essentially historical, sociological, and psychological. In other words, that it is a straightforward empirical inquiry. *Why* do people believe in the existence of God? What are the *causes* or *motives* for this belief? What *needs* or *attitudes* is this belief an expression of? What *kinds of people* and what *kinds of conditions* give rise to such a belief? Who *benefits* by such a belief? Who is *adversely affected* by such a belief? In general terms, what are the *causes* and *consequences* of adherence to such a belief? However, although the questions appear straightforwardly empirical, they are not. These causes, motives, attitudes, conditions, consequences, and so on, are already inextricably entwined with values and theoretical conceptions. He is not undertaking a value-neutral investigation of historical, social, and psychological facts to which considerations of value will independently be applied. To the extent we are faced with a genealogical investigation, the investigation is neither value-neutral nor theory-neutral.

More sense can be made of Nietzsche's approach by considering him as again operating implicitly with types. A central feature of Christian monotheism for him is its basic value orientation to *another world*. The following question is fundamental. What is the nature of a being whose basic value orientation is toward *another world?* The type is grounded in reality and the nature of doctrines that posit other worlds, but it is no mere summary of empirical data, and the relationship between it and empirical data needs to be dealt with in due course. If we take Christianity, for example, it is a complex question how many of its nominal adherents nowadays approximate to this type. No doubt many fail to approximate to it to any significant degree. However, it is more important for him that this overwhelming value orientation toward *another world* is at the core of Christianity; it is central to the Christian scheme of valuation. It is what the doctrine expresses and requires. Of equal importance, the overwhelming orientation toward *another world* is necessarily bound to a cluster of other values. This value cluster can most fruitfully be examined by considering the type in question. The status of this kind of thinking will be taken up later.

Origin

Nietzsche's position can be introduced as follows. In this world there is change, disorder, things come into being and pass away. In this world there is struggle, there is growth and decay, there is instability and unpredictability. There are the weak and the strong. Irrationality and sheer contingency prevail. Pain and suffering appear ineliminable. Everything is permanently in flux. In contrast, God does not change, God is not disordered, God does not come into being and pass away.

> I call it evil and misanthropic, all this teaching about the one and the perfect and the unmoved and the sufficient and the intransitory.
> All that is intransitory—that is but an image! (Z II:2)

God, being omnipotent, has no need to struggle. God does not grow and decline, nor is God unstable and unpredictable. God is always victorious. What impressed itself on Nietzsche is the degree to which God consists of characteristics that are a *negation* of what is found in the world, the very *opposite* of what is found in the world.

For Nietzsche, those who place a higher value on God than on this world must be *despisers of this world* and *despisers of this life*. They are the world-weary, the weak, the ill-constituted, the failures, the powerless, the resentful, those incapable of accepting this world and this life for what it is. "The concept 'God' invented as the antithetical concept to life—everything harmful, noxious, slanderous, the whole mortal enmity against life brought into one terrible unity" (EH XIV:8).

It is not that, having first arrived at belief in God, they then come to despise this world and this life. Rather, first being unable to cope, unable to thrive, and unable to accept this world for what it is, they then created the idea of God as a rationalization of their world-weariness, powerlessness, failure, and devaluation of the world. *This* idea of God issues from a lack of vitality, weakness, an incapacity to cope with a chancy world of constant struggle and change.[5] Thus, he regards God as an ideal produced by the ill-constituted; it is the expression of a depressed and declining life. It is failure to thrive in this world that leads to the construction of another world. Defect, deficiency, and incapacity are the source of Christianity.

There is an evident connection between this and the origin of the slave morality. World-weariness, resentment, and a negative response to the world and life is natural to the slaves. For one, the slaves are the less capable, for another they have to contend with the presence of the masters.

> In my *Genealogy of Morals* I introduced for the first time the psychology of the antithetical concepts of a *noble* morality and a *ressentiment* morality, the latter deriving from a *denial* of the former: but this latter corresponds totally to Judeo-Christian morality. To be able to reject all that represents the *ascending* movement of life, well-constitutedness, power, beauty, self-affirmation on earth, the instinct of *ressentiment* here become genius had to invent *another* world from which that *life-affirmation* would appear evil, reprehensible as such. (A 24)

However, there is another intimate connection with the slave morality. It is not merely an identity of origins. The idea of a single God is closely connected with the idea of morality being equally applicable to all. In other words, it is also connected with the universalizing tendency of morality that is a key feature of the slave morality.

The connection can be explained as follows. In a polytheistic world view there are many ideals of what human beings could be like or what human beings could aspire to. There is a legitimation of diversity. If we take the Greek gods, for example Zeus, Apollo, Dionysus, Prometheus, Poseidon, Athene, and so on, then this very diversity implies there is no unique model suitable for human beings, there is no one way human beings ought to be. Diversity is tolerated, expected, admired, and considered entirely natural. There is diversity, vitality, and dynamic interaction even among the gods.

On the other hand, if we take a monotheistic view of the Christian kind, then matters are clearly otherwise. There is only one higher being, God, and all desirable moral characteristics attach to this being. Thus, there is only one *model* for human beings. There cannot be many types of good human beings. Fundamentally, there can only be one ideal type, namely, that which most closely corresponds to this single model. This dovetails neatly into the slave morality, where the same moral rules are applicable to all, and into the herd morality, which seeks the production of a single type. "The will to a single morality is thereby proved to be a tyranny over other types by that type whom this single morality fits: it is a destruction or leveling for the sake of the ruling type (whether to render the others no longer fearsome or to render them useful)" (WP 315). Indeed, the single Christian God as an ideal is just another facet of the rationalization of a resentment-born desire to impose the same moral rules on all. Monotheism is the veil over a small-spiritedness that cannot tolerate differences.

Many argue monotheism is a more lofty, superior, intrinsically more sublime conception of the deity.[6] Nietzsche's view is the exact opposite. It is polytheism that is the more valuable conception.

> *The greatest advantage of polytheism.*—For an individual to posit his own ideal and to derive from it his own law, joys, and rights—that may well have been considered hitherto as an outrageous human aberration and as idolatry itself. The few who dared as much always felt the need to apologize to themselves, usually by saying: "It wasn't I! Not I! But *a god* through me." The wonderful art and gift of creating gods—polytheism— was the medium through which this impulse could discharge, purify, perfect, and ennoble itself; for originally it was a very undistinguished impulse, related to stubbornness, disobedience, and envy. Hostility against this impulse to have an ideal of one's own was formerly the central law of all morality. There was only one norm, *man*; and every people thought that it possessed this one ultimate norm. But above and outside, in some distant overworld, one was permitted to behold a *plurality of norms*; one god was not considered a denial of another god, nor blasphemy against him. It was here that the luxury of individuals was first permitted; it was here that one first honored the rights of individuals. The invention of gods, heroes, and overmen of all kinds, as well as nearmen and undermen, dwarfs, fairies, centaurs, satyrs, demons, and devils was the inestimable preliminary exercise for the justification of the egoism and sovereignty of the individual: the freedom that one conced-

ed to a god in his relation to other gods—one eventually also granted to oneself in relation to laws, customs, and neighbors. (GS 143)

Nietzsche thought of monotheism as the clearly inferior conception, a point made in the continuation of the same passage:

> Monotheism, on the other hand, this rigid consequence of the doctrine of one normal human type—the faith in one normal god besides whom there are only pseudo-gods—was perhaps the greatest danger that has yet confronted humanity. It threatened us with the premature stagnation that, as far as we can see, most other species have long reached; for all of them believe in one normal type and ideal for their species, and they have translated the morality of mores definitively into their own flesh and blood. In polytheism the free-spiriting and many-spiriting of man attained its first preliminary form—the strength to create for ourselves our own new eyes—and ever again new eyes that are even more our own: hence man alone among all the animals has no eternal horizons and perspectives. (GS 143)

Of course, he distinguishes different monotheistic conceptions, but, in general, the more unified and grand the conception of the deity, the greater the gap between the deity and the world, the more likely it is the product of a small, incapable, resentful, world-negating, and world-weary people. For him, there is an inverse relationship between what he sees as the true stature of a people and the stature of their deity. Those who have the greatest confidence in life, in themselves, and in their own possibilities will have the most diverse gods—gods that are most like themselves. Those who have the least confidence in life, in themselves, and in their own possibilities will have the least diverse gods—gods that are least like themselves. It is the *powerless* who have framed the conception of an *all powerful* god.

Effects

Once such a monotheistic conception is created, it has effects in its own right. Contemplation of it reinforces the negative perceptions and attitudes that gave rise to it. Vague feelings of discontent, failure, disappointment, and resentment are converted into an explicit conception of a better world beyond, and this in turn locks in a perceptual and attitudinal frame where nothing in this world can be of any significant value. Nothing in this world can even approach in value what is in the *other world*. This conception robs us of the capacity to see value in this world. Indeed, the situation is even more serious. The conception arises from a negative valuation of the world and it *both* locks in a negative valuation *and* deepens and strengthens the negative valuation: "The Christian resolve to find the world ugly and bad has made the world ugly and bad" (GS 130).

The implications of this monotheistic conception for the value of human beings and their activities are enormous. No human being can approximate God's goodness. No human being can approximate God's knowledge. No human being can approximate God's power. On this conception the structure of reality itself determines that on every value dimension, human beings can only be a distant second best: "here the highest things are considered unachievable, gifts, 'grace'" (A 21). Of course, even "gifts" can be misleading if we think they can help much. "Gifts" from God will not take us very close in our exemplification of valuable characteristics to their exemplification in God. But even if one regards these characteristics as peripheral and considers the emotions more important the situation does not essentially change. No human love can remotely match God's love, no human compassion can remotely match God's compassion, and so on. It is difficult to see how the conception of what a human being is could fail to be diminished radically in such a comparison.

From the standpoint of value, even the inclusion of free will in this picture is problematic. In one line of reflection on free will, Nietzsche thought of free will as a conceptual instrument, an obvious fiction, to aid the slave morality against those it feared and hated. It is essentially an instrument for blunting tooth and claw, for making human beings tractable. "We no longer have any sympathy today with the concept of 'free will': we know only too well what it is—the most infamous of all the arts of the theologian for making mankind 'accountable' in his sense of the word, that is to say for *making mankind dependent on him*" (TI VI:7). In addition, he was prepared to argue that the notion was conceptually incoherent (BGE 21).

But the issue is worth considering from the standpoint of value, specifically in the context of Christianity. One's free choices, one's goals can only be good if they coincide with God's wishes. If one's free choices and goals run counter to God's wishes then they are automatically bad. What is the point of the power to go counter to God's wishes if any such countermovement necessarily produces something bad? What is the point of free will if its exercise is only good to the degree that it coincides with the will of God? What is the point of free will if any exercise of it contrary to God's will exacts the most fearsome retribution? Only agreement with God is good. Any disagreement with God is bad. "What does 'moral world-order' mean? That there exists once and for all a will of God as to what man is to do and what he is not to do: that the value of a nation, of an individual is to be measured by how much or how little obedience is accorded the will of God" (A 26). That our choices and our plans are *our* choices and *our* plans is of absolutely no valuational significance. Our will has no independent value; it has value only insofar as it agrees with the will of another, namely God. Where can the value be in such a "free will"? Indeed, where can the freedom be in such a "free will"? Where is the freedom when a contrary will extracts a vindictive retribution that imagination cannot surpass?[7] Nietzsche sees "free will" as just a stratagem for the weak to coerce the strong.

If we take specific human activities the situation is no better. Given that a genuine discovery of a truth consists of coming to know what no being has previously known, then no genuine discovery is possible for human beings. For whatever human beings discover is already known to God. On one level, the very effort to discover a truth is pointless. It does not add to what is already known, and it is a mystery why it is not made readily available. "In knowing and in understanding, too, I feel my will's delight in begetting and becoming; and if there is innocence in my knowledge it is because the will to begetting is in it. This will lured me away from God and gods; for what would there be to create if gods—existed!" (Z II:2). Since God is aware of all possibilities, then, just as there can be no genuine discovery, so there can be no genuine creativity. A musical composition can only be a *re*-creation of what God has already contemplated. If genuine creativity requires bringing into existence something that had no previous existence in the universe, then no human being can be genuinely creative if there is an all knowing God. It does not matter whether it is a scientific theory, a literary work, a musical work, a picture, a statue, or a dance piece, it will have been present to God's awareness even before there were human beings.

Consider the following case. Suppose a playwright, totally ignorant of Shakespeare's plays, wrote plays that were word for word identical to the plays written by Shakespeare.[8] How should we regard these as creative acts? No doubt we would regard this person as a remarkable person. On the other hand, we could not help but regard the playwright's activities as a tragic waste; would that this effort and talent had been expended on something else. They produce nothing new; what the playwright does has already been done. The efforts are entirely pointless. We stand to God as this playwright stands to Shakespeare. Whatever we create was already contemplated by the mind of God prior to our existence. There is in principle no way human beings can be the source of genuine novelty in the universe. The best human beings can do is to recreate or rediscover what God has already created or contemplated. For Nietzsche, it is not a source of surprise that art and intellect are not prominent among Christian values.

Without God, it is possible to discover what no being has previously known. Without God, it is possible to have ideas no being has previously had. Without God, it is possible to produce artworks that are genuine novelties in the universe. Without God, it is possible for human beings to make a *unique* contribution to the universe they live in. With God, these possibilities are removed. In a universe with God, both the *actual* value and the *possible* value of human beings is significantly diminished (WP 245), and even this diminished value is derived from another being. God is the great limiter of human possibilities. Further, it is a conception that demotivates the capable from constructive and creative tasks, and invigorates the incapable for repressive and destructive tasks (WP 252).

There is still an important effect to note. Just as this conception is the creation of the weak, the ill-constituted, the failures, the resentful, the world-weary, the world-negators, it is a conception that furthers the interests of this group. The way this operates is central to Nietzsche's negative valuation. It is a vital point that it does not operate by the elevation of this group. It does not seek to increase the health, strength, and vitality of this group; rather it seeks to decrease the health, strength, and vitality of those who have it. "Christianity *needs* sickness almost as much as Hellenism needs a superfluity of health—*making* sick is the true hidden objective of the Church's whole system of salvation procedures" (A 51). Through this conception the ill-constituted seek to gain control by disarming and harming the well-constituted. They turn the well-constituted into the ill-constituted. "Christianity is the revolt of everything that crawls along the ground directed against that which is *elevated;* the Gospel of the 'lowly' *makes* low" (A 43).[9] Incapable of worldly success they seek to destroy the conditions of worldly success in others.

If left merely at a general level, the charges can appear excessive, but if we turn to detail, the charges can look less extreme. A test case is the Christian attitude toward the body. With the invention of the "immortal soul," the body cannot fail to be devalued. But this is not simply an abstract point about logical entailment. Christianity, in fact, has not valued the body highly. The "needs" of the "immortal soul" have always taken precedence over the needs of the body. Indeed, those who have been able to deny their bodies the most have often been held in the highest regard. Values that are within our grasp, dealing with things that we know, are sacrificed on the basis of dubious conceptions. Given the situation of a proven body and an unproven "immortal soul," this stance against the body is a genuine intellectual puzzle (WP 532, 659). Nietzsche not only believes he has an answer to this puzzle, he wants to invert the valuations and accord the body its rightful place.

The Basis of the Case

It is time to be explicit about Nietzsche's methods in his approach to religion. What is so remarkable, if he is right, is that this reference frame where the value of human beings is so significantly diminished is itself a *human invention.* Naturally, there have been contrary views. Both Descartes and Leibniz thought that the idea of God was innate, and they have not been the only ones. Nevertheless, it is surely fair to say that the view that the concept of God is innate is no longer plausible. However, it has an interesting value aspect of its own. What this view supposes is that the human intellect is so weak, so incapable, so puny that it does not even have the power to frame the concept of God, unless God puts it there. It constitutes a neat illustration of the point that this theistic conception contains a frame of reference that almost automatically imposes a negative valuation on human beings and their powers.

A major issue in the revaluation of religion is this. How is the invention of this conception to be explained? If we consult Nietzsche's main work on the issue, *The Anti-Christ,* it is possible to gain the impression that one is dealing with empirical matters of history, sociology, and psychology, but relevant as these may be, they are not the main tools of investigation. The historical, sociological, and psychological data adduced are manifestly too slight for the magnitude of the task. The very insufficiency of the empirical evidence positively invites dismissal of the case as nothing but a parade of prejudices. However, such a response is based on the expectation that a tight empirical case was intended but failed to materialize. But if no tight empirical case was ever intended such a dismissal would be entirely inappropriate. We need to frame a more considered view about the case actually intended before we can sensibly assess it.

A fundamental claim in revaluing Christianity is that the conception of *another world* has been *invented* without evidential warrant (WP 586 [C]). According to Nietzsche, we do not have the transcription of a direct awareness of *another world,* nor do we have a carefully considered, evidentially based, rational inference to *another world.* That the conception is not a transcription of a direct awareness or a soundly based rational inference is neither a historical, nor a sociological, nor a psychological fact. As far as history, sociology, and psychology are concerned, claims of direct awareness have been made, and claims to be advancing a rational case have been made. Whether there has actually been a direct awareness, or whether there has actually been a sound rational case are not matters of either historical, sociological, or psychological fact. That the conception of *another world* must have been *invented* without evidential warrant is the consequence of prior philosophical analysis or investigation.

The fundamental "fact" requiring explanation is neither an established historical nor social nor psychological given. The fundamental "fact" is itself the consequence of theorizing. To say this is not to pass adverse judgment on the claim that the conception of *another world* is *invented* without evidential warrant. It is merely to observe that it is mainly the consequence of analysis and reflection and not of direct empirical investigation, and in the circumstances, it would not be unreasonable to call it a conjecture. This conjecture rules out a priori certain possible explanations of the origin of our conception of another world. A key step in the revaluation of Christianity is the explanation of the *invention* of the conception of another world, but this explanation is an explanation of a conjecture or theoretical supposition and not the explanation of an empirically derived "hard fact."

It is natural to suppose that conjecture or theoretical supposition at the core can only adequately be dealt with by further conjecture or theoretical supposition. Consider the question, What kind of person invents the conception of another world? Nietzsche's answer is that it is a person who is a failure in this world through personal deficiency and who hates it as a consequence. It is a person who lacks the wherewithal to solve his or her life problems in this world. This answer does not report a historical, social, or psychological fact arrived at by any direct empirical investigation. It is a quasi-analytic supposition about what must obtain in the case of a person who takes up an exclusive positive value orientation toward another world. He is again dealing with a type and not with concrete persons. The type that he is implicitly working with is essentially a tool for investigating relations among values; it is not a technique for investigating value-neutral historical, social, or psychological processes. The investigation into the nature of the Christian religion is a highly abstract, theory-laden enterprise, and it is time to bring out more clearly a core aspect of it.

The Conceptual Network

What I call Nietzsche's "conceptual network" occupies an intermediate position between his theory of value and his higher-order values. This conceptual network contains a relatively small number of basic concepts. These are *this world, another world, change, slave, herd, master, autonomous, reactive, resentment, ascending life, declining life, love, hate, revenge, creative, destructive, strength, weakness, ill-constituted, well-constituted, mediocre,* and *will to power.* A series of relations is set up between these fundamental concepts. The slaves are weak, the herd is mediocre, and the masters are strong. The slaves are ill-constituted, and the masters are well-constituted. The strong are autonomous while the weak are reactive. Declining life hates this world while ascending life loves this world. Declining life is weak while ascending life is strong. Ascending life loves change while declining life hates change. The slaves are expressions of declining life while the masters are expressions of ascending life. The slaves hate this world while the masters love this world. The weak hate this world while the strong love this world. Declining life is destructive while ascending life is creative. Thus, the slaves and to a lesser degree the herd are destructive while the masters are creative. The slaves hate and resent the masters, hence the slaves want to revenge themselves on the masters. The masters are indifferent to the slaves and the herd. Declining life hates ascending life while ascending life does not hate declining life. The weak and the mediocre want to curb the power of the strong. The greater the love is for another world the greater the hate is for this world. The greater the love is of this world, the greater the indifference is to another world.

The strong manifest the will to power to a higher degree than the weak or the mediocre. Ascending life manifests the will to power to a higher degree than declining life.[10] These constitute the essential core.

There is a further elaboration adding other notions. The weak seek security and comfort, the strong seek adventure and challenge. The weak seek for a mere continuance of life, the strong seek for an enhancement of life. The weak are content with passivity, the strong seek activity. The weak have a poor self-concept, the strong have a robust self-concept. It immediately follows that declining life seeks security, comfort, a mere continuance of life, that it is content with passivity and has a poor self-concept. On the other hand, ascending life seeks adventure, challenge, enhancement of life, activity, and has a robust self-concept. Further extensions are automatic: if you hate this world you will seek security, comfort, a mere continuance of life; you will be content with passivity, and you will have a poor self-concept. If you love this world you will seek adventure, challenge, enhancement of life, activity, and you will have a robust self-concept. Lower manifestations of the will to power seek ease, higher manifestations of the will to power seek hard tasks. The applications to the slaves, the herd, and the master are immediate and unproblematic, as are the applications to their equivalents—at any rate, near equivalents—plebeian and noble.

The type oriented exclusively toward another world fits directly into this conceptual network. The Christian is identified with this type and a series of consequences immediately follows. The Christian hates this world, is a slave, is weak, is an expression of declining life, is not creative, seeks ease, hates the strong, wants to curb the power of the strong, and so on. To be sure, Nietzsche does not create this conceptual network in a methodologically explicit way. Yet it is this conceptual network that drives the negative valuation of Christianity. Of course, this immediately raises the question of the status of this conceptual network. The problem is pressing since the quasi-analytic character of many of the propositions appears to be at odds with the apparently empirically oriented inquiry into the origins and effects of Christianity.

The conceptual network has a number of features that need clarification before an assessment of it can sensibly take place.

Cohesive

Nietzsche did not think that it was possible for single propositions to be true or false independently of all other propositions. "There are no isolated judgments! An isolated judgment is never 'true,' never knowledge; only in the connection and relation of many judgments is there any surety" (WP 530).[11] So, the conceptual network does not consist, and was never intended to consist of a set of independently verifiable propositions. It would be beside the point to object that not a single one of the above propositions has been independently established, unless one could show that independent verification is in principle possible and appropriate in this case. Now, the attribution of this minimal level of propositional interdependence follows simply from what Nietzsche has to say about judgments in general, but if we look at the above propositions, it is clear that there is a level of conceptual connection in excess of what we expect in narrative history, and is more like the situation in the field of physical dynamics. His conceptual network is a cohesive whole; its basic concepts are tightly interconnected, and its propositions cannot be assessed even in relative isolation. If the conceptual network is to be assessed at all, then it can only be assessed as a whole.

Descriptive

The conceptual network is not narrowly empirical in the sense that sensory perception can directly determine its applicability. But it is descriptive in the minimal sense that one can imagine actual states of affairs to which it would apply and others to which it would not. For example, if those pre-theoretically judged to be the strongest, most dynamic, most successful, most creative invariably had the greatest conviction that there existed "another world," while the weakest, most lethargic, most unsuccessful, most uncreative could on no account be persuaded to believe in the existence of "another world," then it would be fair to conclude the conceptual network had no real application to this world.

Explanatory

The conceptual network is meant to furnish explanations. Why do people come to hate this world?—because of weakness and failure. Why do people invent "another better world"?—because of disenchantment with this world. Why do the weak want to curb the power of the strong?—because it is in their interest and vents their resentment. If we ask about the character of these explanations, it is natural to describe them as a mixture of the causal and the conceptual. In any event, one of its primary roles is to make intelligible fundamental aspects of human valuation.

Evaluative

It is not intended as an exercise in value-neutral social science. For Nietzsche, any knowledge claim whatever is already the expression of some valuation (WP 505). There simply are no value-neutral facts, all facts contain at least covert valuations. But again, there is more to this conceptual network than the covert valuation common to all knowledge claims. It is explicitly evaluative, it contains an evaluative component above that contained in ordinary knowledge claims. If we take the terms "weak," "strong," "slave," "herd," "master," "ascending life," "declining life," "ill-constituted," "well-constituted," "mediocre," and so on, we do not find ourselves in the presence of value-neutral terms to which he has an evaluative response; valuations are already embodied in these terms. On the other hand, they are not purely evaluative either; nonevaluative criteria—insofar as there are such things— also need to be satisfied. The conceptual network is neither purely empirical nor purely evaluative, it is a combination of both.

Abstract

All concepts are abstract in some degree, so the conceptual network cannot fail to be abstract in a minimal sense, but once again more is intended. The concepts of "weak," "strong," "ascending life," "declining life," "power," "ill-constituted," "well-constituted," and so on, are not concepts whose application is restricted to human history, human sociology, human psychology, or human biology, nor are they terms specifically restricted to zoology, botany, or ethology. These are concepts with an application to the whole of life and to the total spectrum of life activities, and hence are inevitably more abstract than the concepts dealt with by the special sciences. Their very abstractness makes the relation between them and observational evidence more problematic, and it positively invites the misconstruction that because the evidence is necessarily not as direct as in the case of the special sciences, it is not evidence at all. The level of abstraction and the valuational aspect suffice to show that the propositions are not simple empirical generalizations.

Attention was drawn previously to Nietzsche's employment of types such as the type oriented exclusively toward the interests of others and the type oriented exclusively toward another world. More sense can now be made of this procedure. Concrete individuals, even if generalizations are made about them, are too complex, too mixed, too varying in the degree to which they exhibit characteristics to ground explanations or to articulate value relations in the conceptual network he sets up. The relevant characteristics need to be isolated, purified, and intensified for the relations between them to become understood, and this is precisely what is intended to be effected when the types are slotted into the conceptual network.

This intellectual procedure is not unusual. In dynamics, we study the relations between mass, force, distance, velocity, acceleration, and so on. Typically, we are not studying concrete cases, nor are we dealing with enumerative inductions from concrete cases; we are dealing with abstract, idealized states of affairs and the relations between them. Even when applying dynamics to a concrete situation, we need to pare away every aspect of the situation that does not feature in the conceptual scheme of dynamics. Put differently, it is only by transforming the individual concrete case into a highly abstracted form, one that will apply to countless numbers of cases differing enormously in theoretically nonrelevant ways, that we can slot it into the general system of relations. Nietzsche's operation with types is analogous. Types must be characterized at a high level of abstraction for the conceptual network to be able to deal with them.

Characterizing a system as descriptive, explanatory, and evaluative at the same time may appear dubious to those raised on the view that there is a clear "fact-value" distinction. But drawing such a distinction depends on controversial epistemological and semantic theses and cannot be accepted as established fact. To use a familiar but apt form of words, it is another dogma of empiricism. If we accept what appear to be the implications of Quinean holism, then we can no more separate factual sentences from evaluative sentences, than we can analytic sentences from synthetic sentences.[12] The capacity to define and determine sameness and difference of meaning is equally implicated in both issues.[13] Without being able to define and determine sameness of meaning, all we could claim is that the interconnected whole enables us to both describe and evaluate, but through the interconnection of sentences it would be impossible to designate individual sentences as purely evaluative or purely factual. It is not my intention to promote a kind of Quinean holism[14] just because it helps

Nietzsche. The aim is simply to point out that there is no proven error in seeking to combine in one system the characteristics Nietzsche seeks to combine. On views currently in high regard, what he seeks to do is undoubtedly feasible.

Let me accept that a conceptual structure combining the characteristics attributed to Nietzsche's conceptual network is possible. This conceptual network is the device that drives the highly negative revaluation of Christianity, and at the same time embodies alternative values. The crucial question now is, what are the grounds for accepting his conceptual network? The answer has already been furnished in general terms in chapters 1 and 2. This conceptual network will have to accommodate the critically scrutinized phenomena of valuation better than its rivals as well as successfully defending its claims about the world. But it is both desirable and possible to go beyond these generalities.

As argued, Nietzsche's conceptual network is not a set of propositions merely expressing his own subjective reactions. If that is all they were, then they may well be subject to rational scrutiny, but the impetus to rational scrutiny would be diminished in the face of what was not intended to be a rational case. No doubt, if one felt the same way one would embrace them, and if one did not, one would reject them. But the matter would not really be one to warrant much rational debate. There are those who have taken him this way and have concluded that there is no rational case to contend with. But this reaction is unwarranted. We are not dealing simply with a set of subjective value judgments. Indeed, there are three major rational constraints determining the acceptability of his conceptual network. First, there is its fit with his theory of value. Second, there is its fit with his higher-order values. Third, there is its fit with the "world." The fit with the first two is straightforward, so let me turn to the third.

Clearly, Nietzsche's conceptual network is not a set of simple empirical generalizations arrived at by enumerative induction. Nor is it easy to conceive direct experiments that could settle its fate. Further, in the sense required by the absolute theory of truth, there is no "fact of the matter" about whether his conceptual network directly mirrors reality. Yet, if the above case is sound, the network has a descriptive aspect. The challenge is to find a model that can accommodate these points and yet permit rational grounds for accepting or rejecting such conceptual networks. There is a model that suits, and given the importance of the status of the conceptual network to the case against Christianity, I proceed to it directly. Indeed, given the novelty of recourse to the model in this context, a deliberate defense of its suitability is required.

The model is geometry, and to aid the discussion let me begin with Euclidean geometry. Although Euclidean geometry is not a collection of empirical generalizations, it was preceded by considerable empirical investigation, particularly by the Egyptians.[15] The codification, systematization, and idealization that is Euclidean geometry did not spring from thin air; it is grounded in well-investigated empirical phenomena. It is this that gives it its descriptive character. But it is also an abstract systematization and idealization, and as such, the epistemic link between it and the material that was the occasion for its conception is problematic. The propositions appear to have a quasi-analytic character, and without adding nongeometrical assumptions, direct experimental tests are not possible. The principal basis for its subsequent acceptance was neither its empirical origins nor its experimental support. The principal basis for its acceptance was that, at that time, nobody could conceive of an adequate alternative.[16] Independent evidential support was simply not a significant issue.

Let me pause for a comparison. Nietzsche's conceptual network does not contain straightforward empirical generalizations, but his own observations of the world form the basis for his abstract systematization and idealization. Its propositions, too, appear to have a quasi-analytic character, and direct experimental tests do not appear possible. However, even if the parallel is accepted up to this point, it is proper to observe that one can readily conceive of alternatives to his conceptual network, and that therefore the issue of its acceptability remains unresolved. So be it, but alternative geometries have also been invented, and we equally have a problem of what the rational basis is for choosing among them. It is here that the crux of the matter is to be sought.

What is the geometry of space? Is it Euclidean? Is it non-Euclidean? At first glance, it is natural to suppose that however difficult the experimental investigations may prove to be, the matter can in principle be settled by experimental investigation alone. Nevertheless, according to one of the strongest candidates for an acceptable answer on this issue, there simply is no fact of the matter as to whether space is or is not Euclidean. The most sophisticated advocate of the position is

Grünbaum.[17] The starting point is that a *pure* geometry is not empirically testable and that specific steps need to be taken before testing can begin. We need to link the geometrical terms with features of the physical world, and even then we can only ever put to test a combination of geometrical claims and physical assumptions. But for Grünbaum, if a geometry combined with a set of physical assumptions passes all experimental tests this does not settle the matter that this is the actual geometry of space. It does not even furnish us with a rational basis for the belief that this is the actual geometry of space.

According to Grünbaum, in the combined testing of the geometry and physical assumptions we also need to make certain stipulations about the behavior of our measuring devices: "And hence there can be no question at all of an *empirically* or factually determinate metric geometry or chronometry until *after* a physical stipulation of congruence."[18] One such stipulation might be that measuring rods neither contract nor expand under transport. Without such stipulations no experimental investigation of geometry can proceed, yet these stipulations themselves are not candidates for truth or falsity; there is no fact of the matter to be settled. Merely to ask the question of how we could objectively determine whether there had been a change of length in our ultimate standard of length is to be immediately confronted with the core problem. For Grünbaum there is no alternative to stipulation, but alternative stipulations are always possible.

In the circumstances of the experimental success of one combination of geometry, stipulations concerning measuring devices and physical assumptions, if we replace the original geometry with another geometry, then provided we furnish the appropriate alternative stipulations about the behavior of the measuring devices, we can have a system that passes all the actual and possible experimental tests of the original. Consequently, mindful of the fact that there is no truth of the matter regarding the stipulations about measuring devices, there is no truth of the matter about the real geometry of space. Grünbaum characterizes space as "intrinsically metrically amorphous"; this means that we have to impose a metrical geometry on space, for there is no metrical geometry intrinsic to space that we can just read off it: "Our concern is to note that, even disregarding inductive imprecision, the empirical facts themselves do *not* uniquely dictate the truth of either Euclidean geometry or one of its non-Euclidean rivals in virtue of the lack of an intrinsic metric."[19] It is important to understand that this is not a mere skepticism about being able to come to know the true geometrical structure of space. Grünbaum maintains that there is no such structure to be known.

Ultimately, the choice of geometry turns on pragmatic and systemic considerations. The geometry providing the simplest, most comprehensible, easiest to use overall system will be preferred. This gives an idea of how to choose between geometries, but it does not tell us why we should choose any in the first place. The answer is readily at hand. We need a systematic conception of spatial phenomena to have any understanding of physical phenomena in general and for the success of the tasks we undertake in space. We can understand more and do vastly more with a geometry than without one. The fact that a metrical geometry is imposed rather than discovered in no way implies that it is easy to create an adequate geometrical structure, or that the choice between geometries is a matter of mere whim. Of course, there are critics of Grünbaum's view,[20] but there is no need for the matter to be definitively resolved. What is of importance is that we have a distinctive model of the rational basis for accepting a certain kind of conceptual structure, and furthermore, a model that is taken with complete seriousness.

It is useful to review briefly the characteristics of a geometry. A geometry is not a system of inductive generalizations, nor is it directly experimentally testable; yet it did arise from empirical observation. It is abstract, and the systematic interconnections it effects render spatial phenomena intelligible. It is applicable to the physical world, useful in human enterprises; yet, if Grünbaum is right, it does not characterize an actual independently existing geometric structure. These are the characteristics that also belong to Nietzsche's conceptual network. It does not consist of empirical generalizations, nor is it directly experimentally testable, yet it arose from his observation of life. It is abstract and the systematic interconnections it effects render valuational phenomena intelligible. It is applicable to the world of human beings; yet, if Nietzsche is right, it does not characterize an actual independently existing structure. Perhaps the *explicitly valuational* components of his conceptual network can be seen to be analogous to the *stipulations* concerning measuring devices in physical geometry.

These observations help to deal with three objections against Nietzsche's conceptual network. First, there is the objection that there are insufficient particular empirical facts and insufficient empirical generalizations to support it. This simply fails to recognize the point that there are conceptual structures that arise from observation of the world but which through abstraction, idealization, and systematization come to be severed from a direct dependence on specific observations and specific generalizations. Euclid's *Elements* constitutes a relevant case; particular empirical facts and specific empirical generalizations are not marshalled as evidence, nor are they required. Second, there is the objection that the conceptual network is nothing but a set of tautologies such as "The strong are expressions of ascending life," and "The weak are expressions of declining life," and so on, and that as such, it does not touch reality at any point. To reply, in an abstract, idealized system there is a greater tendency for propositions to seem tautological when they are merely abstract and idealized. However, even tautologies have a role in making conceptual links explicit, and while there can be no doubt that his conceptual network contains tautologies, the network as a whole has positive content. Circumstances can be envisaged to which it would be inapplicable. Third, there is the objection that the conceptual network is nothing beyond Nietzsche's subjective value reactions, and that as such it may or may not reflect one's own individual feelings, but it does not constitute a candidate for *rational* acceptance or rejection. Remoteness from an observational base, the quasi-analytic appearance of many of the propositions, together with the undoubted fact that his values are expressed in the network, may impel to such a view. But while it clearly contains his valuations, I have sought to show that it is more than that, and that it seeks to make intelligible a range of valuational phenomena. It is fair to conclude his conceptual network is a candidate for application to the world, and that its applicability is subject to rational constraints appropriate to structures of such a kind.

In putting forward this conception of Nietzsche's procedure I am mindful of his observation, "I mistrust all systematizers and avoid them. The will to a system is a lack of integrity" (TI I:26). However, his conceptual network no more exhausts his philosophical views than geometry exhausts our characterization of the physical world. In addition, the following observations ought to be noted. "We have no right to *isolated* acts of any kind: we may not make isolated errors or hit upon isolated truths. Rather do our ideas, our values, our yeas and nays, our ifs and buts, grow out of us with the necessity with which a tree bears fruit—related and each with an affinity to each, and evidence of *one* will, *one* health, *one* soil, *one* sun" (GM Preface, 2). In claiming Nietzsche is operating with this conceptual network I am not attributing to him an all-embracing philosophical system; if he has one, this conceptual network could only be a part of it; and, as the quotation reveals, he thought that the systematic connection and integration of ideas, values, and judgments was both inevitable and desirable. Although I do not claim he self-consciously sets up this conceptual network, I do claim that this conceptual network is latent in the later works, and I do not believe that he would have resisted its characterization as a tightly integrated whole.

Assuming the legitimacy of attributing this conceptual network, two important questions remain. On what basis are we to choose between Nietzsche's conceptual network and its competitors? And, why choose any such network at all? Let me tackle the latter question first. One can no more live without valuing than one can live without movement in space. To be sure, one can move in space without a self-consciously articulated geometry, and one can live without a self-consciously articulated conceptual structure dealing with values, but as one seeks to extend one's understanding of the physical world, and as the tasks one wishes to accomplish in the physical world become more complex, the need for an explicit geometry furnishing a systematization of spatial characteristics becomes more urgent. By the same token, as one seeks to extend one's understanding of the world of valuing beings, and as the tasks one wishes to accomplish in the world of valuing beings become more complex, the need for an explicit conceptual structure throwing light on the valuations of valuing beings becomes more urgent.

Failure to understand one's values and the values of those around one are not notable contributors to the success of one's enterprises. A conceptual structure capable of even modestly increasing understanding here would be welcome. The next step is straightforward in principle, but less so in practice. On what basis are we to decide between Nietzsche's conceptual network and its alternatives? In general terms the answer is simple. We select the conceptual network that gives us the greatest intellectual control combined with the greatest capacity to promote the success of our actions among valuing beings. The basis for choice is substantially parallel to the case of geometry. The criteria are in essence the criteria for selecting the best among available perspectives.

The Aftermath

Nietzsche's attack on Christianity operates on three levels. First, there is a claim that the principal concepts deployed in the Christian belief system have no application to reality. At this level there is no invocation of his conceptual network; it is the kind of criticism that can be made by persons whose theoretical commitments diverge significantly from his own.

> In Christianity neither morality nor religion come into contact with reality at any point. Nothing but imaginary *causes* ("God," "soul," "ego," "spirit," "free will,"—or "unfree will"): nothing but imaginary *effects* ("sin," "redemption," "grace," "punishment," "forgiveness of sins"). A traffic between imaginary *beings* ("God," "spirits," "souls"); an imaginary *natural* science (anthropocentric; complete lack of the concept of natural causes); an imaginary *psychology* (nothing but self-misunderstandings, interpretations of pleasant and unpleasant general feelings, for example the condition of the *nervus sympathicus*, with the aid of the sign-language of religio-moral idiosyncrasy—"repentance," "sting of conscience," "temptation by the devil," "the proximity of God"); an imaginary *teleology* ("the kingdom of God," "the Last Judgment," "eternal life"). This purely fictitious world is distinguished from the world of dreams, very much to its disadvantage, by the fact that the latter *mirrors* actuality, while the former falsifies, disvalues and denies actuality. (A 15)

Fairness requires noting that this is more the program for a critical attack than the critical attack itself. But nothing here suggests that we need to appeal to anything other than the standard criteria for determining the adequacy of a theory to dispose of these conceptions as he would wish. The focus is on the intrinsic cognitive defects of the belief system.

To be sure, the above quotation does not exhaust Nietzsche's case, but however sympathetic one may be to his views it can hardly be maintained that there is sufficient detailed argument to establish his position. It is tempting to conclude that here revaluation has not succeeded, and this is certainly so if definitive refutation is required. But while definitive refutation may be the ideal form of revaluation, it is by no means the only form. The mere claim that these Christian notions are fictions does not establish that they are. However, the claim, even if inadequately supported, does not leave the dialectical situation untouched. The notions may not be decisively refuted, but they have been challenged, and the explicit challenge itself changes the dialectical situation. For the challenge immediately raises the issue of what there is to validate positively the application of these notions. The challenge puts Christianity into a defensive position it may not be able to maintain, and will, in any event, find difficult to maintain. His arguments may not be decisive, but the target is left less secure, and that is itself a significant change of status. Second, there is the recategorization of the function of a religious belief system as primarily articulating a value system rather than an ontological thesis. To the degree that this move is successful it mitigates criticisms of the incompleteness of the arguments on the first level.

The third level of assessment invokes Nietzsche's conceptual network. The emphasis is no longer merely on the intrinsic cognitive defects of the Christian belief system but rather on its valuational defects. The difference is marked by a transition from purely destructive criticism to explanation. Once explanations are proposed his conceptual network comes into play.

> Once the concept "nature" had been devised as the concept antithetical to "God," "natural" had to be the word for "reprehensible"—this entire fictional world has its roots in *hatred* of the natural (—actuality!—), it is the expression of a profound discontent with the actual. . . . *But that explains everything.* Who alone has reason to *lie himself out* of actuality? He who *suffers* from it. But to suffer from actuality means to be an abortive actuality. . . . The preponderance of feelings of displeasure over feelings of pleasure is the *cause* of a fictitious morality and religion: such a preponderance, however, provides the *formula* for *décadence.* (A 15)

Here is an application of Nietzsche's conceptual network. If we reduce the complete application of his conceptual network to Christianity to the bare minimum, we have the following. Christianity is produced by the ill-constituted to promote the interests of the ill-constituted at the expense of the well-constituted. Of course, the ideal case for revaluation requires a demonstration that his conceptual network is rationally superior. Bias need not be invoked to assert that this unqualified rational superiority has not been established. But it would be an error to maintain that this is the only condition in which serious revaluation can take place.

Let me consider representative possibilities. Suppose Nietzsche's conceptual network to have exactly the same level of rational warrant as the Christian belief system. Does this imply the complete failure of revaluation? Surely no such thing is implied. If we return again to the case of geometry, the mere invention of a consistent alternative geometry to Euclidean geometry immediately and dramatically altered its status. Even on the assumption of an equivalent level of rational warrant for the alternative pure geometries, the status of Euclidean geometry is significantly downgraded. The situation is no different here. Even if Nietzsche has only produced a conceptual network with no greater or lesser rational warrant than the Christian belief system, a significant revaluation takes place.

Put generally, the more the rational warrant for Nietzsche's conceptual network exceeds the rational warrant for the Christian belief system the more effective the revaluation. As the rational warrant for his conceptual network falls below the rational warrant for the Christian belief system the less effective the revaluation becomes. But even here there is still a measure of revaluation. A new unrefuted alternative, even if not as well supported as the competitors already in the field, diminishes the status of those competitors. Clearly, if his conceptual network has optimal rational warrant, and the Christian belief system has no rational warrant, then the revaluation has been completely successful. On the other hand, if the Christian belief system has optimal rational warrant, and his conceptual network has no rational warrant whatever, then the revaluation has been completely unsuccessful. But it is a mistake to suppose that something serious can be accomplished only if one of these two extremes is arrived at. There are significant degrees of change of status between these extremes.

When we turn to the substantive issue of the actual comparative rational warrants of the Christian belief system and Nietzsche's conceptual network, we are faced with a situation of great complexity. In support of a claim of superior rational warrant for his conceptual network one might point to his critical attack on the applicability of the Christian concepts prior to the invocation of his own conceptual network. In addition one might contend that his conceptual network furnishes an explanation of the origin of the Christian belief system, while the Christian belief system furnishes no explanation of the origin of his conceptual network, except in the trivial sense that any view contrary to the Christian view would be explained as arising from the human propensity to error or as the work of the devil, or both. But even a warranted claim of explanatory superiority on this point would hardly be enough to establish the case in general. To be sure, his critical observations independent of the invocation of his conceptual network are not without effect; but by the same token his conceptual network might contain its own difficulties.

To summarize. Few would argue seriously that Nietzsche has proved his case, hence the revaluation is not the complete success that it might be, but only the biased would deny that a formidable case has been mounted. His critique has permanently altered the intellectual landscape. It has injected into that landscape a vigorous point of view that, difficult as it may be to prove in its own right, raises doubts about Christianity that are as difficult to dispel as Christianity is to establish. The conceptual network that drives his revaluation is a legitimate intellectual construct whose application is subject to rational assessment. Ideal revaluation would require a demonstration of the incontestable rational superiority of this conceptual network. But a measure of revaluation also occurs in the case where there is simply no demonstration of the nonviability of this conceptual network, even without positive support for it. A superior alternative is not required for a revaluation effect; a viable alternative suffices, but of course, its efficacy is not as great.

The principal steps in the revaluation are the initial reassessment of the function of a religious belief system, the criticism of the cognitive status of the Christian belief system, the deployment of types and Nietzsche's own conceptual network to explain and pass a negative valuation on the Christian belief system and on its values in particular. What is novel from the standpoint of revaluation is the kind of intellectual structure he creates, and the propensity to approach issues of value through types that fit into that structure.

FIVE

Aesthetic Values

The Place of Art

Nietzsche's estimate of art went through several phases. There is great enthusiasm for art in his first work, *The Birth of Tragedy;* there is a noticeable cooling toward art in the period represented by *Human, All Too Human, Daybreak,* and *The Gay Science;* and then there is the return of a positive attitude in the later writings. Although this later positive attitude is strong, it never matches the original enthusiasm. The later views are central to the enterprise of revaluing values, and it is largely these that will be considered. In any event, his later sympathy for the arts is still as unmistakable as his antipathy to slave morality and Christianity. There is a connection between the two attitudes. Slave morality and Christianity arise from a negating, incapacity-driven rejection of this world; their orientation is to another world and they are antithetical to the arts for this reason. On the other hand, positively to embrace the arts is positively to embrace what is offered by this world.

> Our religion, morality, and philosophy are decadence forms of man. The *countermovement: art.* (WP 794)

> In the main, I agree more with artists than with any philosopher hitherto: they have not lost the scent of life, they have loved the things of "this world"—they have loved their senses. (WP 820)

The arts are a sphere where attitudes of life-affirmation naturally flourish. But of course that does not imply an uncritical acceptance of all art.

The potential of art to enhance life is ranked above that of morality and religion throughout Nietzsche's reflections on the matter. But morality and religion are seen in extremely negative terms, and the question naturally arises of how art stands in relation to values he regarded more positively. Knowledge is the most obvious case to take;

it is typically held in high regard, but its relative position also varies. In his early period, art is clearly rated above knowledge. In the middle period, the relation changes and knowledge is valued above art. In the final period, art is once again placed above knowledge, though not as far above it as in the first period.[1] In any event, there is no question that, in the final period, art is regarded as a positive value of the first rank.

Given that the potential of art to enhance life is placed above that of morality and religion, it is noteworthy that we are already faced with an important attempt to reverse prevailing Western systems of value that place morality and religion above the arts. However, the ordering challenged is neither universal nor inevitable: "traditional Japanese culture was structured, so to speak, with its aesthetic values at the center. Aesthetic concerns often prevailed even over religious beliefs, ethical duties, and material comforts."[2] On the other hand, Nietzsche's positive attitude toward the arts has the consequence that his revaluations here appear less dramatic and less incisive than elsewhere, and this impression is reinforced by the fact that there were important changes in his views on art. But if we keep in mind that his attitude toward morality and religion is negative, while his attitude toward the arts is largely positive, we will not be misled into supposing that just because his revaluations appear less radical here that they are either unimportant or ineffective.

There is a further factor contributing to the impression that Nietzsche's revaluations are less revolutionary here, and that is that subjectivism about aesthetic values appears more natural and has always been more widely spread than subjectivism in morality. Insofar as he can be seen to be supporting some form of subjectivism, he will not seem to be supporting anything especially revolutionary. But we need to be careful here. In the chapter on moral values two levels of subjectivity were distinguished, that belonging to perspectival truths in general, and the higher level of subjectivity belonging to moral and religious claims. For him, aesthetic judgments do not belong to the highest level of subjectivity, but equally they do not belong to the highest level of objectivity attainable by perspectival truths. Judgments of aesthetic value do not have an entirely inferior cognitive status, but they are not as objective as it is possible for judgments to be in his general framework.

Let me amplify the last point. For Nietzsche, thinking about the world in terms of "subject," "object," "attribute," "cause," and so on, may be unavoidable for human beings (WP 487). Neither the weak, the mediocre, nor the strong may be able to frame acceptable perspectives without these concepts. He is prepared to allow there may be features of the human perspective we cannot vary at will. By contrast, what is beautiful for the strong will not typically be beautiful for the weak or the mediocre, and what is beautiful for the weak or the mediocre will not typically be beautiful for the strong (WP 804, 852). Take a mundane example. The judgment that something is a tree will be more objective than the judgment that a sonata is beautiful. Agreement in judgment is to be expected on the former, but not on the latter. Nevertheless, the judgments of beauty will not be pure fictions or inventions either, and the acknowledgment of variability does not entail complete subjectivity.

Nietzsche is no more a radical subjectivist about aesthetic claims, in which anybody's claim is as good as anybody else's, than he is a radical subjectivist about truth claims, although it is difficult to deny that he is more of a subjectivist about beauty than truth. There are, then, two aspects to the superiority of art over morality and religion. On the one hand the substantive values art yields are greater than those of morality and religion, and on the other the cognitive status of aesthetic claims is superior to that of morality and religion. One way of putting it is this. While morality and religion are pure fictions, or pure inventions, aesthetic claims are grounded in the real world, and while they may not be candidates for the maximal objectivity attainable in his framework, they are not ranked with the maximally subjective either.

It may be thought unnecessary to introduce a further category for aesthetic judgments, but it fits Nietzsche's views. He emphasizes that art does not function the way science, or morality, or religion do. Indeed, he asserts that art saves us from truth. It is hard to see how it could do so, if aesthetic awareness and aesthetic judgments simply embody truth on a par with scientific truth. Equally, it is difficult to accord aesthetic judgments the same purely subjective, fictional status accorded moral and religious judgments that have no grounding in this world. A key point about art lovers is their strong attachment to the things of this world, and this requires that aesthetic characteristics be grounded in this world in some way.

Although Nietzsche's positive attitude toward art declined in the middle period and recovered in the later period, there is a relative constancy in that his attitude toward art remained basically favorable. However, there is one major change in his views on art. In the early *The Birth of Tragedy*, art gives meaning or value to life: "I am convinced that art represents the highest task and the true metaphysical activity of this life" (BT Preface). To be sure, not just any art does this, but it is in art and nowhere else that the answer lies. Put another way, the value of life is held to be a problem, and art is advanced as the solution. In the later writings, such as *Twilight of the Idols,* the very attitude that puts the value of life in question is forcefully attacked: "For a philosopher to see a problem in the *value* of life thus even constitutes an objection to him, a question-mark as to his wisdom, a piece of unwisdom" (TI II:2). In his later thought the value of art is a problem, and art finds its value in the stimulus to life it furnishes. Put simply, in the early view art justifies life, in the later view life justifies art. Put another way, in the early view life derives its value from art, in the later view art derives its value from life. Of course, this is a dramatic change in his valuation of art, but in either phase it leaves the value of art above morality and religion. These later views invoke his higher-order values and aspects of the conceptual network identified in the last chapter.

More detailed consideration of Nietzsche's revaluation strategies here requires identification of what he opposes. In some cases the targets are plainly identified, but in others, as in the case of truth, what he opposes needs reconstruction from indirect observations and the prevailing views of the time. Since my focus is on his later views, my approach does not require strict chronological exposition, but relevant changes in his views will be noted.

The Principal Elements

To lend form to the discussion, let me chart a conceptual map independently of Nietzsche by reference to which views on art can be more clearly understood. Five elements and the relations between them are crucial to providing an adequate account of the arts. They are the *artist,* the *artwork,* the *real world,* the *art audience,* and the *background society.* It is a noteworthy characteristic of the great theories of art that have dominated thinking on these issues that they have focused on some of these factors to the almost total exclusion of the rest.

The imitation or representation theory[3] provides an account of art primarily in terms of the relation between the *artwork* and the *real world,* while the expression theory, and its subvariants such as the freudian theory of art provide an account in terms of the relation between the *artist* and the *artwork.* The institutional theory provides an account in terms of the *artwork* and the *art audience,* while the marxist theory provides an account in terms of the relation between the *artwork* and the *background society.* The most austere of the major theories, the formalist theory, provides an account solely in terms of the intrinsic characteristics of the *artwork* itself.[4]

Although Nietzsche's position changed over time, it is useful to begin by characterizing his mature stance on one of the major theories of art in the Western world, namely, the representation theory. According to the simplest form of this theory the principal function of art is to imitate or represent reality with as great a fidelity as possible. The less the artwork deviates from the reality it seeks to depict, the better it is as an artwork. The theory has its most immediate and intelligible application to the visual arts and literature, but can be applied to all the arts. It is a theory about the function of art, and it embodies a criterion of what constitutes good art. This theory is substantially at variance with Nietzsche's later thoughts on art.

To take the visual arts as a critical example. According to Nietzsche, the way we are perceptually aware of the world is already a creative act. In perception we do not simply read off reality the way it is in itself; the human species has forged a way of representing the world perceptually to suit its own kind. An imitation or representation in art of what we are already perceptually aware would be totally pointless. It would be an uncreative act of copying what was itself the result of a prior creative act. But in addition, the human perceptual point of view is forged principally for practical purposes; utility for the species is the key consideration. The *re*-presentation of the world conceived in this way simply has no serious point.

Clearly, the representation theory also implies a most unflattering conception of the artist. The artist not only is not creative, the artist must not be creative. To the extent that creativity implies deviation from what is merely presented, to that extent creativity is bad. An artist may, perhaps, be creative about techniques, but he or she may not be creative about content. On this view there cannot be any more to a good artist than technical skill in imitation. Further, it should be noted that this theory is not just a philosopher's invention. Consider the following remarks of Leonardo da Vinci, where the theory appears to be unreservedly espoused: "When you wish to see whether the general effect of your picture corresponds with that of the object presented by nature, take a mirror and set it so that it reflects the actual thing, and then compare the reflection with your picture and consider carefully whether the subject of the two images is in conformity with both, studying especially the mirror."[5] The inapplicability of the suggestion even to such pictures as Leonardo's own *The Last Supper* makes the grip of the conception puzzling, but one cannot avoid its implications. The artist is a passive transcriber of an independently fixed scene and has no positive contribution to make. This view is far removed from Nietzsche's conception of the nature and proper role of the artist: "Nature, artistically considered, is no model. It exaggerates, it distorts, it leaves gaps. Nature is *chance.* To study 'from nature' seems to me a bad sign: it betrays subjection, weakness, fatalism—this lying in the dust before *petits faits* is unworthy of the *complete* artist. Seeing *what is*—that pertains to a different species of spirit, the *anti-artistic,* the prosaic. One has to know *who* one is" (TI IX:7).

The implications for the art audience, and for the value of the artwork, are no better. The art audience is a mere passive contemplator of what is presented to it. But more seriously, the very contemplation of art appears pointless. On this view, the art audience is not presented with anything new it does not encounter in everyday life; it is presented with just the same once again. Art has no distinctive contribution to make to the values of life if the unmodified representation theory is correct. No enhancement of life can be gained from the contemplation of art that cannot just as readily be gained from the contemplation of the reality it depicts. Aristotle suggests that it is natural for human beings to take pleasure in imitation as such.[6] But even allowing that such pleasure constitutes some enhancement of life, it is difficult to see such enhancement as in any way major.

It is useful to relate this to Nietzsche's early views in his first book, *The Birth of Tragedy.* There the notions of the Apollinian and the Dionysian are introduced. The Apollinian factor is that in human beings which brings dreams, seeks to individuate and discriminate, seeks to control and impose order, seeks security, repose, and familiarity. It is the factor underlying the urge to individuation, differentiation, the quest for objectivity, and clearheaded self-knowledge and self-possession. The Dionysian factor is that in human beings which seeks intoxication and ecstasy, seeks for an obliteration of distinctions, seeks an abandonment of controls, seeks participation and action, seeks forgetfulness and change. Sculpture is the characteristically Apollinian art form, while music is the characteristically Dionysian art form, although the ideal for the art of tragedy is a balance between the two. Naturally, there are difficult issues here about the ontological status of these factors and the legitimacy of the distinctions. However, several points can be extracted of concern to the present enterprise.

There is a trace of the representation theory in Nietzsche's conception of art at this stage, and in particular of tragedy, for the Dionysian factor is credited with a capacity for revealing the tragic nature of reality at a more fundamental level than is gleaned from commonsense observation or scientific investigation. In this two-tier view, imitation or representation is in some measure rescued from triviality by having the most significant level of reality as its object. Yet already this is not the most important aspect of art for him. What is crucial is the way art can deal with this revelation. It is the capacity to celebrate in the face of terrifying existence that constitutes the positive contribution of art, and of tragedy in particular. "That life is really so tragic would least of all explain the origin of an art form—assuming that art is not merely imitation of the reality of nature but rather a metaphysical supplement of the reality of nature, placed beside it for its overcoming. The tragic myth too, insofar as it belongs to art at all, participates fully in this metaphysical intention of art to transfigure" (BT 24). The mere representation of a terrifying existence is not valued in its own right. It is what art can do beyond mere representation that is important to it. Thus, even in his earliest work there is a clear trend away from any simple representation theory.

The point is reinforced by Nietzsche's suggestion in *The Birth of Tragedy* that the meaning of human existence lies in art rather than knowledge. This clearly requires a conception of art that does not merely attribute to art the function of imitating or representing reality with the least possible deviation. It requires a conception of art as making its most important contribution either independently of, or at most in conjunction with, imitation and representation. An additional point is that both the Apollinian and Dionysian factors are seen as essentially creative, the Dionysian as the basic source of emotional content, and the Apollinian as the active producer of rationality and form. These conceptions, with their implications of creativity, are not compatible with the representation theory unless it is heavily qualified.

Nietzsche expressed dissatisfaction with his early views in a later preface to *The Birth of Tragedy*, and the form in which he expressed this dissatisfaction suggests limits to what can profitably be derived from these earlier views; but they are useful as indicators of modes of thinking that persist in later theorizing. In any event, the gap between Nietzsche and the representation theory only increased with time. The degree of adherence to the representation theory in his early work is dependent on the concurrently espoused two-tier conception of reality. The abandonment of the two-tier view of reality implicit in *The Birth of Tragedy* is important, for it robs imitation or representation of the possibility of any higher task.

While it is useful to locate Nietzsche in relation to the major theories of art, and more of this will be done later, such a location is dependent on what is implicit rather than what is explicit. Typically, his focus is on more specific issues, and it is these that now need to be considered, but it must be kept in mind that these issues are closely related to each other and to more general positions.

The Artist

Undoubtedly the principal feature of Nietzsche's revaluation in the arts is the centrality he attributes to the role of the artist.[7] Consider the following elevated picture of the tragic artist: "*What does the tragic artist communicate of himself?* Does he not display precisely the condition of *fearlessness* in the face of the fearsome and questionable?—This condition is itself a high desideratum: he who knows it bestows on it the highest honors. He communicates it, he *has* to communicate it if he is an artist, a genius of communication. Bravery and composure in the face of a powerful enemy, great hardship, a problem that arouses aversion—it is this *victorious* condition which the tragic artist singles out, which he glorifies" (TI IX:24). In Nietzsche's value system invigoration and enrichment are what finally count. Where the greater activity and creativity lie, there lies the greater value; conversely, where the lesser activity and creativity lie, there lies the lesser value. It is essential to his conception that the artist *creates* and that creation is an *active* enterprise. It is here that we must begin: "all I wish to underline is that Kant, like all philosophers, instead of envisaging the aesthetic problem from the point of view of the artist (the creator), considered art and the beautiful purely from that of the 'spectator'" (GM III:6). Of all that is involved in art, it is the artist that is the most active and creative element, and it is the creativity of the artist that is the most important element. What matters most to art is the artist. Flattering as this is to artists, there is at least an element of paradox here.

Let me take up this point. Almost automatically one assumes artworks themselves are the most important components in art and that the artist is merely a means to their production. But on further reflection it is natural to regard the artworks not as ends in themselves but as means, that is, as the furnishers of rewarding aesthetic experiences, with the experiences themselves as the final ends. Irrespective of their ultimate correctness, completely natural processes of thought lead to the conclusion that in art it is only aesthetic experiences themselves that can be ends. If this much is granted, then there immediately arises the issue of whether the aesthetic experiences of each individual are equally valuable. It is in relation to this issue that a crucial aspect of Nietzsche's views about the position of artists can best be understood.

For Nietzsche, there is no doubt that some persons possess a greater capacity for valuable aesthetic experiences than others. The essential point is this. Just as the production of art requires creativity and vigor, so also does its contemplation. Further, the higher the degree of creativity and vigor involved the more valuable the experience is. "All art exercises the power of suggestion over the muscles and senses, which in the artistic temperament are originally active: it always speaks only to artists" (WP 809). This leads immediately to the issue of what the differences are between the experiences of the artist and the ordinary art contemplator. According to Nietzsche, the art contemplator should seek to enter the same creative state that gave rise to the production of the artwork, "the effect of works of art is to *excite the state that creates art*—intoxication" (WP 821). The ideal is for the art contemplator to experience what the artist experienced. But if we grant him that the genuine artist is more dynamically creative than the ordinary art contemplator it is difficult to see how the art contemplator could ever match the intensity of the artist's experience. The creative visions of the artist are not matched in the art audiences' contemplation of art, "whoever cannot give, also receives nothing" (WP 801).

It is the artist and the artist alone who experiences the artwork to its fullest; it is the artist alone who can derive from art the maximum it can offer. Thus, even if we do not regard the artwork as an end in itself but merely as a means to the production of aesthetic experiences, so that what justifies art is these experiences, this does not relegate the artist to the status of a mere cog in the production machine. If the point of art is the quality of the aesthetic experiences it furnishes, then the quality of the aesthetic experience had by artists outweighs those had by ordinary art contemplators. Only artists can wring from art the full value it contains. Put another way, artists are not only the best producers of art, they are also the best consumers of art.

Consider the following observations of what is required of artists and artistic production:

> *Towards a psychology of the artist.*—For art to exist, for any sort of aesthetic activity or perception to exist, a certain physiological precondition is indispensable; *intoxication*. Intoxication must first have heightened the excitability of the entire machine: no art results before that happens. . . .

> The essence of intoxication is the feeling of plenitude and increased energy. From out of this feeling one gives to things, one *compels* them to take, one rapes them—one calls this procedure *idealizing*. Let us get rid of a prejudice here; idealization does *not* consist, as is commonly believed, in subtracting or deducting of the petty and secondary. A tremendous expulsion of the principal features rather is the decisive thing, so that thereupon the others too disappear. (TI IX:8)

> In this condition one enriches everything out of one's own abundance: what one sees, what one desires, one sees swollen, pressing, strong, overladen with energy. The man in this condition transforms things until they mirror his power—until they are reflections of his perfection. This *compulsion* to transform into the perfect is—art. (TI IX:9)

It is hardly to be expected that the ordinary art contemplator can match the states that went into its production. The great importance attached to artists is reflected in two of Nietzsche's specific reactions. The great and almost unwavering admiration for Goethe is not just an admiration for the totality of his works, it is an admiration for the man (TI IX:49). The works are a sign of the greatness of the man, they do not exhaust it. By the same token, the lashing of Wagner in *The Case of Wagner* is not just a critique of his works, it is a disappointment in the man who produced them. The works are signs of a nature gone astray. It is difficult to explain the vehemence on any assumption other than that Nietzsche had an elevated conception of the nature and role of the artist, and that he perceived a gap between the real and the ideal.

The elevation of the artist to the predominant position in art is a major aspect of Nietzsche's revaluation,[8] but it is important to see that this is not just an idiosyncratic personal preference. The according of a superior position to the artist is intimately bound to fundamental aspects of Nietzsche's philosophy and with a specific analysis of art. More of this will be revealed in what follows.

The Artwork

Just as Nietzsche disclaims absolute truth and absolute goodness, so he disclaims absolute beauty: "*The* beautiful exists just as little as does *the* good, or *the* true" (WP 804). On the other hand, there is no doubt he thought of beauty as extremely important, and the only other aesthetic characteristics to which he devotes anything like the same amount of interest are style and form. He is a subjectivist of sorts about beauty, but he is not a radical subjectivist; he does not maintain that anybody's view on what is beautiful is as good as anybody else's. An analogy he has recourse to in explaining the nature and status of beauty in art is the perceptual alteration that occurs in romantic love. The emotion entirely transforms perceptions of the object of that emotion: "Love is the state in which man sees things most of all as they are *not*. The illusion-creating force is here at its height, likewise the sweetening and *transforming* force" (A 23).[9] The love object comes to be seen to possess a radiance, a splendor, a magnetism that it normally lacks. The transformation is grounded in, and inextricably bound to, the actual characteristics of the love object, but the emotion is not a reaction to these characteristics neutrally perceived. What is actually seen has a luster and enchantment it would otherwise lack.

Of course, lovers think of themselves as merely responding to perfectly independent, objective characteristics in the love object that, somewhat surprisingly, otherwise normally intelligent persons are too obtuse to discern. No doubt, if the lover were to become fully self-conscious of being the principal author of the splendid vision, ardor would cool. But equally, there is no doubt it is the lover who is in large part the author of this enchanting scene, even if we must accept that something is given, that what we are dealing with is transformation rather than free invention. I have maintained that Nietzsche is not a radical subjectivist about aesthetic characteristics; however, if the case of the lover is a model for the awareness of beauty in the arts as he appears to intend, then it is natural to wonder how extreme subjectivism can be avoided. This issue needs to be addressed.

The first point is this. The transformation of an otherwise mundane object into a vision of splendor in the way indicated is a genuine creative act. It introduces into the world an intensity and enchantment it previously lacked. There is something new of positive value in the world. Take a case with important parallels. Pain is not a characteristic attaching directly to objects, as shape and size are, it is subjective; the pain I feel nobody else feels. Things that are painful to me, even in the most direct biological sense, may be pleasantly stimulating to others. But pain is no illusion or fiction or pure invention; it is both real, and discounting its functional payoffs, typically a positive disvalue. Nor are anybody's judgments about who is in pain, or about the nature of that pain, as good as anybody else's. For Nietzsche, beauty is just as real as pain, except that beauty is the consequence of creative activity, and constitutes a genuine enrichment of life. Further, beauty requires a significant input from its creator. Not just anything can be a candidate for beauty. Beauty can only be found in the output of the dynamic and well-endowed (TI IX:8, 9). The finger paintings of three-year-olds, or the random paint dribblings of thirty-year-olds, or the stackings of bricks on gallery floors simply do not rate as candidates for beauty. A certain origin is essential for beauty. Of course, this does not mean that no one will judge the three-year-old's finger painting as beautiful, but for Nietzsche, the judgment would be as worthless as its object. Judgments of beauty are certainly not all on a par.

The second point is this. The capacity of persons to find things beautiful, the capacity of persons to transform things creatively, will vary from person to person, but not in a random fashion. The strong, the vital, the well-endowed will have this capacity, and the weak and ailing will not. The capacity for beauty is not the same in everyone. Contemplate pain once more. Some persons feel no pain at all, and whatever the resultant life problems are, there is no doubt about the objectivity of the condition. In general, the intensity of the pain for any given stimulus can be varied almost at will with either anaesthetics or with substances that block the action of anaesthetics whether natural or otherwise. The capacity to respond with no pain, or mild pain, or intense pain in the face of a given stimulus is objectively based, however subjective the pain itself is. Similarly, some will experience no beauty, some will have only mild experiences of beauty, and only the exceptional will have intense experiences of beauty.

The final point is this. The experiences of beauty themselves are not all equal. Just as a mild and tolerable pain is not the same disvalue as an acute and intolerable pain, so a modest and mildly engaging experience of beauty is not of the same value as an intense and completely enthralling experience. Of course, the intensity of the experience will be determined by the creative power of the person in question. Those with no creative powers—in his terms, the weak, the decadent, the overburdened, the ailing, the world-weary—cannot generate experiences of beauty of any intensity; only the strong, the vital, and the dynamic can do so. Put bluntly, the transforming visions of the weak will be neither as beautiful nor as valuable as the transforming visions of the strong. These observations clarify in some measure the sense in which Nietzsche is an objectivist about beauty and the sense in which he is a subjectivist. I hope to shed further light on the issue in what follows.

Naturally, the status of beauty is not the only interesting thing about it, and it is fair to say Nietzsche attempts some analysis of the notions of beauty and ugliness; but the analysis is only partial. According to him, what increases strength, vitality, and fitness is beautiful, what decreases strength, vitality, and fitness is ugly. Clearly, these must be regarded as necessary rather than sufficient conditions of beauty and ugliness for him. One thirsts to know what the other conditions are, and he has things to add: "'Beauty' is for the artist something outside all orders of rank, because in beauty opposites are tamed; the highest sign of power, namely power over opposites; moreover without tension;—that violence is no longer needed; that everything follows; obeys, so easily and so pleasantly—that is what delights the artist's will to power" (WP 803). But the thirst for enlightenment is unquenched, for without extensive concrete examples such remarks are too unspecific to unravel. The passage can be construed as implying that beauty requires variety, intensity, balance, and harmony, but even such a gloss is of little assistance without concrete examples. However, even this minimal level of analysis makes it plain that beauty and ugliness are not mere matters of whim.

To be sure, there is a measure of subjectivism in Nietzsche's position. What is beauty for the strong and dynamic will not be beauty by the weak and weary, and what is beauty by the weak and weary will not be beauty for the strong and dynamic. It is also plain that only what is beauty for the strong and dynamic is taken as an important positive value, and that what is beauty for the weak and weary is either an unimportant value or no positive value at all. "What serves the higher type of man as food or refreshment must to a very different and inferior type be almost poison" (BGE 30).[10] There will be irremediably different judgments of beauty, but they will certainly not be on a par. Indeed, properly speaking, what appears beautiful to the weak and weary will not really be beautiful at all, for it will lack any significant propensity to increase strength, vitality, and fitness.

One may ask why what increases the strength, vitality, and fitness of the weak and weary should not also be called beautiful, thus permitting a simple and univocal account of beauty. It might be a lesser beauty, but real beauty nevertheless. From Nietzsche's side, there are two points to be made. On the one hand he did not regard the weak and weary as capable of significant improvement in strength, vitality, and fitness. On the other hand he thinks the strong and dynamic naturally select the healthy alternative, while the weak and the weary naturally select the unhealthy alternative. Thus the weak and the weary have a propensity to call beautiful what is in fact inimical to vitality and well-being, and little propensity to call beautiful what is conducive to vitality and well-being. For him, the weak seek what weakens; the strong seek what strengthens (CW 5).

The novelty of Nietzsche's views lies in the connection between beauty and broadly biological values. Certainly, that art may be either good for a person or bad for a person is not new. Plato, his bête noire, argues for the exclusion of specific forms of art from the state depending on whether they are harmful or beneficial.[11] But clearly, harm and benefit are there construed in basically moral terms and not in broadly biological terms.

The Art Audience

Nietzsche is intent on combating two major conceptions of the relation between artworks and the art audience. The first conception is that the art contemplator is disinterested or detached in the contemplation of art, that the art contemplator's desires, needs, passions, inclinations, or aversions are not and ought not to be aroused, engaged, or satisfied in the contemplation of art. On this view, the proper pleasure to be derived from an artwork depends entirely on awareness of the intrinsic characteristics of the artwork and not on the specific emotional make-up of the art contemplator. The view implies that only a fraction of any human being is involved in the contemplation of art, and that fraction merely passively registers the characteristics of the artwork and derives what pleasure there is to be obtained from such a registration. Both Kant[12] and Schopenhauer[13] defended this type of view, and both were Nietzsche's targets.

This claim that the art contemplator must be disinterested and detached in the contemplation of art is at variance with Nietzsche's views on several levels. At the metaphysical level it presupposes that there is a "real person" distinct from an individual's desires, needs, passions, inclinations, aversions, and so on, and that this "real person" can be *subject* while the artwork is *object* in the contemplation of art. For him, such a "real person" is nothing but a fiction. The person simply is the totality of desires, needs, passions, inclinations, aversions, sensations, thoughts, and so on. There is no person or substance that exists independently of these things and merely *has* them and who can disengage himself or herself from them; the person is these things. Just as there is no "pure knowing subject" in the acquisition of knowledge, no "pure moral agent" in human actions, so there is no "pure aesthetic subject" in aesthetic contemplation. From the standpoint of revaluation strategies, this objection is an objection to a factual presupposition of the view that places such a high value on disinterested and detached aesthetic contemplation.

There are other objections at the level of value. This conception of the relation between art and the art contemplator cuts art off from the well-springs and dynamics of life itself. Art is simply irrelevant to what a person is, does, and feels; it is irrelevant to most of a person's life. What a person feels most deeply and passionately about must in no way intrude in the contemplation of art. If art must be contemplated disinterestedly and with complete detachment, then this places art firmly on the periphery of life, and positively debars art from affecting the mainstream of life. For Nietzsche, even if such aesthetic contemplation and such a role for art were possible, it would not be in the least bit desirable. Involvement is essential: "By means of music the passions enjoy themselves" (BGE 106). For him, art worthy of the name must be capable of profound effects; it must be able to engage the whole person; it must be able to engage what matters to a person; it must be able to increase strength and vitality. In his later thought, the capacity of art to affect life beneficially beyond the mere disinterested contemplation of it is absolutely central. "Art is the great stimulus to life: how could it be thought purposeless, aimless, *l'art pour l'art?*" (TI IX:24).

A further undesirable consequence of this model of aesthetic contemplation is that a specific artwork must have the same value or the same meaning for each art contemplator. No artwork can hold a special value or meaning for any individual. With this approach, art, too, is ruled out as a possible candidate for contributing a unique meaning to one's own existence. Whatever makes a person unique, individual, different, must be rigidly excluded from the disinterested and detached attitude appropriate to aesthetic contemplation. No individual idiosyncrasies or personal leanings are permitted to intrude. Everyone must derive the same enjoyment from a specific artwork, if aesthetic enjoyment is at issue. Nietzsche never could see any value in this kind of uniformity (BGE 43). Even if it is possible, it is not desirable. He was unwilling to countenance that a specific artwork could or should have the same meaning for the strong and dynamic as for the weak and declining: "Books for everybody are always malodorous books: the smell of petty people clings to them" (BGE 30). Good art for the exceptional individual will contain little for the unexceptional individual, and good art for the unexceptional individual will contain nothing for the exceptional individual.

In addition, the conception requires the art contemplator to be entirely passive. No effort, no contribution, no activity is expected or allowed. Any intrusions from the self on passive receptivity are aesthetically inadmissible. Nietzsche is opposed to any enterprise that requires passivity, but he is specifically opposed to it in the contemplation of art. "All art works tonically, increases strength, inflames desire (i.e., the feeling of strength), excites all the more subtle recollections of intoxication—there is a special memory that penetrates such states: a distant and transitory world of sensations here comes back" (WP 809). There are two aspects to this effect on the art contemplator. On the one hand Nietzsche holds that to contemplate an artwork one must in some measure match the creativity of the artist. Without this matching creative activity on the part of the art contemplator, the artwork simply cannot be understood; its whole point will be missed. The proper contemplation of art is *re*-creation. On the other hand he regards art as a celebration of life, and a part of what this means is that the art contemplator is an active participant in a celebration. There is a world of difference between a passive spectator of a celebration and an active participant in a celebration, and it is to the latter rather than the former that the artist and the art contemplator ought to aspire.

The second view Nietzsche opposes can be called the therapeutic conception, namely, that the artwork relieves the art contemplator from some undesirable condition. Both Aristotle's views on tragedy and Schopenhauer's views on art in general fall into this category. For Aristotle, one function of tragedy is to purge the spectator of fear and pity, and this is considered as relief from something undesirable.[14] For Schopenhauer, the contemplation of art furnishes respite from the otherwise unremitting demands of the will; this again is conceived of as relief from an undesirable condition.[15] In both cases, art removes a purely negative condition from the art contemplator; apparently it has little of a positive nature to contribute in its own right.

Nietzsche has objections to both views. Against Aristotle he makes the point that this conjectured therapeutic purpose could not succeed. The venting of an emotion may provide immediate relief from it, but repetition merely strengthens the emotion. The frequent spectator of tragedies would eventually become more fearful and pitying rather than being freed from fear and pity (WP 851). Similarly, in the case of Schopenhauer the disengagement required to furnish relief from the demands of the will is simply not possible (WP 851). But the essence of the objection to these views does not depend entirely on the inefficacy of the proposed therapies or to the defects of their psychological presuppositions. The fundamental objection is that they embody an impoverished conception of the possibilities of art. For him, art has the potential for making a major contribution to life, whereas these conceptions necessarily relegate it to a minor and peripheral role.

So far the focus has been on the negative, on erroneous ways of conceiving the contemplation of art, but implicitly the substance of the positive conception has already emerged. The contemplation of artworks requires the engagement of the whole person, and this, of course, includes the emotional make-up of the person. The contemplation of artworks requires a positive creative act on the part of the art contemplator. Only those whose active and creative powers approach those of the artist will be in a position to appreciate the artwork. Proper contemplation of art increases the activity and involvement of the art contemplator rather than decreasing it. In addition, the art contemplator enters new states that he or she has never been in, states that affect the whole person. The essence of art is to bring something new to life. The articulation of this conception makes it more intelligible how art can be a tonic and relevant to life in general.

Comparisons and Contrasts

Nietzsche's departures from the representation theory of art have already been noted. On the basis of his views about key aspects of art, it is possible to suppose that he is implicitly a proponent of the expression theory of art, and the suggestion merits consideration. The simplest version of the expression theory is propounded by Tolstoy.[16] According to Tolstoy the function of an artwork is to convey as simply, clearly, and directly as possible the emotions of the artist to the art audience; the aim is to have the art contemplator feel exactly what the artist felt. Nietzsche, too, holds that the art contemplator must seek to recreate the state the artist was in on the occasion of the artwork's creation, but there is still a significant difference between the two views.

Tolstoy's emphasis is on the direct, unaltered, unadorned transmission of ordinary emotions that occur naturally in the life of the artist. There is no suggestion that either invention or elaboration or transformation is in the least bit desirable; indeed, they are to be avoided. The skill of the artist consists in transmitting emotions as simply and directly as possible. Further, the emotions that ought to be transmitted, according to Tolstoy, are the emotions that are had by and can be understood by everybody. On this view, it is difficult to see how art can constitute any significant enrichment of life, although Tolstoy certainly thought that it did. It appears that art adds absolutely nothing new; the emotions that it transmits are already available in the natural course of life. To be sure, one might derive emotional experiences from art it would be impractical to experience directly, but even here all art would furnish is a practical second best.

Nietzsche is opposed to such a view on several counts. First, it is important that art furnish something new and something unobtainable outside of art. This entails that the artist must either create or invent or transform his or her material. The mere transmission of the normally encountered adds nothing. Further, to restrict art to the transmission of those emotions that everyone can feel or understand is to reduce art to the lowest common denominator. In effect, it is saying that the only real art is the art of the "herd." Proposals like this always elicited his inexorable scorn. In addition, the feelings that present themselves to consciousness in the normal course of life are typically only of secondary importance. The indulgence of individual emotion merely constitutes an objectionable romanticism. According to him, art must deal with what is important; art must have a serious purpose; art must foster the growth, development, and thriving of life. It is difficult to see how the transmission of ordinary emotions could have any serious role in the fulfillment of such a purpose. Tolstoy also thought that art must have a serious purpose, and that was the teaching and reinforcement of universal moral values. Naturally, this is a purpose Nietzsche repudiates. For him, the morality involved is essentially anti-life, hence it would make art essentially anti-life, whereas it ought to be the great promoter of life.

Certainly, Nietzsche is not an adherent of the expression theory of art in the simple form articulated by Tolstoy. But there are more sophisticated versions of the expression theory, and it is more difficult to differentiate him from these. R. G. Collingwood is a major exponent of a more sophisticated version of the expression theory.[17] According to Collingwood, although the essential function of art is the expression of emotion, neither emotion nor expression can be understood in the simple-minded way Tolstoy appears to understand them. Emotions are not fully determinate and clearly apprehended in the way sensations are, and further, the process of unadulterated transmission, as envisaged by Tolstoy, is impossible.

According to Collingwood, the expression of an emotion in an artwork serves to shape, form, define, and give character to the emotion itself. The very act of expression has a role in determining what the emotion is. Expression is not transmission, it is transformation, it is making the indeterminate more determinate. Put another way, the emotion is in part what it is, because of the way it is expressed. One important implication is that the emotion expressed in an artwork cannot be felt *as such* independently of that artwork, for that particular expression is essential to that specific emotion. Take an example. It is simply not possible to experience the emotions expressed in Beethoven's Ninth Symphony independently of the symphony itself. The form and the emotional content are essentially and not merely accidentally linked; the emotional content cannot be had apart from the form it is embodied in. Our only access to specifically those emotions is through the symphony itself. On this view, artists create new ways of feeling that do not exist independently of their artworks.

Unquestionably, Nietzsche's view fits better with this conception. On the one hand it attributes to artists a genuinely active and creative role; art is a source of truly novel feelings, and as such it allows for art to make a contribution to life unobtainable outside of art. It allows art to constitute a true enrichment of life. On this view, the art contemplator must seek to feel what the artist felt, as he also requires. On the other hand, beyond this addition to life, the view can readily accommodate his further conception that art must celebrate life and embody affirmative attitudes to life. If artists can create new ways of feeling, then, of course, they can create new feelings of celebration and affirmation. In addition, it fits well with his conception that worthwhile creation requires shaping, molding, and imposing form. Given this degree of similarity of view, one may wonder where the differences lie.

Collingwood, like Tolstoy, maintains that the function of art is to express universally shared emotions, and like Tolstoy he explicitly disavows the kind of elitism in art that is at the basis of Nietzsche's reflections.[18] But the disavowal is not a consequence of the general theory of art that sits quite comfortably with elitism. The theory of expression itself is compatible with the expression of the rarest emotions of the rarest individuals. Collingwood's disavowal of elitism appears to embody a personal value orientation that lies outside the core of the theory itself. Indeed, there is a high level of compatibility between the theory of expression itself and Nietzsche's views. If one wanted to highlight differences, one could say that for Collingwood expression is central to art and everything else is peripheral, whereas for the later Nietzsche, causing life to thrive is central and everything else, including expression, is peripheral. But it is unhelpful to try to make the differences too sharp. The problems each set himself were different, and we ought not to compare the solutions as if they were solutions to exactly the same problems. A fairer assessment would be that while there is by no means an identity of views, there is a significant level of complementarity as far as key aspects are concerned. Collingwood's theory of the inner workings of art dovetails neatly with Nietzsche's views of what the outer workings of art ought to be. At the same time, it sits comfortably in the general framework of Nietzsche's philosophy. It is too strong to say that Nietzsche is explicitly committed to an expression theory of Collingwood's kind, but if the implications of Nietzsche's observations are teased out it is not unreasonable to say that it fits better with such a theory than with any of its alternatives.

A consideration of formalism, a theory Nietzsche is at least by implication opposed to, also clarifies his views. Formalism fits best with the conception of the art contemplator as detached and disinterested in the contemplation of art, hence, it is not surprising that Kant embraced both at the same time. It is difficult to see how the contemplation of form alone could require the engagement of an individual's desires, needs, passions, inclinations, aversions, and so on. "Art reminds us of states of animal vigor; it is on the one hand an excess and overflow of blooming physicality into the world of images and desires; on the other hand, an excitation of the animal functions through the images and desires of intensified life;—an enhancement of the feeling of life, a stimulant to it" (WP 802). At least it must be allowed that in the contemplation of form alone a lesser engagement of the whole person is expected than in the contemplation of something more comprehensive. In formalism the senses and the emotions have little or no role to play, and this is the source of conflict with his views.

For Nietzsche, art must stimulate the senses, art must engage the emotions, in short, art must involve the whole person. Insofar as formalism denies this, it is unacceptable. An important point remains. Art must act in the service of life, art must promote the thriving of life. Of all the major theories of art, formalism looks the least promising in offering an account of how this may occur. If formalist art had such an effect, it would be surprising, and in any event it would be a purely accidental outcome. What Nietzsche sought was a theory of art with intelligible connections between the contents of artworks and promoting the thriving of life. It is more natural to regard formalist art as involving, if not an active stance against the senses and the emotions, then at least a deliberate disregard for them. Nietzsche regards this as anti-life, and it forms one of his basic objections to it.

Let me draw the threads of these comparisons together. Of theories that deal with the inner workings of art, the formalist theory is the theory Nietzsche's views are most directly opposed to. But this does not imply form was not an important aspect of art for him. Form was certainly important in his thinking about art, but not to the exclusion of everything else. Further, he clearly does not accept simple forms of the representation theory of art, or simple forms of the expression theory of art. A sophisticated version of the expression theory is what he appears to be closest to. However, this requires at least the following caveat: more sophisticated and highly qualified versions of the representation theory of art can be difficult to distinguish from sophisticated versions of the expression theory. Thus, while we can be certain that he was not a formalist, and confident that he did not espouse simple versions of the representation theory, or simple versions of the expression theory, and have some grounds for saying that he is committed to a sophisticated version of the expression theory, his views do not exclude positively a sophisticated and highly qualified version of the representation theory.

Art and Life

Unquestionably, Nietzsche's conception of the relation between art and life is a prominent feature of his revaluation in this sphere. It is central to his conception that art must enhance life. But how this is to be understood is not immediately transparent, but it is easier to clarify his views indirectly rather than directly. When we take theories of art that deal more with the role of art in life rather than with the inner workings of art itself, the theory of art his position initially appears closest to is the play theory of art. The characteristic strategy of play theories of art is to settle on an account of what positive contribution play makes to life, and then to propose that art serves the same function. Consequently, there are as many play theories of art as there are theories of play.[19] Consider a number of the most important ones. There is the "discharge of surplus energy" theory of play, and its mirror image the "recuperation" theory; there is the "learning a behavioral repertoire for later life" theory; there is the "increasing fitness through exercise" theory; and there is the "optimal arousal" theory. There is some similarity between the last two except that one is mainly oriented toward the fitness of the body, while the other is more oriented toward the fitness of the perceptual and control systems. However, none of these are quite what Nietzsche has in mind.

Take the "discharge of surplus energy" theory of play that forms the basis for Spencer's theory of art.[20] Spencer sees the surplus energy as potentially damaging, and its release as having a preventative and therapeutic role. Nietzsche, too, sees the best art as arising from a superabundance of energy, but the expression in art of this energy does not have a primarily preventative or therapeutic role. Neither are the "learning a behavioral repertoire for later life" nor the "increasing fitness through exercise" conceptions he espouses. The "optimal arousal" theory looks more promising. According to this theory, the function of play is to create an optimal level of readiness and efficiency for dealing with life-problems that subsequently present themselves. But this is not exactly his view either; it embodies a too narrow conception of the benefits of play, and the envisioned level of readiness is set at too basic a biological level.

Let me state more generally why none of these conceptions fit. The problem is this. Although Nietzsche has a strong biological orientation in his later reflections on art, the above suggestions place too much emphasis on the directly biological. Since this is bound to appear paradoxical, some explanation is warranted. A major difficulty for play theories of art is to explain why in adult life both play and art coexist. Or, to put it slightly differently, why is the extension of play into adult life not sufficient? Or again, why is art by itself not sufficient? Take Spencer's theory as a case in point. Surely, a game of tennis or golf has far greater potential for the release of surplus energy than sitting through an opera or reading a novel. Why have apparently inefficient means of releasing surplus energy, when efficient means are available? On the other hand, if we take the "recuperation" theory, then sitting through an opera or reading a novel appear to furnish a far greater potential for recuperation than a game of tennis or football. Why have both kinds of "play"? Such considerations naturally lead to the supposition that art has a function different from that of play. In any event, it is reasonable to suppose that this is what Nietzsche thought, and his position is ripe for explication.

Typically, theories of play are framed within a broadly biological perspective that encompasses not only human beings but also other playing species. By and large, the goal is a general theory of animal play. In such a context it is not surprising that what is common between human beings and other species is emphasized, and the way human beings differ from other species is ignored or underplayed. But here the differences may be more important than the similarities. Many species play, but only human beings have both play and art. At the very least, this suggests that art may have a function distinct from play. Thus, there is a problem: does Nietzsche, who is also operating within a broadly biological perspective, have in mind some function for art that differentiates it from play? It is my view that he does.

It is useful to recall that Nietzsche requires art to enhance life, to promote the thriving of life. But the thriving of human life requires both the thriving of the human spirit as well as the thriving of the human body. Of course, the terms "spirit" and "body" only refer to two different aspects of persons, and he sees no commitment to ontological dualism in their use: "'Since I have known the body better,' said Zarathustra to one of his disciples, 'the spirit has been only figuratively spirit to me; and all that is "intransitory"—that too has been only an "image"'" (Z II:17). If this point is granted, then his position can be put. The most important function of art is to promote the thriving of the human spirit.[21] On the other hand, play is more directed at the thriving of the body, although overlap is inevitable. But then, art, in promoting the thriving of the human spirit, must deal with and have as its subject matter the human life-world; it must deal with human problems and human prospects. In art's celebration of life, life itself must be identified as the ground for celebration. Art must have a subject matter that pertains to the human spirit. "A psychologist asks on the other hand: what does art do? does it not praise? does it not glorify? does it not select? does it not highlight? By doing this it *strengthens* or *weakens* certain valuations. . . . Is this no more than an incidental? an accident? Something in which the instinct of the artist has no part whatever? Or is it not rather the prerequisite for the artist's being an artist at all. . . . Is his basic instinct directed towards art, or is it not rather directed towards the meaning of art, which is *life?* towards a *desideratum of life?*" (TI IX:24). Play, by contrast, typically has no subject matter at all. Neither tennis nor golf nor football is about anything; they have no subject matter, and as such they do not require the same engagement of the spiritual aspect of human beings. However, these observations do not deny that good art may also have a direct tonic effect on the body and that bad art may have a direct deleterious effect. "The effect of the ugly can be measured with a dynometer. Whenever man feels depressed, he senses the proximity of something 'ugly.' His feeling of power, his will to power, his courage, his pride—they decline with the ugly, they increase with the beautiful" (TI IX:20).

To understand Nietzsche's position better, his observations on the notion of "art for art's sake" need attention (TI IX:24). What these observations imply is that the thriving of the human spirit that art promotes cannot simply be identified with the production and contemplation of art itself. The production and contemplation of art may be a part of this thriving of the human spirit art promotes, but it cannot be equated with the whole of it. The additional effect art must have is to promote a love of life. Of course, art may increase our bond to life simply because of our attraction to the beauties it itself furnishes, and while this is undoubtedly part of what he had in mind, he also had in mind that it should increase our bond to life beyond art. Art ought also to increase our enthusiasm for living, it ought to give us zest for plans, projects, and shaping the future over and above our involvement with art. It hardly needs pointing out that these effects involve both the spiritual and the physical aspects of human beings. It is the potential of art to contribute to both invigoration and enrichment that leads to its high ranking.

Nietzsche's emphasis on the dynamism, vitality, and creative power of the artist becomes more intelligible in this framework. It is difficult to see how we could become energized or enthused by artworks unless considerable energy and effort went into their production in the first place. It is hard to imagine being moved to a greater love for life by anyone not already fully in love with life. The depressed, the embittered, the disappointed, the exhausted, the defeated, the indifferent, the spiritually anemic are not types capable of stimulating a great love for life. If anything, their effect is likely to be the opposite. His emphasis on the full involvement of the art contemplator in the contemplation of art also becomes more intelligible in this context. For art to have a significant effect on one's outlook on life, it will have to be capable of engaging and energizing the whole person.

This covers the major aspects of Nietzsche's later theorizing about art that I propose to deal with; but, of course, it leaves areas of his interest in the arts untouched. Specifically, it does not deal with his interest in particular artists, particular art forms, or particular artworks. Anyone aware of the extent of his preoccupation with Wagner alone, for example, will immediately recognize the gap.[22] But it is not my aim to offer an exhaustive coverage of his reflections on art. Principal revaluations are the focus. At this point, an assessment of their effectiveness is in order.

As a prelude, some observations about art and theories of art may help. A good deal of theorizing in the arts centers around the notion of function: What is the function of an artwork? What is the function of the artist? and so on. The great traditional theories of art can be seen as answers to these questions concerning function. For the representation theory, the function of art is to represent the real world; for the expression theory, the function is to express the emotions of the artist; for the formalist theory, the function is to exhibit aesthetically pleasing forms. There are two important points to note. First, each is a single function account, and second, each implicitly limits in a general way what aspect of a human being art is addressed to. Representational art is principally addressed to the senses; expressionist art is principally addressed to the emotions; formal art is principally addressed to the intellect.

The theories of the past have assumed that these functions are somehow fixed independently of us, as if we had no say in the matter. This is surely quite implausible. It is in large measure up to us what function we want art to serve. In this context Nietzsche sets up a noble and inspiring conception of the function of art; it is a function that we could well seek art to fulfil. It presents a genuine ideal of art, and, as such, it is difficult to criticize. But there is a possible difficulty nevertheless. The difficulty turns on distinguishing the function of art considered collectively from the function of artworks considered individually. For some theories of art there is no significant difference. For example, for the representation theory the function of art both individually and collectively is to imitate or represent reality. But there could be a difference between individual and collective function and we need to ask specifically whether there is in Nietzsche's case.

The art that fulfils its potential, when considered collectively, has the function of invigorating and drawing us more closely not merely to the artworks themselves but also to life beyond art, in short, it has the function of promoting the thriving of life. But must each single artwork considered individually have the function of promoting the thriving of life? There is ground for holding that Nietzsche thought so. The castigation of Wagner's works in *The Case of Wagner* appears to be predicated in part on just such an assumption, as if each artwork had to carry the whole meaning of art within itself. However, such a position faces a weighty counterargument. According to that argument, there is no single function that can be imposed on each artwork or that it is desirable to impose on each artwork. If the meaning of art lies anywhere, it lies in the diversity of the functions that individual artworks can fulfil. Artworks can stimulate, entertain, inspire, console, shock, disturb, delight, puzzle, unsettle, provoke, imitate, exhibit form, express emotion, inform, present new ways of looking at things, and so on. There simply is no one thing that each artwork must be doing.[23] On this argument, by seeking an elevated function for art, Nietzsche is charged with ignoring its more modest functions. He assumes that an artwork must contribute to the thriving of life. But surely artworks can exist and furnish rewards by doing many other things.

The natural reply to the argument is that all the specific things listed above that individual artworks can do unproblematically fall under the formula of promoting the thriving of life. We do not have different functions here, rather, we have different *ways* of fulfilling the same overall function. Consequently, it can be argued that Nietzsche has no problem in accommodating art from the lightest to the most weighty and as diverse as Schubert's *Dances,* the drawings of Escher, and Voltaire's *Candide,* as well as Mozart's *Don Giovanni,* Raphael's *School of Athens,* and Tolstoy's *War and Peace.* But a problem remains. There may be artworks that individually denigrate and vilify life, and considered individually have the tendency to depress and devitalize, but that may be vital to art collectively having the function that Nietzsche seeks for it. If we had available only the writings of Samuel Beckett and only the paintings of Francis Bacon, we would not have much to invigorate us or draw us more strongly to life, but their presence among other artworks may well intensify the capacity of other artworks to do precisely that. Art considered collectively may be able to promote the thriving of life better, if artworks considered individually are not all required to do so. To require of art collectively that it contribute to the thriving of life beyond the production and contemplation of art itself seems reasonable, although it is contestable. To require of each artwork individually that it contribute to the thriving of life beyond its production and contemplation seems less reasonable.

In claiming Nietzsche has succumbed to the supposition that there is a single function that each artwork must fulfil, namely, promoting the thriving of life, I am mindful of the fact that he warns against such assumptions elsewhere, in particular concerning the institution of punishment. "Today it is impossible to say for certain *why* people are really punished: all concepts in which an entire process is semiotically concentrated elude definition; only that which has no history is definable" (GM II:13). But I believe this perspective may have eluded him in considering art, and if this is so, it constitutes a definite flaw.[24] But while Nietzsche may have fallen into the trap of requiring of artworks individually what can only reasonably be demanded of art collectively, the flaw is not fatal. It may be inappropriate to demand of each single artwork that it palpably strengthen our bond to life, that each single artwork constitute a celebration of life, although some will anyway, but the conception of art collectively as a crucial element in drawing us more powerfully to life, of being an essential part of the celebration of life, of promoting the thriving of life, is of enduring importance and a worthy candidate for acceptance.

To sum up, five main aspects of Nietzsche's revaluation of aesthetic values have been addressed. First, there is the attack on the objectivity and universality of such major aesthetic concepts as beauty. Second, there is the elevation of the artist to a paramount position in art, together with the demand that the artist be dynamic, vital, and endowed with exceptional creative force. Third, there is the attack on the disinterested or detached ideal of aesthetic contemplation and the insistence on the engagement of the whole person in the contemplation of art. It is of note that the disinterested or detached ideal for aesthetic contemplation has continued to have a considerable following even since his time. Nevertheless, in recent times there has been a strong attack on this conception by George Dickie.[25] However, Dickie does not mention Nietzsche; had he done so, he might well have found additional ways to support his case. Fourth, there is the insistence that art have an aim beyond art itself, that art promote a love of, and enthusiasm for, life not only in art but beyond it. Finally, there is the valuation of art not only above morality and religion but also above knowledge.

The revaluations in art are not rich in new techniques or methods of revaluation. There is not the diversity of methods or of arguments that can be found in the revaluation of truth, morality, and religion. Of course, this is perfectly natural; one marshals one's most fearsome weapons against one's greatest enemies, and art is not among them. On the other hand, we must not suppose that what is here is merely a disconnected set of observations about art. Indeed, Nietzsche's conclusions concerning art are the consequences of his view of reality, his higher-order values, and to a lesser degree the conceptual network identified in the previous chapter.

SIX

New Directions

Beyond the Hammer

Nietzsche uses the vivid metaphor of philosophizing with a hammer. Clearly, he has in mind the smashing of old and outworn ideals and idols, but what exactly the hammer is to be identified with is not as clear. One might simply seek to identify it with the collection of revaluation strategies already considered and with others that may have been omitted; nevertheless, this does not go far enough. Three aspects need to be taken into account. First, there is a hard, uncompromising attitude, an unrelenting determination to subject every sacred cow to rigorous critical scrutiny. Second, there is an array of critical stratagems that show up the weaknesses of the old values. Third, there is a system of positive valuations, including his higher-order values, that is used as a weapon against the values to be deposed. The "hammer" must be conceived of as an amalgam of attitude, negative devices, and positive devices.

Destruction is the aim of philosophizing with the hammer. One uses it to eliminate the outworn and the unacceptable. But once that task is accomplished, more remains than a total value vacuum. Positive conclusions emerge, as in the case of art, and there are the values forming part of the hammer itself. Although the ground is not left entirely bare after the negative task is accomplished, a significant constructive task is required. Thus the task of revaluation has two distinct components, destruction on the one hand, and construction on the other. It is time to turn to the constructive phase. Nietzsche thought of himself, at the time of *Ecce Homo,* as having furnished the constructive component first in *Thus Spoke Zarathustra,* but while this overlooks the preceding critical works, it illustrates the importance he attached to positive construction.

Besides the theory of value and the higher-order values, Nietzsche's most important positive conceptions are the *Übermensch* and the eternal recurrence. I have no intention of covering every aspect of these topics, nor of resolving some major issues of interpretation. My concern is with what revaluation strategies rival interpretations imply, more than with the ultimate correctness of those interpretations; but I am concerned that the interpretations I consider be plausible in their own right. My focus is on how the conceptions can function as strategies for erecting new values. To venture a general observation, the negative part of revaluation appears to be more immediately effective, but the positive part, particularly if his theory of value and higher-order values are included, is the more richly intriguing and likely to be of more lasting worth.[1]

The *Übermensch*

It is vital to recognize that the *Übermensch*[2] is not primarily a stand-alone ideal; it is not an arbitrary ideal erected in the context of a neutral, undisturbed, and unproblematic valuational background. The *Übermensch* has an important role as a specific solution to a specific problem. Indeed, the *Übermensch* is a response to what Nietzsche sees as a value crisis. This crisis arises out the circumstance characterized by the proclamation that *God is dead:* "The time has come when we have to pay for having been Christians for two thousand years: we are lost for a while. Abruptly we plunge into the opposite valuations, with all the energy that such an extreme overvaluation of man has generated in man. Now everything is false through and through, mere 'words,' chaotic, weak, or extravagant" (WP 30). There are two aspects to this crisis. On the one hand it spells the death of what had been conceived of as the major and indispensable values of Western culture, and as such creates a value vacuum. On the other hand it does not leave us with flat ground to build on. The overwhelming orientation to another world that this, now defunct, theistic conception entails has produced a denigration, a slander, a belittlement, a vilification, a devaluation of this world. Thus we do not just need new positive values, we also need to overcome the ingrained negative valuations left behind. It is not entirely clear why the negative valuations fail to evaporate simultaneously as completely as the deposed metaphysical-religious conception and its purportedly positive values, and indeed, he raises the possibility himself (GM II:20), but the view is immediately dismissed (GM II:21). The position appears to be that since a great effort was required to put these values in place initially, they have become so ingrained that a great effort will be required to replace them. For this we need the *Übermensch* (GM II:24).

The solution to this value crisis is required to perform two distinct tasks. First, it must furnish new positive values, and second, it must remove the residual negative valuations. Of course the tasks are not necessarily unrelated; the new positive values may simply blast away the remaining negative valuations, but that is only one possibility. Perhaps no new positive values can take hold until the remaining negative ones are eliminated. That what we are dealing with here is a *solution* to a *problem* is a point of fundamental importance, but it is of equal importance to determine for *whom* it is a solution. Naturally, it appears that the solution is primarily for people in that culture in which the now largely disintegrated and disintegrating Christian world view once prevailed. In *Thus Spoke Zarathustra*, Zarathustra says in the encounter with the saint, "I am bringing mankind a gift" (Z Prologue, 2). And plainly, the "gift" is the doctrine of the *Übermensch*. Having presented the doctrine, Zarathustra warns the people that time is running out for the solution; their cooperation is required in bringing forth the *Übermensch*. There is the danger of becoming the *Ultimate Man*, and if that happened, they could no longer bring forth the *Übermensch*:

> It is time for man to fix his goal. It is time for man to plant the seed of his highest hope.
> His soil is still rich enough for it. But this soil will one day be poor and weak; no longer will a high tree be able to grow from it.
> Alas! The time is coming when man will no more shoot the arrow of his longing out over mankind, and the string of his bow will have forgotten how to twang!
> I tell you: one must have chaos in one to give birth to a dancing star. I tell you: you still have chaos in you.
> Alas! The time is coming when man will give birth to no more stars. Alas! The time of the most contemptible man is coming, the man who can no longer despise himself.
> Behold I shall show you the *Ultimate Man*. (Z Prologue, 5)

The implication is that the solution is for mankind in general, and that mankind should help to bring it forth. However, the reception Zarathustra receives leads him to modify his original intention of presenting his doctrine to mankind in general; he narrows his aim in how the doctrine is to be communicated: "To lure many away from the herd—

that is why I have come. . . . 'I will make company with creators, with harvesters, with rejoicers: I will show them the rainbow and the stairway to the Superman'" (Z Prologue, 9). What is not entirely clear is whether there has merely been a change in whom the doctrine is presented *to*, or whether there has also been a change in whom the doctrine is a solution *for*. Is the solution now only for the "many that are lured away from the herd"? But whether the solution is a solution for some smaller group, or whether it is addressed to all persons who embrace or embraced the Christian theistic world view that has now— whether they know it or not—disintegrated in their embrace, the solution is for current persons who are themselves not *Übermenschen*, and who are in a value crisis.

The *Übermensch* is a solution to this problem for these people. But just what is this solution? Just what is this *Übermensch*? To begin, the *Übermensch* is a superior person, not merely superior *among* current persons, but superior *to* current persons. This will be a more powerful, more dynamic, more creative, more disciplined, more intense, more severe, more capable person. This will be a healthier, stronger, harder type; this will be a type with boundless love and enthusiasm for this world and for this life. There is a crucial ambiguity in this picture. We need to know whether the *Übermensch* is already a complete embodiment of the new values, or whether the *Übermensch* is an essentially incomplete embodiment of the new values, the point being that the *Übermensch* will, from superior endowment, create the substance of the new values. The point is important enough to reformulate. Is the *Übermensch* already the new value? Or, is it the capacity of the *Übermensch* to generate new values that really matters?

Support for both interpretations can be found in the texts. I take the interpretation that there is an essential value-creating role for the *Übermensch* as the more central, but both possibilities will be considered. The difference in interpretation can be important. A commonly voiced complaint is that the ideal of the *Übermensch* is too unspecific from the standpoint of positive values.[3] This may be a complaint of real substance against the conception of the *Übermensch* as already completely embodying the new values, but it is of less substance as an objection to the conception of the *Übermensch* as essentially having the role of creating new values. My focus will be on how the *Übermensch* constitutes a solution to the value crisis. To facilitate the discussion, let me call the first interpretation of the *Übermensch* the value-embodiment model, and the second interpretation the value-creation model.

The Value-Embodiment Model

This model in turn generates two solutions to the value crisis. First, there is the *replacement* solution. Nietzsche's observation that the *Übermensch* will stand to man as man stands to the apes implies that the *Übermensch* is conceived of as a replacement for current human beings, at any rate, as far as the order of value is concerned. Current human beings in value crisis will not be given new values; they will simply be replaced by a group of more valuable, value crisis free beings. "What is the ape to men? A laughing-stock or a painful embarrassment. And just so shall man be to the Superman: a laughing-stock or a painful embarrassment" (Z Prologue, 3). Just as the existence of human beings is not what makes life valuable for apes, so the existence of the *Übermensch* is not going to be what makes life valuable for us. Second, there is the *veneration* solution. "I want to teach men the meaning of their existence: which is the Superman, the lightning from the dark cloud man" (Z Prologue, 7). Here it is not replacement that is suggested; we ourselves are to see our own meaning in this new being:

> Could you *create* a god?—So be silent about all gods! But you could surely create the superman.
>
> Perhaps not you yourselves, my brothers! But you could transform yourselves into forefathers and ancestors of the Superman: and let this be your finest creating. (Z II:2)

We venerate great musicians, artists, thinkers, athletes, leaders, and so on; and unquestionably, many find life to be significantly enriched through their presence. On a more modest note, there are parents for whom fulfillment in some measure consists in the recognition of the higher level attained by their children. In these cases, the existence of other valuable persons is seen as increasing the value and significance of one's own life. Put abstractly, the recognition that the human species has produced outstanding types can certainly increase the sense of the worthwhileness of life. The outstanding do, after all, inspire people. The *Übermensch* will be more outstanding than even the most outstanding types hereto, and it is the veneration of this new type that will resolve the value crisis. We will once again find value in the world through seeing the *Übermensch* as highly valuable.

There are problems for both solutions. Let me consider the first solution. It is worth being reminded that we are not, in the first instance, assessing the desirability of human beings being replaced by a superior species as a straightforward thesis in its own right; we are considering it as a solution to a value crisis. This value crisis is a crisis for *those* who have lost the capacity to believe in the Christian world view. But, this "solution" does absolutely nothing for these people; it leaves them to dangle with their value crisis until the day they die. An underlying presupposition in the characterization of the value crisis is that it is a bad thing that those who have lost their values have lost them and that it would be a good thing for *them* to acquire new and healthier values. The replacement model simply does not furnish a solution to the initial problem. It does not just miss; it is not even in the race. And this remains so, irrespective of the intrinsic merits of the proposal to replace human beings by superior beings.

But there is also an important argument that the proposal to replace human beings with superior beings has acute problems of its own. The imputed difficulty could be called the paradox of generalized excellence; the claim is that excellence generalized ceases to be excellence.[4] Suppose that a super-race, in which every person could write a Shakespearean play before breakfast, a Mozartean opera before lunch, paint a *Guernica* and then run the marathon in half an hour before dinner, play the piano like Liszt after dinner and conceive a Newton-quality theory of the universe in the evening, supplanted human beings. Think of how desperately dull and commonplace all this would eventually be. Who would want to see a Shakespearean play? Who would want to listen to a Mozartean opera? Who would care if you played like Liszt? The claim is that excellence is essentially a positional concept. To excel is to surpass others. While the *Übermenschen* are excelling *us* there is no problem, but once they themselves become the new reference class, the very same charges of the commonness of it all, and the general mediocrity of it all, must again arise, requiring an *Über-Übermensch* for its solution, and so on ad infinitum. In a nutshell, the problem is, so the argument runs, that an essentially relational concept—excellence—is being treated as if it were nonrelational.

There are several replies open to Nietzsche. First, his higher-order values, particularly as expressed in the criterion of coherent multiplicity, preclude the situation envisioned above. He is nowhere in favor of the multiplication of identical human beings even if they are high performing human beings. The *Übermenschen* would have to be individually outstanding in different spheres, and no "higher-level" commonness or "higher-level" mediocrity or "higher-level" herd is either implied or required. Second, the objection fails to note the attitude component in the conception of the *Übermensch*. If the *Übermenschen* are strongly drawn to this world and affirm and celebrate it, while we are completely disenchanted and see no value in it, then from the standpoint of value it makes more sense they should possess it than that we should. Nor is there anything radical or unusual in such a judgment. It is simply valuational good sense that an object be possessed by those who cherish it rather than by those who hate it or are indifferent to it. Finally, there must be something wrong with the objection in virtue of the unacceptable consequences it brings in its train. If we look down rather than looking up, the implication is that human beings are of no higher value than sheep—all that we have managed is a new commonness—that if human beings were taken from the world but sheep remained nothing of value would be lost to the world. But this looks very much like a reductio ad absurdum of the objection. If we are prepared to accept that human beings are more valuable than sheep, then it is difficult to see what could preclude the possibility of there existing a group of super beings standing to us, in value terms, as we stand to sheep. It is difficult to see how we could avoid the conclusion that it would be better for such beings to exist rather than not exist. Thus the fact that the replacement solution is not a real solution for those in the value crisis does not mean that the proposal itself is intrinsically untenable.

The second solution by way of the veneration model is immediately on stronger ground, for it actually has something for those undergoing the value crisis. According to this solution, those in value crisis will actually come to feel that life is more worthwhile once they come to venerate these new outstanding types or once they become committed to their production. But here we need to look at the process that will elicit the veneration. Veneration is itself a value-guided process; one venerates because of the values one holds. In light of this, we can pose an uncomfortable dilemma. If the *Übermensch* embodies values contrary to the values of those in the value crisis, then the *Übermensch* cannot be an object of veneration for them. On the other hand, if the *Übermensch* embodies values those in the value crisis already hold, then there cannot be a real value crisis. Those purportedly undergoing a value crisis must have sound values after all. Put another way, without already having the right values, one cannot venerate the *Übermensch*.

One needs to be clear about the argument. It is not argued that the veneration of superior types cannot increase the sense of the worthwhileness of life in those who venerate; it clearly can, but it requires a specific value setting. In a setting of no values, or completely decayed values, or unhealthy values, those who embody healthy values cannot be objects of veneration. The veneration of the *Übermensch* can only arise in a society whose values are already healthy. Veneration of the *Übermensch* may come after the value cure, but it presupposes such a cure and cannot itself constitute it.[5] It is only a cure for the already cured. Thus, neither of these solutions is an adequate response to the initial problem. The first one does not address itself to the patient at all, while the second only offers a cure to the patient provided that the patient is already well. Let me see whether other alternatives fare better.

The Value-Creation Model

This model sees the essential point of the *Übermensch* in the new values that the *Übermensch* will create. "A change in values—that means a change in the creators of values" (Z I:15). Of course, the *Übermensch* will be a remarkable and superior being prior to the creation of the new values, but it is the new values to be created that matter most. In a section that begins with the mention of the *Übermensch* Nietzsche finishes the section as follows: "Like the sun, Zarathustra also wants to go down: Now he sits here and waits, old shattered law-tables around him and also new law-tables—half-written" (Z III:12, 3). The phrase "new half-written law-tables" is repeated several times and the context makes it compelling that the *Übermensch* is not the complete embodiment of the new values, that at least half of them are yet to be created. These new values will presumably be values for those in the value crisis, and will replace those lost with the withering of the Christian worldview.[6] The salient point concerns the mechanism by which those who have lost their values will be led to adopt the newly created ones. We can readily dismiss rational persuasion alone as a means that Nietzsche had in mind. This leaves two principal solutions, the attraction model and the imposition model.

Let me begin with the *attraction* model. In the past there have been individuals who have produced belief systems and value systems with an enormous capacity to attract people. Buddha, Mohammed, Confucius, and Jesus are outstanding examples. Countless millions of persons over many centuries have been drawn to these belief systems and have been willing to shape and organize their whole lives around them and their conceptions. No doubt coercion is not entirely missing from the picture, but attraction surely predominates. Viewing this phenomenon in Nietzschean terms, we are bound to conceive of these types as concentrated embodiments of the will to power, the level of concentration being such as to enable the production of these powerfully attracting conceptions. To be sure, other factors will have played a part in the embrace of these conceptions, in particular the nature of those who are attracted to them, but their intrinsic capacity to attract must be taken to be of prime importance.

Those who have lost their values in the value crisis will actually get new values from the *Übermensch*. Clearly, this model furnishes a more adequate solution to the initial problem than the previous two; those in the value crisis are actually catered to. But one can legitimately query the manner of acceptance of the new values. The main point is that we cannot conceive of this as a rational process. It is the inherently powerful drawing capacity of the conceptions themselves that will lead to their embrace. There are three reasons why it cannot be primarily a rational process. First, we have no suitable model of how a rational transition is possible from a state of having no values to a state of having values, or from a state of having values to a state of having values that are their antithesis. Second, there is Nietzsche's settled view that power is required to effect great changes. Third, on his theory of value, attraction and repulsion lie at the very basis of value.

If we accept that it is the intrinsic drawing power of the conceptions embodied in, for example, Buddhism, Islam, and Christianity rather than the hard rational case in their favor that basically explains their embrace, then we ought not to have difficulty in accepting the possibility of a similar process in the spread of the *Übermensch*'s new values. Of course, we know Nietzsche was attracted to this model. The basic idea behind *Thus Spoke Zarathustra* is just that of a superior type bringing new values to those in value-loss, value-degeneration, and value-confusion. Naturally, it does not follow that just because this is the idea behind *Thus Spoke Zarathustra*, that it must also be the idea of the *Übermensch* in *Thus Spoke Zarathustra*, but the point is worth making nevertheless. In any event, there is little doubt that Nietzsche had leanings toward this kind of solution, whatever other leanings he may have had. Looking at the solution as a whole, it is a pleasantly benign view of what might eventuate, but it is not the only view; another important possibility remains.

There is also the *imposition* model. In this solution, the *Übermensch* both creates the new values and imposes them by force. While religion may be a useful place to seek parallels for the attraction model, politics is a more useful place to seek parallels for the imposition model. Stalin can be taken as an exemplary case. No human cost was too great in the quest to have his new values take hold. There is no reason to believe the *Übermensch* would be more restrained, or even as restrained, in the imposition of the newly created values (WP 1027, 1028). One needs to keep in mind that the *Übermensch* will be "beyond good and evil." The *Übermensch* will not be activated by pity, sympathy, or "slave morality" conceptions of justice, equality, fairness, rights, sanctity of the individual, and so on:

> And if you will not be fates, if you will not be inexorable: how can you—conquer with me?
>
> And if your hardness will not flash and cut and cut to pieces: how can you one day—create with me?
>
> For all creators are hard. And it must seem bliss to you to press your hand upon millenia as upon wax,
>
> Bliss to write upon the will of millenia as upon metal—harder than metal, nobler than metal. Only the noblest is perfectly hard.
>
> This new law-table do I put over you, O my brothers: *Become hard!* (Z III:12, 29)[7]

From the standpoint of the old morality, the *Übermensch* may show no moral restraint whatever. It is a matter of regret that often Nietzsche's sympathizers do not recognize this possibility and his opponents recognize no other.

The picture can be softened a little. It is alien to Nietzsche's conception that the *Übermensch* take pleasure in cruelty for cruelty's sake. The *Übermensch* would not flaunt power in this way; the truly well-endowed and powerful, confident of their power, have no need to flaunt it or dissipate it uselessly. The petty use of power is fundamentally alien to this conception. But while this softens the picture a little, it does not soften it much. The "higher purpose" may still permit just about anything, and to say that they would not be gratuitously cruel is not to say that they would not cause great suffering if required. Surely, one would have to be absolutely certain that the "sickness" was extreme before acquiescing in cures with such drastic possibilities. To be sure, there is legitimate uncertainty that this is his preferred solution, but it is a possibility that cannot be explicitly ruled out. Further, although the attraction and imposition models have been dealt with separately, they are not mutually exclusive, and it is possible to construct a solution combining both. However, since such a solution does not raise any new problems or embody new advantages, it is sufficient merely to draw attention to it.

The time has come to assess the value-creation model. Both versions of the value-creation model are superior to the value-embodiment model *as solutions* to the initial problem. First, those in the value crisis, those who have lost their values, will get new values. The core of the problem is thus directly addressed. In addition, there are intelligible models of how the new values could be transmitted. But being a better solution does not necessarily entail being a good solution, and this issue also needs consideration. One can reason as follows. If there is a genuine value crisis and the continuation of this crisis poses a real threat to the well-being of the human species, then a cure is highly desirable, and it is difficult to see how it could be effected other than by exceptional persons inventing values that command assent or to which assent is commanded. This is as much as Nietzsche appears to be saying. But this is merely to diagnose a problem and indicate the direction in which the solution must lie. However, even if we do not quarrel with the diagnosis of the value crisis, there is no substantive solution here. The situation might be improved if there were positive steps to take to enhance the prospects of the *Übermensch* being produced, but, although we are enjoined to do so, there really are no concrete measures we can take.

There are seemingly paradoxical suggestions that conditions in which it is most difficult for superior beings to arise ought to be set up, for the truly superior being can only emerge in a struggle against the greatest difficulties. Consider the following observation that does not specifically mention the *Übermensch* but that is clearly relevant: "*Evil.*— Examine the lives of the best and most fruitful people and peoples and ask yourself whether a tree that is supposed to grow to a proud height can dispense with bad weather and storms; whether misfortune and external resistance, some kinds of hatred, jealousy, stubbornness, mistrust, hardness, avarice, and violence do not belong among the *favorable* conditions without which any great growth even of virtue is scarcely possible. The poison of which weaker natures perish strengthens the strong—nor do they call it poison" (GS 19). But this does not really help. Should we really make life exceptionally difficult for promising persons? Perhaps we can take the matter one step further and make life as easy as possible for promising persons. After all, one could argue that it is conditions in which life is as easy as it possibly can be that it is most difficult for the truly superior being to emerge. They would have to face the most difficult challenge of all, that of having no real challenges. To the extent that we are ignorant of what positive steps we can take to bring the *Übermensch* into existence, to that extent we have merely the form of a solution and not its substance. To call the expectation of the arrival of the *Übermensch* wishful thinking may be unkind, but it is not entirely inaccurate.

There are two further issues worth taking up, and both are concerned with the relation of these considerations to general aspects of Nietzsche's philosophy. One concerns the value crisis itself and the other concerns the *Übermensch*. It is something of a puzzle why Nietzsche thought that the "death of God" brings about such a grave value crisis requiring such a dramatic solution. The Christian God and the slave morality are two sides of the same coin; they are life-denying; they are other-world oriented, and they act in the interests of the ill-constituted. It is difficult to see why the "death of God" should not be welcomed by Nietzsche as a wonderful cleansing of the air. What is lost is simply a pernicious world view linked to equally pernicious values. Profound relief at the liberation seems the appropriate response. Since when is a special solution required for what must amount to a part of the real cure in its own right?

Of course, one might claim that the Christian world view and its associated values are not all bad, and that with the "death of God," the good is lost while the bad remains, and this is the basis for the value crisis. The problem with this is to identify anything that Nietzsche regards as good about Christianity that has now been lost. There are suggestions that the crisis is due to Christianity raising unrealizable expectations of what constitutes an answer to the problem of the meaning of life, and that these unrealizable expectations persist even after the "death of God" (WP 30). But it is difficult to see why the cultural and cognitive conditions that lead to the "death of God" should not inevitably lead to the death of such unrealizable expectations. For my part, it is something of a mystery why he did not regard the "death of God" as already, in its own right, constituting a return to healthier values. Naturally, it is possible that even healthier values may be improved upon, but if there really was a desperate value situation, it was surely the situation before the "death of God" rather than after. Thus, in the broader framework of his philosophy, the necessity for the *Übermensch* as a solution to a crisis may not be as great as generally conceived.

Further consideration of the relation of the *Übermensch* to other aspects of Nietzsche's philosophy is in order. The *Übermensch* fits best with his conception of the will to power. Indeed, we can characterize the *Übermensch* as the optimal human expression of the will to power. Given the permissibility of the connection, the *Übermensch* can less problematically be considered the embodiment of the highest values, quite independently of its functioning as a specific solution to a specific value crisis. But, of course, it is its role in the latter that leads to the positing of the connection with the will to power rather than the other way around. Nevertheless, it is worth further inquiry how well this ideal fits with other aspects of his philosophy.

Let me make some preliminary observations. In *On the Uses and Disadvantages of History for Life* (UM II) Nietzsche makes the point that too great an absorption in the past can be inimical to a current, healthy, dynamic, thriving life. One ought to limit one's interest in the past to what can be put in the service of life in the present. To have too great an orientation toward the past is to have too little orientation to the only thing that matters, the life we live now. Put abstractly, preoccupation with absent things can draw our attention away from the vital concerns of life. Next, consider a key point made against Christianity, namely that it constitutes a rejection of *this world* and an embrace of a fictional *other world*. Once again, we have a misdirection of attention from the here and now, from the vital concerns of life, and naturally, this is regarded as detrimental to life. But if we turn to the *Übermensch* in this context, we find that this being does not now exist. If it is to exist at all, it will be at some unknown time in the future. But surely, to pay too great an attention to this possible future event is potentially just as inimical to life as to pay too great an attention to past events; both rob us of energy for, and intensity of involvement in, the present.

Arguably, the fit between the doctrine of the *Übermensch* and his affirmative philosophy is not as tight as it could be.

It remains to consider how the *Übermensch* fits into the enterprise of revaluing all values. Of specific interest is the question of exactly what is new here. The *Übermensch* is not the articulation of a radically new value. The high valuation of superior persons is a pervasive feature of valuation independently of Nietzsche. The *Übermensch* is an extension, intensification, and refinement of such modes of valuation, and his higher-order values play a crucial role in the process. The principal difference is the weight attached to creativity and affirmation within the cluster of admirable characteristics, but even this is not unique. When it comes to the role of the *Übermensch*, it is revealing to compare Nietzsche's views with Christian conceptions. The *Übermensch* is a being not currently part of this world, but superior to beings that are currently part of the world, and the coming of the *Übermensch* to this world is required for this world to have any value. On standard Christian conceptions, God is a being not currently part of this world, but superior to beings that are currently part of this world, and a special relation of God to this world is required for this world to have any value. The parallel is quite marked.

The plight of the world without the *Übermensch* may not be deemed quite as bad in Nietzsche's picture as the plight of the world is without God in the Christian picture, but the difference is principally one of degree. As a solution, the *Übermensch* is from outside the world as it is now constituted, perhaps not as radically outside as God, but outside nonetheless. For all Nietzsche's reputed radicalism, the underlying positions are remarkably similar. No special malice is required to see in the *Übermensch* a small god, and to see in God a large *Übermensch*. Contrary to common perceptions, the *Übermensch* is not a radical breaking with the valuations of the past, although it purports to be. The desire for strong leaders in times of crisis is well-nigh a human universal. But then, in fairness to Nietzsche, he did not regard the *Übermensch* as his most important conception;[8] he reserved that estimate for the eternal recurrence.

The brunt of my criticism has been directed at the *Übermensch* as a solution to a specific problem. These criticisms do not apply to the *Übermensch* considered independently as an ideal type of human being and apart from the role of furnishing a solution to the purported value crisis. The ideal of a more dynamic, more disciplined, more creative, more life-affirming type than seen hitherto is not easily dented, nor do I see any reason to try. Indeed, if the *Übermensch* can properly be construed as the embodiment of the maximally affirmative attitude toward life and this world, then it is an ideal worthy of being taken with great seriousness.

The Eternal Recurrence

The underlying conception of the eternal recurrence is of the world repeating itself endlessly in identical cycles. According to the most natural interpretation, Nietzsche took the idea of eternal recurrence to be of enormous importance to questions of value.

> *The greatest weight.*—What, if some day or night a demon were to steal after you into your loneliest loneliness and say to you: "This life as you now live it and have lived it, you will have to live once more and innumerable times more; and there will be nothing new in it, but every pain and every joy and every thought and sigh and everything unutterably small or great in your life will have to return to you, all in the same succession and sequence—even this spider and this moonlight between the trees, and even this moment and I myself. The eternal hourglass of existence is turned upside down again and again, and you with it, speck of dust!"
>
> Would you not throw yourself down and gnash your teeth and curse the demon who spoke thus? Or have you once experienced a tremendous moment when you would have answered him: "You are a god and never have I heard anything more divine." If this thought gained possession of you, it would change you as you are or perhaps crush you. The question in each and every thing, "Do you desire this once more and innumerable times more?" would lie upon your actions as the greatest weight. Or how well disposed would you have to become to yourself and to life *to crave nothing more fervently* than this ultimate eternal confirmation and seal? (GS 341)

While this is a key passage it is only one of a number, and exactly how this doctrine is to be taken and how it bears on issues of value are matters of dispute. My intention is to consider two major strands of interpretation and assess their impact on values.

The Realistic Interpretation

It is central to this interpretation that the eternal recurrence is articulating a genuine hypothesis about the world.[9] This general interpretation encompasses several variations. In the first variation, the eternal recurrence is simply taken as a fact without a direct valuational message for the conduct of life.[10] In the second variation, it is the knowledge that eternal recurrence is a *fact* that is taken to have value consequences directly affecting conduct.[11] In the third variation, it is the *possibility* that eternal recurrence could be a *fact* that is taken to have value consequences directly affecting conduct. The underlying idea in the last two variations is that the recognition of either the fact or the possibility, either will alter the way we choose or must alter the way we choose, or will furnish an important ground for altering the way we choose. In these interpretations, impact on choice is paramount. The arguments for the eternal recurrence as fact or as real possibility are certainly important but they will not be considered; my concern is simply with the relevance to values.

It is important to understand how eternal recurrence can function in its impact on choice. One way is as follows. Eternal recurrence serves to multiply the consequences of our choices. We will get the consequences of a given choice not just once, but again and again and again. We can characterize it as an infinite multiplier of the consequences of our choices, or, if we wish to be more conservative, it is a multiplier without limit of the consequences of our choices. Take a mundane illustration from life. The decision what to have for lunch just for today may be important, but it is a decision that pales into insignificance when compared to a decision that would commit one to having exactly the same lunch every day for the rest of one's life. Put in a nutshell, eternal recurrence would make each decision vastly more momentous than we normally hold it to be; it vastly increases the pressure in making choices.

There are formidable arguments denying that eternal recurrence could have any effect on choice. Let me begin with one of the strongest. The supposition embodied in eternal recurrence is that each cycle is identical to every other cycle:

> "I shall return with this sun, with this earth, with this eagle, with this serpent—*not* to a new life or a better life or a similar life:
> "I shall return eternally to this identical and self-same life, in the greatest and in the smallest, to teach once more the eternal recurrence of all things." (Z III:13, 2)[12]

There are no special cycles, not this one, not the one before it, not the one after it, nor any other one. From this simple assumption, we can run the counterargument in several ways with essentially the same upshot. If we have real choice in this cycle, then we must have real choice in each cycle. But then a choice in this cycle does not fix anything for subsequent cycles; it does not set in concrete anything for subsequent cycles to repeat. Put simply, if the choice in this cycle is independent, then the choice in each cycle is independent. The situation is then parallel to my choosing a dish for lunch today and being just as free to choose the same dish tomorrow. Whatever freedom there is to choose in this cycle, the very same freedom must exist in every other cycle. Consequently, there is no additional pressure on current choice at all.

Consider the argument from the other direction. If in cycles subsequent to this one I have no freedom of choice, then I could not have had freedom of choice in this or any other cycle. The choices that I have made in an indefinite number of preceding cycles I will continue to make in this, and in an indefinitely increasing number of subsequent cycles. The contemplation of the number of cycles either has no effect, or has already had its effect in every preceding cycle and will continue to have its effect in every subsequent cycle whether I pay any attention to it or not. Put simply, if there is no choice in subsequent cycles, then there is no choice in this or in previous cycles. Let me pull the two strands together. If we are free to choose in each cycle, the pressure on our choice is off. Equally, if we have no choice in any cycle, the pressure on our choice is off. Yet each cycle must be identical, and either we are free to choose or not.[13]

For the "multiplier of consequences" pressure to eventuate, there must be something *special* about this cycle. We must be able to make choices in this cycle that become *fixed* in subsequent cycles. We must be free in this cycle in a way we are not free in subsequent cycles. Unfortunately, the impact on choice requires at least one special cycle, whereas the doctrine itself specifically precludes this. There can only be urgency if this cycle is different, but there is no way this cycle can be different. It is hard to see any way of circumventing this difficulty, nor is it the only difficulty. Problems also exist concerning memory and identity.

Let me take memory first. If the cycles are identical to each other, there can be no memory in one cycle of any previous cycle, for this would constitute a way the cycle with memory added differed from the previous cycle that lacked such a memory. It is then argued that it can be of no concern to me what happens in the next cycle, if in the next cycle I have no recollection of what happened in this cycle. Of course, if it can be of no interest to me what happens in the next cycle, then *a fortiori* it can be of no interest to me what choices in this cycle commit me to as far as the next and other cycles are concerned. Thus, the intended urgency entirely evaporates. While an intuitive grasp of this argument is not difficult, the underlying assumptions are not entirely clear. The crucial assumption appears to be this. The multiplier effect of the repetition will be defeated if there is no cumulative registration of the repetitions within conscious awareness. Of course, cumulative registration of the repetitions within conscious awareness is just what is precluded by the non-overlap of memory between cycles.[14]

Let me distinguish two levels of knowledge. First, there is the general proposition that an endless, identical repetition of cycles takes place. It is possible for this proposition about the sequence of cycles to be known in each cycle. Certainly, it could only get to be known by argument and inference, but that is irrelevant as long as it gets to be known in exactly the same way in each cycle. Second, there is the specific knowledge of what occurs in one cycle that is then carried over to the next cycle, which is then carried over to the next cycle, and so on. This is what I have called the cumulative registration of repetition in conscious awareness. Without doubt, the latter is precluded by the nature of eternal recurrence. The memory objection can now be put another way. If all we have is the general knowledge of the repetition of identical cycles, then the multiplier effect, though actual, is irrelevant to any issue of choice. This is an interesting claim and deserves attention.

Consider a number of possible cases. Suppose that I become the captive of an evil power called Nomem who confronts me with the following situation. Information is extracted of what I regard as the perfect, the most desirable way to spend one month, and of what I regard as the most horrific, the least desirable way to spend a month— a month of pure pleasure and a month of pure pain as I conceive it. Next, I am to perform an arduous task. If I do well, I will be granted the month of pure pleasure; if I do poorly, I will be inflicted with the month of pure pain. Call this case one. Naturally, in these circumstances, I will try hard to do well.

Now, suppose that Nomem has invented an anti-memory pill that can remove all memories of previous life experiences without impairing skills or comprehension in any way. Imagine that Nomem upgrades his offer in the following way. If I do well, then I will get the month of pure pleasure repeated indefinitely; if I do poorly, then I will get the month of pure pain repeated indefinitely. But there is a proviso, at the end of each month I will be given the anti-memory pill whatever the outcome. Call this case two. If the memory objection to the eternal recurrence is sound, then I ought to regard both case one and case two as absolutely equal, and I ought not to try any harder in the second case than I do in the first. But such a suggestion seems to me utterly fanciful; I would be vastly more concerned about my performance in the second case than in the first.

Next, suppose that Nomem offers me a further variation. Again there is the arduous task, the endless months of pure pleasure or pure pain with the anti-memory pill at the end of each month, except for the first month. In the first month, I am to have a perfectly ordinary month irrespective of my performance of the task, at the end of the month I receive the anti-memory pill, and the sequence of months of pure pleasure or months of pure pain begin depending on my performance on the task. Call this case three. If the memory objection to the eternal recurrence is correct, I ought not to be concerned about this case at all. In any event, I ought to be less concerned about it than about case one. But this seems to me quite wrong. I would be far more concerned about case three than about case one.

The principle these cases embody is this. It is the *totality* of pain to be experienced, or the *totality* of pleasure to be experienced, that is central to choice and action. It is the *actual occurrence* of pain and pleasure that is crucial, rather than the *cumulative representation* of them in a single unified conscious awareness. Of course, one cannot expect proof here, but further argument is possible. It is worse for two people to be in agonizing pain than for one person to be in agonizing pain, even worse for three, and so on. The fact that these pains do not occur in the same consciousness, or that there is no cumulative representation of them in one conscious awareness is hardly relevant. I simply ought to try harder to prevent the horrible suffering of three than to prevent the horrible suffering of one. Now, if, in thinking of others, the sheer quantity of pain is relevant irrespective of whether it occurs in one consciousness or whether it is sequentially remembered by any one person, why should the sheer quantity cease to matter in my own case just because the quantity is segmented by memory failure?

Putting it this way is liable to draw the following response. The segmentation of experience by the kind of memory loss imagined destroys personal identity. Consequently, the successive experiences of pain or pleasure separated by memory loss are the experiences of pain or pleasure of different persons, and while we may have some obligation to minimize the pain of others, it lacks the same urgency as minimizing our own. On this argument, eternal recurrence may affect choice, may have an impact on values, but it removes all personal urgency, for it will not be literally me in the next or subsequent cycles. But such a reply clearly shifts ground; here the crucial defeater is held to be failure of personal identity and not mere failure of memory. Failure of memory apparently only furnishes the basis for failure of personal identity.

Let me summarize the argument. Provided personal identity is preserved, then, even with the regular kind of memory loss envisaged in the Nomem cases, the memory loss itself does not remove a vital, legitimate concern for our own condition after each successive memory loss. The concern about what happens to me is still more direct and pressing than a concern about the fate of other persons. Memory loss on its own does not defeat the multiplier effect of eternal recurrence. In my terms, the multiplier effect is not contingent upon cumulative representation in conscious awareness; abstract knowledge of recurrence is sufficient provided that personal identity is preserved. Thus, the issue of personal identity is of some importance, and it is to this that I now turn. However, if my arguments are correct, then, while failure of personal identity may remove a great deal of the additional pressure from choice, it will, nevertheless, not remove all the additional pressure.

The claim that personal identity is not preserved in the cycles of the eternal recurrence has its supporters.[15] My response to the Nomem cases indicates that I do not regard memory non-overlap to be sufficient for the nonidentity of persons. But while I do not propose to undertake a comprehensive investigation of personal identity, there are observations worth making. Leaving the issue of memory aside for the moment, let me take one of the main arguments against the preservation of personal identity over successive cycles of the eternal recurrence. The essence of the case is as follows. The qualitative identity of persons is not sufficient for numerical identity, and eternal recurrence can never furnish more than the qualitative identity of persons over the successive cycles. Put another way, it is impossible to find sufficient conditions for personal identity across the cycles of recurrence.

To amplify the point, suppose that concurrently with this world and over its entire history there exist an indefinitely large number of qualitatively identical parallel worlds. Every object, every person, every event, indeed every feature is repeated exactly in each of these worlds. Suppose, however difficult it may be to do this consistently, that what I choose in this world occasions a corresponding choice by my qualitatively identical counterparts in the other concurrent worlds. Since these qualitatively identical counterparts are either located in different parts of space, or indeed, in different spaces altogether, the case is rock solid that I am not numerically identical with these counterparts. Consequently, I have no reason to feel the same sense of urgency about the fate of these counterparts that I now feel over my own fate. I have literally no reason to regard each of these counterparts as me. The claim then is that in the case of eternal recurrence the identity of myself and my qualitatively identical counterparts in the successive cycles is no better than the identity between myself and the qualitatively identical counterparts in concurrent worlds.

Undeniably, this is an important argument, but it is by no means conclusive. In the concurrent worlds, either the nonidentity of spatial location, or the nonidentity of the locating space, or the nonidentity of the material of composition is sufficient for the numerical nonidentity of myself and my qualitatively identical counterparts. But these nonidentity occasioning factors are absent from the successive cycles of the eternal recurrence. In the next cycle, "I" will be composed of just the same "stuff" or ontologically basic constituents that I am composed of in this cycle, and the successive spatial positions that "I" occupy in the next cycle will in no way differ from the ones that I occupy in this cycle. Of course, this raises the question of whether the numerically identical "stuff" or ontologically basic constituents[16] occur in each cycle, and while this would have to be argued, it appears to be the most natural assumption.

Let me draw these considerations together. Provided that the numerically identical "stuff" or basic ontological constituents occur in each cycle, and "I" am composed of the numerically identical "stuff" or basic ontological constituents in each cycle, the case for me being regarded as the same person in different cycles is a good deal stronger than for me and my qualitatively identical counterparts being regarded as the same person in the concurrent worlds. My qualitatively identical "I" in the next cycle will be composed of numerically the same "stuff" or ontologically basic constituents that I am composed of in this world. In clear contrast, the qualitatively identical counterparts to myself in the concurrent worlds cannot be made of numerically the same "stuff" or ontologically basic constituents that I am made of here.

Put generally, there is no more than qualitative identity in the concurrent worlds, whereas there is both qualitative identity and numerical identity of ultimate constituents in the successive cycles of the eternal recurrence. This does not conclusively establish that personal identity is preserved in the successive cycles. But it counters the claim that nothing beyond mere qualitative identity can be furnished by eternal recurrence. Something more than mere qualitative identity is possible, but whether that "more" is sufficient for personal identity across the cycles is another matter. Nevertheless, I take the following conclusion to be warranted. While there may be an arguable case, there is certainly no conclusive case that personal identity cannot persist over the successive cycles in eternal recurrence.

Returning to my central concern, if my previous arguments are correct, then the multiplier effect of the eternal recurrence obtains, if there is identity of persons across the successive cycles, even if memory is not preserved. On the other hand, if personal identity does not persist across the cycles, this does not entirely eliminate the multiplier effect of the eternal recurrence; the multiplier effect may be diminished, but it is not eliminated. For example, suppose that I make a bad choice that condemns me to an enormous amount of suffering, and thus also condemns the indefinite number of the qualitatively identical counterparts to myself in the successive cycles to an enormous amount of suffering. The consequences of my decision are multiplied in both cases. In the one case, they are multiplied for myself alone; in the other case, they are multiplied for myself and an indefinitely large number of qualitatively identical counterparts. Naturally, it makes the decision more momentous in both cases, though not necessarily equally momentous.

In summary, let me recall an earlier distinction. It could be either the knowledge of eternal recurrence as *actual* that is intended to impose urgency on our decisions, or it could be the mere *possibility* of eternal recurrence that is intended to impose urgency on our decisions. The principal difficulty for the former case was that it requires one cycle to be special; *this* cycle must fix matters for the successive cycles. It was argued that one cycle being special was incompatible with the nature of the arguments in favor of the actuality of eternal recurrence, and this constitutes a major stumbling block to its efficacy as a consequence of choice multiplier. On the other hand, if *mere possibility* is at issue, we can simply imagine the sequence of cycles with *this* cycle as special in the required way. In this way, the difficulty of the inconsistency of a special cycle with the arguments for the actuality of eternal recurrence is avoided. Regrettably, what we gain on one side, we lose on the other. Pure possibilities may have some capacity to exert pressure on our choices, but this capacity can in no way be equal to that of known actualities. It is difficult to see how the pure possibility option can maintain the required urgency and impact. After all, nonrecurrence is also possible. How do I incorporate the possibility of nonrecurrence into my choice alongside the possibility of recurrence? Does one have to give both possibilities equal weight?

Independently of the previous consideration, the last two interpretations also face considerable additional difficulties concerning choice. The model of choice that is required for these interpretations appears to be one that Nietzsche is explicitly opposed to: "But even when the moralist merely turns to the individual and says to him: '*You* ought to be thus and thus' he does not cease to make himself ridiculous. The individual is, in his future and in his past, a piece of fate, one law more, one necessity more for everything that is and everything that will be. To say to him 'change yourself' means to demand that everything should change, even in the past" (TI V:6). The implication is that one cannot simply deny and evade one's past and base one's action entirely on some current calculation about the future.[17] A major difficulty for interpreting the eternal recurrence as a guide to action is that it is required to be the kind of guide to action that Nietzsche did not regard as able to be acted on.

While the doctrine encounters formidable difficulties on this interpretation, it is still instructive to compare it to other conceptions. Nietzsche's view is not the only one that contains a consequence of choice multiplier. The Christian conceptions of Heaven and Hell are essentially consequences of choice multipliers. The consequences of "good" choices will be augmented by heavenly rewards; the consequences of "evil" choices will be augmented by the punishments of Hell. There is, of course, the additional parallel that the consequences go on forever. However, despite these similarities there are major differences, far more than in the case of the *Übermensch*.

On the Christian conception, the rules are laid down by an all-powerful being; they come from outside us, and we have absolutely no say in the matter. In addition to the natural consequences of human action, this all-powerful being deliberately attaches consequences that have no intrinsic connection with human actions in question. But what is most significant is the scale of the attached non-natural consequences. If we go counter to the rules of this all-powerful being, we are threatened with an eternity of the most horrible pain and suffering. No more extreme or coercive threat is imaginable. To suggest that we are free to obey or not obey in this context is a manifest absurdity. If this is freedom, what would compulsion look like? On Nietzsche's conception, we decide, we do, we face the natural consequences of our actions, and only these. Even if they are repeated endlessly, the responsibility is entirely our own. On his view, we have persons, as autonomous as it is possible for human beings to be, facing hard choices; on the Christian conception, we have persons in the shadow of an all-powerful God with his own agenda for everyone and irresistible means of enforcement. The contrast is undeniably striking.

There is another quite different conception that also furnishes an instructive contrast. In addition to there being consequences of choice multipliers there are also consequences of choice or life situation minimizers. The following is a standard case. We human beings are tiny specks of dust on a small rock in an unimaginably vast space, and even the longest life is but a brief flicker in the unimaginably vast extension of time. Typically, this picture is deployed to minimize the impact of some misfortune or pain; it does so by emphasizing the utter insignificance of these occurrences in the broader scheme of things. There can be little doubt that many people find such a conception of real use in times of distress; it works. But there is one significant drawback to this conception: if our pains and misfortunes are rendered insignificant, so are our joys, our accomplishments, our good fortune, indeed any of our positive values. It is a conception that minimizes the impact of good fortune just as effectively as misfortune. It may be medicine when times are bad, but it is poison when times are good.

Here, also, are important points of contrast with Nietzsche. On the one hand, there is his opposition to anything that would seek to diminish the value of life or this world. Insofar as this conception promotes such a diminution, it is inconsistent with his views. On the other hand, on a more specific level, he would regard the effort to make our problems and difficulties seem smaller as cowardice; far better to love life even in clear sight of the greatest difficulties. Put briefly, this conception seeks for an attenuated vision of life and its value; his conception seeks for an intensification of life and its value.

However, the conception that focuses on the minuteness of life in the vastness of space and the brevity of life in the immensity of time can be exploited in a more positive fashion. The very minuteness of the possible value that might be derived from the universe, given our own minuteness in it, makes it imperative—so it can be argued—that we extract the maximal value that we can from it, for there is not a droplet of value to waste.[18] Thus, this conception too can be seen as increasing the importance of choice. In eternal recurrence, it is the possibility of being overwhelmed by the consequences of choice that is the spur; in the conception just considered, it is the possibility of being underwhelmed by the consequences of choice that is the spur. Which one could exert the greater pressure on choice, and which one fits best with an affirmative attitude toward life are points that could well be pursued further, but it is time to return to the main issues.

The relations of eternal recurrence to other aspects of Nietzsche's philosophy are worth considering. Let me start by taking the realistic interpretation in its strongest form. This assumes that eternal recurrence actually takes place. As has frequently been pointed out in discussion, this doctrine does not fit well with perspectivism. It requires each cycle to be exactly the same as the cycle before it independently of any conceptualizations of the world by human beings or other species. It appears to require the world-in-itself have a completely articulated structure down to the finest detail independently of any knowing subject. Of course, a reply seeking to evade this consequence and reconcile the doctrine with perspectivism is possible. A perspectivist can argue that according to the best perspective we have managed to hammer out after the most strenuous efforts, the world repeats itself endlessly in identical cycles. Naturally, we are constrained to act on the best perspective available. However, the implication that it must be possible for there to be perspectives as good as our own that do not contain the doctrine of eternal recurrence can leave a sense of unease. If we take the realistic interpretation in its weaker form as confronting us merely with the possibility of eternal recurrence, the appearance of incompatibility diminishes significantly. These are only brief observations, but the following seems a fair summation. A considerable task is required to reconcile perspectivism with eternal recurrence on the above interpretations. The task might succeed, but that it will is by no means obvious.

If we relate the realistic interpretation of the eternal recurrence to the *Übermensch*, we again find that the fit is not optimal. The *Übermensch* is projected as the solution to an urgent value crisis. But if eternal recurrence obtains, then in *previous* cycles the *Übermensch* will already either have occurred or not occurred, and the very same will be repeated in *this* cycle. Indeed, the arguments in favor of the eternal recurrence contain the assumption that the cycles contain all that can possibly occur. Thus, if the *Übermensch* is possible, it will inevitably occur: if the *Übermensch* is not possible, it will inevitably not occur. There simply cannot be any urgency in the issue of whether the *Übermensch* comes about or not. Here it has to be kept in mind that each cycle must exhaust the possibilities, for if it does not, then the next cycle may contain previously unactualized possibilities and hence be different and not a recurrence at all.

A further point flows naturally from the previous consideration. There is a great deal of emphasis in Nietzsche's philosophy on activity, energy, change, on shaping, creating, imposing new forms, on the open possibilities for life. Both ontologically and valuationally the bent is away from the static, the unchanging, the uncreative, and the limited; the bent is toward nonrigid, nonregularized, constantly transforming ways of thinking rather than mechanical ways of thinking. The will to power is itself an embodiment of these ways of conceiving things. The eternal recurrence does not fit well with these ways of thinking. To begin, the number of possibilities is limited; they constitute a fixed finite number. Every real possibility will be actualized as a consequence of the ultimate constitution of reality. But why such an emphasis on creativity, if there are only a finite number of possibilities? Why such an emphasis on creativity, if every real possibility must be actualized? Furthermore, the overall conception is one of extreme rigidity and order; it warrants being called "clockwork" if anything does. Just as the hands of the clock go round, so do the cycles of the world. Of course, one can always legitimately observe that the intracyclical processes are not typically conceived of in such a rigid and ordered fashion, but this merely reinforces the point about an uncomfortable fit.[19] Nietzsche himself sees the doctrine as a reconciliation of mechanistic and Platonic modes of thought (WP 1061). But why he should be pleased by this—as he appears to be—is unclear, for elsewhere he shows little regard for either mode of thinking.

Turning to the valuational implications, on the grand scale the universe is totally fixed and unchanging; there is nothing other than an endless, numberless, monotonous repetition of the same.[20] If we recall Nietzsche's arguments that what is common, what occurs in a large profusion cannot really be valuable, then it is difficult to see how the conclusion can be avoided that the world is worthless. A completely unique world would appear to fit his general scheme of values better. There is surely a difficulty here. At the very least, one would like to have some explanation. Why does wholesale intracyclical repetition diminish value, while wholesale repetition of cycles themselves does not? Of course, he recognizes some of the valuational difficulties inherent in his conception: "'The man of whom you are weary, the little man, recurs eternally'—thus my sadness yawned and dragged its feet and could not fall asleep" (Z III:13, 2). The continuation of the passage appears to suggest that songs and singing may constitute a cure for Zarathustra's disgust, and one could take this to mean art in general or one could take this to mean the cultivation of an affirmative attitude. If the latter is intended, then the position embodied in the interpretation that follows may be being obliquely put. Again, I do not want to overplay the point, but on the realistic interpretation, the dissonance of his views appears to be more in evidence than their harmony.

The Attitude Portrayal Interpretation

On this interpretation, the function of eternal recurrence is to furnish a graphic characterization of the maximally affirmative attitude to this world and to oneself.[21] This interpretation has considerable independent support, but it is also to some extent a reaction to the perceived difficulties of the realistic interpretation. Concerning *Thus Spoke Zarathustra* Nietzsche writes, "The basic conception of the work, the *idea of eternal recurrence*, the highest formula of affirmation that can possibly be attained—"(EH IX:1). The maximally affirmative attitude is so strong it incorporates a love of life extending not only to its joys and good fortune, but also to its pains and misfortune. It embraces a love of *all* the aspects of life to the extent of eagerly welcoming their eternal recurrence in their entirety. Undoubtedly, this is an important conception. If one advocates, in the abstract, that one ought to have a maximally affirmative attitude toward life, it is hard to disagree; but by the same token, it is hard to know exactly what is meant. The eternal recurrence can be used to furnish one vivid conception of such an attitude.

To many, the eternal recurrence is the encapsulation of a highly inspiring attitude, but even as an attitude it has its criticisms. Considering the most important of these will help to clarify the conception. One objection is this. It is *irrational* to have a strong positive attitude toward one's pains and misfortunes. It is one thing to face them with courage and resolution, but it is quite another to wish their eternal recurrence. The rational course is to wish for their nonoccurrence in the first place, and for their nonrepetition in the second. The idea underlying this objection is the following. Occurrences in life each have a value in their own right independently of each other, and the rational course is to apportion our positive and negative attitudes accordingly. Pain and misfortune are independently bad, and we *ought* to have a negative attitude toward them; we *ought* to wish for their nonoccurrence and nonrepetition.

The objection depends on a specific conception of value that Nietzsche disclaims. For him, values arise from our own nature; they arise from our positive and negative orientations, from the power that draws to or repels from things. It is we who are the source of our own values; we are value makers not value takers.

> Evaluation is creation: hear it, you creative men! Valuating is itself the value and jewel of all valued things.
> Only through evaluation is there value: and without evaluation the nut of existence would be hollow. Hear it, you creative men! (Z I:15)

The values of the occurrences of life are determined by us. The value of pain and "misfortune" are not independently fixed givens; what value they have for us is at least in part up to us. Thus, having the strong positive attitude toward pain and "misfortune" that this conception of the eternal recurrence entails is not irrational in its own right. It is entirely consistent with the contextual nature of value embraced in his theory of value. Naturally, his theory of value may turn out to be unacceptable, but without that being demonstrated there is nothing obviously absurd in the above attitude.

But this is not the only issue concerning values. Also at issue is the whole question of how to evaluate one's life. We can distinguish two models for assessing value, a combinatorial model and a holistic model. On the combinatorial model, one takes individual life experiences independently of each other, assigns a certain positive or certain negative value to each experience, and then performs a summation operation to determine the value of the life as a whole. On the holistic model, what one evaluates directly is the life as a whole, the value of the whole is not derived from a prior, one by one, valuation of the parts. The holistic mode of valuation is typically the one employed in the arts. For example, the idea of dividing a picture into a thousand cells and independently aesthetically evaluating each cell, and then combining these valuations into an valuation of the picture as a whole is a manifest absurdity. Given that the models are bound to yield divergent results, it cannot be a matter of indifference which model is suitable in the evaluation of one's life.

The dominant motif in the eternal recurrence is on the repetition of one's *whole life* irrespective of the character of the parts. It is natural to take this as both implicitly operating with the holistic model and advocating its employment. If the holistic model is appropriate, then there is no difficulty in taking a highly positive attitude toward one's life as a whole without even regarding it as sensible to evaluate the parts independently. If we return to the case of evaluating a painting, there is nothing absurd in judging a picture to be a fine picture while at the same time regarding it as valuational nonsense to pass independent aesthetic judgments on each of the individual cells that it might be divided into. It was argued in chapter 3 that Nietzsche is committed to an aesthetic value-model for evaluating human beings, and the holistic model for evaluating a life can be seen as simply another application of it.[22]

Indeed, there are more fundamental reasons to suppose Nietzsche is committed to a holistic model. His theory of value commits him to the view that goals cannot be evaluated independently of their relations to other goals, so the combinatorial model is ruled out at a basic level. The employment of the holistic model constitutes an important step in rendering the maximally affirmative attitude embodied in the eternal recurrence intelligible. Those who wish to maintain that the maximally affirmative attitude embodied in his conception is absurd have a task ahead of them to show this. Not only will they have to demonstrate the acceptability of an alternative theory of value, but they will also have to argue a successful case for their own specific model for evaluating a life.

Another important point concerns personal identity. To wish that the pains and misfortunes of one's life had not occurred either presupposes that one could still be the same person that one is without these occurrences, or else that one actually wishes to be another person. Taking the first case, for Nietzsche there is no "pure self" that is only contingently related to its life-experiences, or "real self" that is essentially related to some of its experiences and only contingently related to others. The self is the totality of what one does and undergoes.[23] Hence, one cannot literally wish to be the same person and yet not have undergone the pains and misfortunes that one has. The only real option here is to wish to be a different person. To be sure, this is a person that resembles one quite closely but does not undergo the pains and misfortunes that one has undergone. But for Nietzsche, to wish to not be the person that one is constitutes the extreme limit case of a negative attitude. With this in mind, it is easier to understand how the eternal recurrence involves not only the maximally affirmative attitude toward this world but also a maximally affirmative attitude toward oneself. One's attitude toward oneself is so affirmative that one wishes for one's own eternal recurrence that must, of course, be without change. Indeed, he thought only the greatest persons were capable of so affirmative an attitude: "My formula for greatness in a human being is *amor fati:* that one wants nothing to be other than it is, not in the future, not in the past, not in all eternity. Not merely to endure what happens of necessity, still less to dissemble it—all idealism is untruthfulness in the face of necessity—but to *love* it . . ." (EH II:10). For some, a ground for espousing the attitude portrayal interpretation in preference to the realist interpretation is that it is perceived as avoiding the principal difficulties of the latter. This perception is only partly correct. Personal identity across the cycles of the eternal recurrence is certainly one of the crucial problems for the realist interpretation. However, what has not been equally noted is that it is almost as great a problem for the attitude portrayal interpretation. To have a coherent desire, or a willingness, or a positive attitude toward having one's life repeated over endless identical cycles requires it to be conceptually coherent that it is actually oneself in each of these cycles, and not a merely qualitatively identical counterpart. If all that was logically possible was to have a maximally affirmative attitude toward an unending sequence of nonidentical but qualitatively indistinguishable counterparts, then much of the appeal of the notion would be lost. The logical coherence of the attitude requires the logical coherence of the intentional object of that attitude. If personal identity across cycles is logically incoherent, then it is logically impossible for me to adopt an affirmative attitude toward the endless repetition of *my* life in such cycles. One cannot positively welcome a conceptual impossibility. In considering the realist interpretation I argued that the impossibility of personal identity across the cycles of eternal recurrence had not been established. Thus, I am not urging the point as an objection to the attitude portrayal interpretation. The case I am putting is simply that the attitude portrayal interpretation does not necessarily evade the problem of personal identity, and its having done so cannot unequivocally be counted among its advantages over the realist interpretation.

Having considered objections to this interpretation, let me turn my attention to its more positive aspects. What we have is essentially a picture, a picture of a maximally affirmative attitude toward life. But what is the use of a picture? Philosophers in particular, who typically have it hammered into them that everything needs to be supported by arguments, are usually not impressed by the mere presentation of a picture. Can there be a serious point to the presentation of such a picture? It is useful to consider the point by relating the maximally affirmative attitude to a broader philosophical context. In thinking about the meaning of life, especially under the influence of Christianity, the view has developed that the answer must somehow consist in the espousal of some doctrine. One will understand what the meaning of life is, once one accepts the right doctrine or theory or view. That is, the meaning of life will itself be given by way of some articulatable cognitive construct. But for Nietzsche, all cognitive constructs are limited constructions constrained by biology, experience, temperament, time, and place. Such fleeting fragments produced by life itself could not possibly furnish the meaning of life. Or, put directly, there is no intellectual solution to the "problem" of the meaning of life; indeed, there is no intellectual problem of the meaning of life. How could a mere fragment of life—a thought, a transitory state of life itself—put the whole value of life in question? "One must reach out and try and grasp this astonishing *finesse, that the value of life cannot be estimated*" (TI II:2).

Insofar as there is a real difficulty at the root of our unease, the resolution is to be sought in attitude rather than intellectual inquiry.

For Nietzsche, the whole quest for the meaning of life is misconceived if it is conceived as the quest for an intellectual answer. The maximally affirmative attitude toward life replaces the misguided search for intellectual solutions. Thus, the maximally affirmative attitude toward life is not simply one value among a number of his values; it is that attitude whose embrace constitutes the only resolution that is possible in feelings of disquiet about the meaning of life. Of course, he is not unique in seeing the resolution of the felt difficulty in attitude rather than doctrine; Zen Buddhism takes much the same position, even if its conception of the attitude involved is quite different. Nevertheless, Nietzsche's conception ranks among the few of real importance on this issue.

To return to the role a picture of the maximally affirmative attitude can play in the acceptance of values, it is useful to remember that basic values cannot be established by argument, for there are no more basic value premises from which they could be derived. In this regard, Nietzsche is in no worse a position than anyone else. It is not, and cannot be, underpinning arguments that are the ground for the acceptance of basic values; it must be the drawing power of the values themselves. For those like him who wish to replace old values with new values, there are fundamentally only two tasks: to destroy the old values and to present new values with an inherent power to attract. The basic new values can no more have underpinning arguments than the basic old values had. Success depends entirely on the drawing power of the new values. It is here that "pictures" can be important. To advocate a maximally affirmative attitude toward this life in abstract terms is to advocate something so tenuous as to be almost contentless. The concrete representation of such an attitude by way of the eternal recurrence is certainly more compelling.

For Nietzsche, new values must be articulated in a way that engages the whole person and not just the "intellect": "What has first to have proved itself is of little value" (TI II:5). The "intellect" is an abstraction, and even then of only part of a person. The "intellect" is not excluded from this value acquisition process, but it is secondary to the rest of one's nature; one's emotions, desires, passions, senses, capacities and so on all need to be involved: "One chooses dialectics only when one has no other expedient" (TI II:6). He regarded *Thus Spoke Zarathustra* as articulating his positive values, and it is manifest that it is far more a deliberate attempt to beguile than a deliberate attempt to convince rationally. But rather than regarding this as a failure to do what ought to be done, there is a strong case for regarding it as the only thing that can be done to get new values accepted.

Naturally, this does not entail that values are immune to rational processes. The issue really is of when, where, and how rational processes come into play. On one model, the initial advocacy of values, even basic values, must be rational in the sense that reasons, grounds, evidence, more basic judgments, or the like, must be adduced in favor of these values from the beginning. With a little malice this could be called the "stilts" model of rationality: no proposition can walk on its own legs but always requires the "stilts" of other evidentially supporting propositions. The model is highly problematic in its own right, for the "stilts" need "stilts" that in turn need "stilts" ad infinitum. But when we are dealing with basic values, we are by hypothesis dealing with something that cannot be supported by anything more basic, for there is nothing more basic to act as support. The "stilts" model is clearly inappropriate as a model for the advocacy of basic values.

There are, of course, other models of rationality. On another model, the rationality of claims depends not on the quality of antecedent reasons, but rather on the capacity of claims to survive subsequent critical onslaught; it is survival capacity and not ancestry that matters.[24] This is a far more suitable model for the advocacy of basic values, and one that I take Nietzsche to be implicitly operating with. Once propounded, values may be dissected, criticized, and compared; their fit with what we are independently prepared to accept may be assessed; presuppositions may be unearthed; consequences may be extracted; alternatives may be proposed, and so on. But to begin their life, basic values do not antecedently need to be propped up by anything; nor could there be anything to prop them up with.

If this is correct, it is a mistake to require that Nietzsche furnish rational grounds for his conception of a maximally affirmative attitude. Given that the maximally affirmative attitude is one of his basic values, it is simply inappropriate to require it to be supported by reasons that cite more basic values. The point is this. It is not rational to reject this conception *just because* it has not been antecedently supported by reasons, for it cannot be supported by reasons that articulate more basic values. From this standpoint, presentation of a compelling "picture" may indeed be the appropriate means of launching basic values. But there are other kinds of "reasons" than more basic values that can be adduced in defense of the maximally affirmative attitude, the principal one being his own theory of value. If we raise the question, for whom is the world most valuable? then in terms of his theory of value the answer is that the world is most valuable to those who are most powerfully drawn to it. Thus, the ideal of the maximally affirmative attitude is not floating free and unconnected to anything else, it is fully in tune with his theory of value.

While I have not sought to resolve the issue, the attitude portrayal interpretation seems to capture what is central to Nietzsche's thinking better than the realistic interpretation. In addition, there is a notably better fit between the attitude portrayal interpretation and other major aspects of his philosophy. For example, it does not conflict with perspectivism; it does not imply strictly limited creative possibilities; it lends more point to the conception of the *Übermensch*, and so on. Of course, there are other interpretations. In one recent interpretation, the eternal recurrence is seen neither in realistic terms nor directly in attitude terms but rather as an ongoing challenge to self-creation in the here and now.[25] But doubts about where the impetus to self-creation is to come from if the recurrence is not real, and the lack of affirmation of the world beyond the self place limits on the persuasiveness of the interpretation.

SEVEN

A Survey of Strategies

The Current Position

Representative cases of revaluation have been considered, but there has been as much focus on the substance of the revaluations as on the underlying strategies. This has created a setting where the strategies can be considered directly. By far the most important instruments of revaluation are Nietzsche's own higher-order values. They give the whole enterprise a shape and direction it would otherwise lack and unify the consideration of areas as diverse as knowledge, morality, religion, and art. The higher-order values are themselves grounded in his theory of value, although they are not reducible to it. Both the higher-order values and the theory of value are subject to rational assessment, and hence their employment constitutes no barrier to the intelligibility of the enterprise of revaluing the highest values and the enterprise of revaluing all values. However, the importance of the higher-order values to the project of revaluation ought not blind us to the importance of other strategies whose existence is vital to the intelligibility of the project overall. His higher-order values and theory of value have been considered in chapter 1, thus the ensuing focus is on the remaining strategies, although aspects of the higher-order values come into play as well.

It is difficult to develop a satisfactory classificatory scheme for revaluation strategies, and a residual level of arbitrariness appears to be ineliminable, but the effort is worthwhile for it can facilitate understanding. Apart from the application of higher-order values, the revaluation strategies can be seen as falling into four groups. First, there are those strategies that promise destruction from within the attacked value systems. Theoretically, these are important cases both for the revaluation of the *highest* values and for the revaluation of *all* values, for they offer the prospect of revaluation without utilizing substantive auxiliary value assumptions. Second, there are those strategies that furnish challenges from without the attacked value systems. Naturally these appear to be the most problematic cases. Seemingly, if the external material contains values, then these values must be higher than those attacked and not themselves subject to attack, in which case neither the *highest* nor *all* values could be being revalued. Third, there are those strategies that involve a reorientation of inquiry, that invite considering value issues from new points of view. Finally, there is the explicit advocacy of new values to replace the old.

Destruction from Within

Value systems are as subject to internal defects as any other kind of system. Nietzsche exploits both traditionally acknowledged defects and adds some of his own. In considering these strategies I propose to take them in order of potency.

Contradiction

The value system that contains absolute truth as its peak value presupposes the consistency of the concept of a knower who can become aware of independent states of affairs without the knower's own nature influencing the content of awareness. For Nietzsche, such knowing requires an interaction that is not an interaction. In other words, the concept of such a knower is contradictory.

> Henceforth, my dear philosophers, let us be on guard against the dangerous old conceptual fiction that posited a "pure, will-less, painless, timeless knowing subject"; let us guard against the snares of such contradictory concepts as "pure reason," "absolute spirituality," "knowledge in itself": these always demand that we should think of an eye that is completely unthinkable, an eye turned in no particular direction, in which the active and interpreting forces, through which alone seeing becomes seeing *something,* are supposed to be lacking; these always demand of the eye an absurdity and a nonsense. (GM III:12)

It would be absurd to advocate as an ideal something that it is logically impossible to attain. Whether he is correct that the concept of absolute truth presupposes such a concept of a knower, or whether he has shown it to contain a contradiction is arguable, but I take him to have presented a good case. If we grant that he is right about the connection and the contradiction, what can we conclude about the project of revaluation?[1]

Establishing that a value system contains a contradiction certainly appears an ideal revaluation strategy, but there are points to consider. The first one concerns scope. Could the contradiction generating assumption simply be removed while preserving the rest of the value system? Take the case of set theory. The proposition that there is a set containing all and only those sets that do not contain themselves is contradictory. But of course this did not spell the end of set theory. The contradiction was traced to an unrestricted axiom of set existence; this was modified and the bulk of set theory was preserved.[2] Perhaps the contradiction in the absolute theory of truth is like this, requiring only a minor adjustment to be rehabilitated. After all, there are stratagems, such as Tarski's ban on semantically closed languages,[3] to avoid the generation of other contradictions involved with truth. If these are sound parallels, the discovery of a contradiction can simply be a prelude to fine-tuning rather than to overthrow. Nietzsche would hardly be happy with the suggestion that all he had shown was that the absolute theory of truth required fine-tuning.

However, the parallels may not be as great as they initially appear. While there may be instances where contradictions are easily dealt with, there are other cases where they are more serious. Suppose, for example, that a contradiction had been found not just in the concept of one special set, but rather in the concept of "set" itself, in the concept of any set whatever. In that event, we would surely have to abandon set theory itself. Nietzsche's finding a contradiction in the case of the absolute theory of truth looks more like the devastating latter case than the milder case considered before. Nor is Tarski's case exactly parallel. According to Tarski, the unrestricted application of the truth predicate generates contradictions such as the liar paradox. But the contradiction does not arise from the analysis of the content of the concept of truth in its own right; it arises simply from the unrestricted application of a predicate, irrespective of whether we have analyzed the underlying concept. Nietzsche's case is different.

Contradiction may have a minor impact or it may have a major impact; it depends essentially on the centrality to the system of the contradictory notions. Consider another case. If we were to find both that the concept of *point* was contradictory and that the concept of *line* was contradictory, we would surely have to alter our conception of the status of geometry radically. It is reasonable to maintain Nietzsche conceived of the defect in the concept of absolute truth as having as basic and central a role in the absolute theory of truth as the concepts of point and line have in geometry. While it is not my intention to make final judgments about the success of his strategies, it is important to note that contradiction can sweep away whole systems at a time, and this is surely important if one is seeking to revalue *all* values. The unearthing of contradictions must be regarded as a major strategy in such an enterprise.

Another aspect of the enterprise needs consideration, namely, the revaluing of the *highest* values. Can contradiction be effective against the *highest* values? To be convincing, we must deal with the argument that contradiction cannot touch the highest values, because it itself presupposes a commitment to values. The argument proceeds as follows. When we reject a system that contains a contradiction, we do so on the grounds that we espouse consistency as a value. Hence, rejecting systems on the basis that they contain contradictions is not a value-neutral procedure. Let me explicate the value-model involved with an apparently parallel case. We regard health as a definite positive value; smoking is an independently identifiable activity that we may reject because we value health. We regard consistency as a definite positive value; a system with contradictions is independently identifiable and one that we may reject because we value consistency.

One can argue that if consistency was the peak value in a system of cognitive values, it can never be threatened or dislodged by the discovery of a contradiction, for the positive value *consistency* would itself be used to reject a contradiction when it was found. Consistency would still remain the peak value. Put another way, if we do not value consistency and continue to value consistency, contradiction is powerless to force the rejection of anything whatever. Indeed, in this way of conceiving the matter contradictions are rejected for a reason; contradictions cannot work to reject if that reason is absent. Contradiction *by itself* could not overthrow consistency as a value; contradiction moves nothing when consistency as a value is not in force. This looks as if it poses a serious threat to the enterprise of both revaluing *all* values and of revaluing the *highest* values. If there are values even contradiction cannot overthrow, then the prospect for revaluing *all* values is not promising.

To my mind, there is a flaw in this argument. The core assumption is that contradictions are rejected for a *reason*, that reason being an independent embrace of the value of consistency. What I propose to argue is that contradictions are not rejected for a reason, or at any rate, not for an independent reason that lies outside of the contradictions themselves. Consider the following case. My bank manager says to me, "I am categorically offering you a million dollar loan and I am categorically not offering you a million dollar loan." What am I supposed to do? Think of how absurd it is to say, "I am rejecting your offer because I value consistency." The plain fact is that I am not confronted with anything that is even a candidate for rejection, much less a candidate for rejection for a reason. What the bank manager said is self-canceling or self-voiding; no further reason for canceling or voiding is required or possible.

What I am arguing is that talk of rejecting a contradiction is misleading; properly speaking, there is nothing to reject. Suppose that I have a sheet of paper blank on one side and "Five is a number and five is not a number" written on the other side. Certainly, I cannot reject what is on the blank side because I value consistency; there is simply nothing to reject. But equally, there is nothing for me to reject on the other side either; whatever was being attempted to be said was simultaneously being withdrawn. Of course there is a sentence there, but there is no rejectable claim. Suppose that my faith in consistency waned, could I go back to the bank manager and accept his offer? But there is no offer. We do not need *reasons* to reject contradictions. Contradictions are *self-canceling* or *self-voiding;* they themselves effect a situation where there is nothing to accept or reject; no higher values need be or can be invoked to do their job for them. The efficacy of contradiction does not reside in the embrace of a higher value. To make a formerly unnoticed contradiction explicit is to show that what was taken to be a matter of substance is in fact empty.

If this account of contradiction is correct, then there is no special problem about contradiction reaching even the highest values. Contradiction cancels without appeal to other values. Thus, the intelligibility of the enterprise of revaluing all values gains additional support. No value system is immune from collapse through contradiction. Contradiction is a value-free means of revaluing values and its scope is unlimited. However, there is a qualification concerning contradiction that needs to be mentioned. I have dealt only with the negative employment of contradiction. I have not addressed interpretations that see Nietzsche as deliberately employing contradiction to convey a "positive" position impossible to convey in any other way. Whether there are such self-conscious uses of contradiction to present a positive position in Nietzsche, and whether theoretical sense could be made of such uses are not issues I propose to take up. I am not convinced that there are such uses, and my own analysis of contradiction is not sympathetic to such a procedure.

False Presupposition

Disinterested contemplation as the ideal of aesthetic contemplation presupposes that human beings are capable of disinterested contemplation. But according to Nietzsche it is false that human beings can disengage themselves from their desires, passions, and so on, in aesthetic contemplation. The value requires a fact to obtain that, as it turns out, fails to obtain. We can put the point in more graphic terms: the "pure aesthetic contemplator" is a fiction. He employs this strategy widely. For example, in the previous section reference was made to his view that there was a contradiction in the concept of a knower required by the absolute theory of truth, but there is also an empirically based argument that all knowing in this world is an interaction between the knower and the known, the nature of the knower coloring the product with its own nature. Putting the conceptual incoherence of contradiction aside, there is also the fact that we cannot in this world come to know in the way required by the absolute theory of truth. The "pure knower" is a fiction. Thus, the "pure knowing subject" is not only a fiction on conceptual grounds, the "pure knowing subject" is also a fiction on empirical grounds.

Nor are these the only cases. Altruistic action requires the ability to detach ourselves completely from our own interests and have our action guided by a single, entirely independently functioning motive, namely, the good of another. For Nietzsche, the way we are constituted does not allow for such a detachment. The "pure disinterested agent" is a fiction. Free will that is intimately connected with the value of punishment requires an action to issue from an agent in such a way that it is not merely the inevitable consequence of either a part or the totality of what the agent is. But in this world what we do is a consequence of what we are. The "pure moral agent" is a fiction. As in the previous case, the "pure moral agent" is not only a fiction on conceptual grounds, the "pure moral agent" is also a fiction on empirical grounds.

What makes these cases important is this. Value systems frequently contain presuppositions about the world. To reject the value system it is not always necessary to attack the purely valuational component; showing the factual presuppositions to be untenable is sufficient in many cases for a collapse of the system as a whole. Here we apparently have another case where values can be revalued without recourse to other values. Certainly, it furnishes a strategy whereby aesthetic values can be revalued without employing other aesthetic values; whereby moral values can be revalued without using other moral values; whereby religious values can be revalued without using other religious values, and so on. In light of this, it might be supposed that we have here another entirely value-free means of revaluing values. But in an important sense this is not so. The efficacy of the strategy relies on truth being a value. No particular account of truth is mandated, but without truth as a value the machinery will not move. The strategy is powerless against those with no interest in truth. Those who hold that they are entitled to believe whatever makes them feel good are unlikely to be troubled by this strategy.

The strategy can also be deployed against cognitive value systems that embody specific conceptions of truth, but it still requires commitment to truth as a value. However, this point ought not to be overplayed. While the strategy relies on cognitive values, it provides a moral-value-free means of revaluing moral values: an aesthetic-value-free means of revaluing aesthetic values; a religious-value-free means of revaluing religious values, and so on. The existence of this strategy graphically illustrates the point that in the revaluation of moral values, for example, one is not restricted simply to confronting one set of substantive moral values with another set of substantive moral values. Thus, insofar as Nietzsche's critiques deploy this strategy, they cannot be rejected on the grounds that he is merely using his own values to reject values incompatible with them. His arguments concerning the facts of the matter need to be assessed.

Self-undermining Advocacy

Near the end of my consideration of altruism in chapter 3 I pointed out that, according to Nietzsche, altruism is advocated for unaltruistic reasons.[4] Those who advocate altruism do so to serve their selfish interests, and he takes this to constitute a form of self-refutation. To discuss the underlying strategy, let me simplify the case. Suppose that altruism had only ever been advocated for selfish reasons. It is natural to feel that the status of altruism as a value would be significantly diminished if this were true, but it is rather more difficult to account for this feeling. Certainly we do not have a straightforward contradiction. It is closer to what has been called pragmatic self-refutation, but it is not quite that either. Take a standard case of pragmatic self-refutation. A person utters in English the sentence "I am not now uttering an English sentence." The very act of utterance furnishes the sufficient ground for the falsity of the content of the utterance. The refutation is decisive; there is nothing left to argue about. On the other hand, one who utters the sentence "Altruism is good" with the definite, but not necessarily publicly revealed, intention to secure a benefit for oneself and oneself only does not refute the content of the utterance in anything like the same decisive fashion, if indeed at all in the individual case.

Pragmatic self-refutation as it is usually understood furnishes too strong a model of what is involved. Nevertheless, it is surely right to feel that if altruism were universally advocated for selfish reasons only, this would seriously weaken its status as a value. Let me uncover the basis for this feeling. To begin, we need to distinguish two different accounts of the nature of value judgments such as "Altruism is good." On the objectivist account, the judgment is a straightforward candidate for truth and falsity, and the independently existing valuational facts make it one or the other. Here it looks as if the motives underlying the advocacy of a particular value are irrelevant to the truth or falsity of the value judgment in question. Strictly speaking this is correct, but the matter is conceived too narrowly. There is not only the question of truth, there is also the question of the grounds for believing something is true.

Typically, if everyone believes something to be true this furnishes some ground for believing it is actually true. Similarly, if everyone believes something to be false this furnishes some ground for believing it is actually false. Take a hypothetical case. Suppose that there was a claim that a UFO landed in the stadium at half-time during the Super Bowl. If we interviewed every person present and each one believed the claim to be true, we would have some ground to believe it was true. If we interviewed every person and each one believed the claim to be false, we would have some ground to believe it was false. The grounds are not conclusive and everybody could be wrong, nevertheless unanimity gives a ground for belief. Correspondingly, if everyone other than myself genuinely believes it to be true that altruism is good, then this gives me some ground to believe that it is true. By the same token, if everyone other than myself genuinely believes it to be false that altruism is good, then this gives me some ground to believe that it is false.

Now if altruism has only ever been advocated for selfish reasons, then on any occasion "Altruism is good" is uttered, the utterer does not believe it to be true that altruism is good; they believe that promoting self-interest is better. If it is in fact held not to be good by all those who appear to be saying it is good, and these constitute the majority of persons, then this furnishes a ground for not believing it to be good. If we discover that universally people have feigned to espouse a particular value, while in fact espousing its opposite, then we have some ground for espousing this latter unfeigned value. Put simply, the more people there are who do not believe that altruism is good, the more reason we ourselves have to believe that it is not good. Let me call this "evidentially undermining advocacy." When this takes place it may still be true that altruism is good, but our grounds for believing it to be true are lessened. Even if values are objective, detected hypocritical advocacy is evidentially undermining.

But we have dealt with only one conception of the nature of value judgments, namely the objectivist one, and we need also to deal with a subjectivist conception. On the subjectivist conception, the sentence "Altruism is good" when sincerely uttered is merely an indicator of the utterer's positive orientation toward altruism. Here the problem for someone trying to decide about values is different. The problem concerns whether one should take a positive attitude toward altruism. Suppose that I am in doubt about whether to take a positive orientation toward altruism or not; what kinds of considerations could be of help in making up my mind? One way to begin is to restate the problem. Would I feel there to be more value in my life if I adopted a positive attitude toward altruism rather than a negative attitude? Introspection by itself is powerless to settle the matter, and the only other place I can look is to other people.

If it turns out that all of those people who appear to be advocating altruism do not have a positive attitude toward it but rather the reverse, and it turns out that these people are in the majority, then it is reasonable for me to conclude that the majority of people do not feel that the value of their lives is increased by adopting a positive attitude toward altruism. Unless I know myself to be different from other people in a relevant respect, the facts I am confronted with give me ground to believe that if I adopt a positive attitude toward altruism, this would not lead to my feeling that the value in my life had been increased, and may well lead to the opposite feeling. The fact that the majority of others have judged that altruism can make no positive contribution to their lives gives me ground to believe that it will also make no positive contribution to my life.

If altruism has always only been advocated for selfish reasons, then it has only ever been advocated by persons who do not have a positive attitude toward it. Such advocacy, should it be discovered, undermines the attraction of altruism. Clearly, it has no attraction to those who appear to be advocating it. Let me call this "attraction undermining advocacy." When this takes place, it may still be the case that my taking a positive attitude toward altruism would make a worthwhile contribution to my life, but the indications are against it. Thus, whether one is an objectivist or a subjectivist about values, the selfish advocacy of altruism damages the value, and Nietzsche is within his rights to employ this as a revaluation strategy. At the same time, let me make it clear that I have no reliable information about whether in some, most, all, or no cases altruism has been advocated for selfish reasons. Naturally, the success of the strategy requires fact rather than conjecture concerning the motives behind the advocacy of altruism, but my central point is that the strategy can make serious inroads on values, if we had the required facts. Perhaps the strategy cannot have quite the strong impact that Nietzsche thought that it did, but that is a relatively minor consideration.

Means and Ends Confusions

The attack on altruism as the highest value proceeds in part by pointing out that the worth of altruism derives from the benefits that the aided individuals derive. Conceptually, altruism is a means requiring other values as ends. This point cannot damage altruism to the point of dictating its abandonment, but it furnishes the basis for a convincing case that altruism cannot be the highest value. After all, revaluation can just as readily lead to downgrading as to rejection. Indeed, downgrading is the best result that can be expected from the commission of this error alone. As a revaluation tool, it is less drastic than the first two.

Altruism is not the only place where means and ends confusions are exploited. Nietzsche denies that pleasure and pain are ultimate ends, in part as a consequence of his biological orientation. For the body, pleasure and pain are means to bodily well-being. This fact surely requires those who wish to maintain that pleasure and pain are ends in themselves to demonstrate what it is about these states that warrants mere means for the body being converted into ultimate ends for the person. Doctrines that hold to pleasure and pain as ultimate ends and have no answer to this point are definitely weakened by it. Clearly there is real scope for revaluation based on a detection of this confusion.

Related to but conceptually distinguishable from means and ends are the notions of cause and effect. Nietzsche thought that the confusion of cause and effect, with effects being taken for causes and vice versa, was a major source of error in thinking, particularly in thinking about the mind (TI VI). It is particularly important in the devaluation of consciousness, for the whole realm of consciousness is seen as the arena of mere effects and not of causes. The point is also exploited in the attack on free will that is, of course, heavily implicated in the "moral values." The parallel reveals a systematic aspect in his approach. In this instance, it shows itself in the detection of formally similar reversals in apparently unrelated areas. Just as, in some cases, means have been mistaken for ends, so, in other cases, effects have been mistaken for causes.

Before turning to another group of revaluation strategies, let me make some observations about this group as a whole. It should be plain by now that revaluation is not simply confronting one substantive value system with another substantive value system. Value systems can be impaired by a variety of internal defects; nor is it necessarily an easy matter to discern these defects. Imagination and something close to genius are required to unearth the difficulties in some views. There is nothing automatic or mechanical about the application of the strategies discussed so far. Considering the soundness of value systems is earnest intellectual activity. Further, although Nietzsche is not a radical subjectivist, subjective value systems are just as subject to internal defects as objective ones. Being a subjectivist does not exempt one's own value system from the possibility of gross error: subjective value systems are liable to contradiction; subjective values can rest on false factual assumptions; subjective value systems may contain means and ends confusions, and so on. It is simply not correct that worthwhile intellectual activity stops where subjectivism begins.

Challenge from Without

Challenges to a value system from without are typically challenges from other value systems, but this can occur in more than one way and these need to be distinguished.

Advancing a Superior Alternative

Nietzsche's system of specific values is embedded in his conceptual network, which in addition to its evaluative component also contains descriptive and explanatory components. A value-encompassing explanatory conceptual network is one apt way to characterize it. He clearly regards his own conceptual network to be superior to the Christian world view. But we do not have a mere juxtaposition of world views; he is prepared to argue vigorously for the weakness of the Christian world view. He not only seeks to expose the weakness of the valuational component, he also seeks to establish its descriptive and explanatory inadequacy.

The criteria for selecting the superior view are, by and large, the standard criteria for determining when one theory is superior to another.[5] Certainly, choice of the best theory from a number of competing theories relies on cognitive values, so this is not an entirely value-free strategy for the revaluation of values. Although this is a limitation, it still leaves the strategy with considerable scope. With only cognitive values presupposed, we can decide between theories embodying moral values, or religious values, or aesthetic values, or any others. This reinforces the point that there are other ways of seeking to revalue, for example, moral values than by merely pitting one set of moral values against another.

An important point about this strategy is that it is explicitly a rejection and replacement strategy. The inferior theory is rejected and replaced by a superior theory. This is, of course, exactly what Nietzsche sought. The demonstration of the weaknesses of the Christian world view is intended to lead to its rejection and replacement by his own sounder conceptual network. Another important point concerns the status of the cognitive values presupposed in this kind of theory selection. To be able to revalue all values these cognitive values must themselves be able to be revalued. It was argued previously that these were especially difficult cases, particularly for this kind of strategy. The discussion of the choice between rival theories of truth in chapter 2 amply illustrates this. But not every kind of strategy has to work against *every* kind of value. If we can employ cognitive values to revalue every other kind of value, then we have taken a considerable step toward the possibility of revaluing all values.

Advancing an Awkward Alternative

Let me begin by explaining what I mean by an awkward alternative. By an awkward alternative I mean a competing theory that has no currently known decisive objection to it of either a factual, valuational, or conceptual nature. One way a theory can be weakened is simply by advancing an awkward alternative. Take a simple case. According to utilitarians, happiness is a higher value than autonomy; according to Nietzsche, autonomy is a higher value than happiness. Nietzsche's view is an awkward alternative; there is no known decisive objection to it of either a factual, valuational, or conceptual nature. Where formerly there may not have been doubt, there must now be doubt.

The advancing of an awkward alternative does not in itself warrant a rejection and replacement of the original theory. Obviously, this is a less potent strategy than the previous one; it merely weakens a theory. On the other hand, its potency ought not to be underestimated. To show that a theory is no better than some competitor constitutes a serious undermining of a theory. However, as a strategy it is variable in its effects. A theory with many known awkward alternatives will not be much shaken by the addition of another one. A theory with no known awkward alternatives will certainly be shaken when one is advanced.

It is instructive to compare the last two strategies. It was pointed out that the previous strategy depends on cognitive values. One must be able to assess in what ways one theory is *better* than another, particularly if one is seeking its replacement. The current strategy is slightly less dependent on specific cognitive values. Simply being confronted with an alternative one cannot fault is enough to cause difficulty for the original theory. Naturally, the latter judgment will exploit some cognitive values, but these need not be either as explicit or as extensive as those in the previous case. Thus, when it comes to revaluing cognitive values themselves, this strategy holds out more promise than the previous one.

There is a further point about these strategies. According to conventional wisdom, criticism is an essentially negative, destructive, and uncreative enterprise. Given that the revaluation of values is seen as a critical enterprise, it is easy to assume that it, also, is purely negative, destructive, and uncreative. But this is mistaken. The highest order of intellectual creativity is required to produce better alternatives to widely entrenched theories, and a significant order of creativity to produce their equal. Insofar as the revaluation of values relies on these strategies, it is a highly creative enterprise. Inventing a better theory is harder work; one must meet tougher standards; and naturally the rewards are greater. Inventing a theory that is merely no worse is easier work, but, of course, the rewards are less.

Value-Model Alternatives

This strategy is closely related to the previous two, but it is sufficiently important to merit independent mention. It was argued in chapter 3 that Nietzsche seeks to replace the moral value-model with an aesthetic value-model for assessing human beings. It is not exactly that aesthetics itself ought to replace morals as such, but rather that certain formal characteristics of aesthetic valuation ought to be at the basis of the valuation of persons, and, of course, this means the rejection of many current moral judgments. The warrant for the replacement is the superiority over its rivals of his underlying theory of value, his higher-order values and his conceptual network that incorporate this mode of valuation. But while replacement is clearly intended, replacement is not required for a significant revaluation effect. Provided that there is no known cogent objection to utilizing the aesthetic value-model instead of the moral value-model, then, although this is not a sufficient warrant for replacement, it is sufficient to damage the authority of the moral value-model.

It has been emphasized that to revalue, for example, moral values, one is not simply restricted to counterpoising a given set of moral values with an alternative set of moral values. In the strategy under consideration the challenge comes from evaluative criteria entirely outside the moral realm. The mere possibility of applying other criteria sets an intellectual task to either defend or replace the original criteria. Of course it might be suggested that there is a conceptual error involved in applying an aesthetic value-model instead of a moral value-model in the domain in which the moral value-model has traditionally been applied. But while the suggestion can be made, it is not self-validating, and it needs to be shown that an error has occurred, and without such a demonstration the challenge posed by another model is real.

New Scales

Two main interpretations of the eternal recurrence were considered and both furnish something new for the weighing of values. If the realistic interpretation of the eternal recurrence is correct, then in at least two variations of it we are furnished with new scales that we can apply to values across the whole spectrum of values. Naturally, there are difficult problems here, but even if they should all prove to be intractable we are still left with something. We can still ask of anything, would I like *this* repeated forever? There can be little doubt that the careful consideration of such a question can significantly alter one's valuations, and if it does so, it does so without presupposing the acceptance of other values. It is not other substantive values, but rather the placement of choice within a special context that effects the change.

On the attitude portrayal interpretation, we are offered a striking image of a maximally affirmative attitude. With this image available we can inquire of any value to what degree it is in consonance or dissonance with this image. Even if one does not embrace this as one's preferred articulation of a maximally affirmative attitude, can one be exposed to it and not have one's attitude toward, for example, complaining and complainers altered? Unlike the previous cases, this advances a positive value in its own right. But whether this positive value is actively embraced or not, seeing values in this new context furnishes the potential for changing our valuations. New contrasts frequently bring new judgments in their train.

Reorientation of Inquiry

By and large, the strategies considered so far are not uniquely Nietzschean strategies, however distinctive his manner of application may be. We now come to a range of strategies that arise largely from his own vision of the issues and how to deal with them. They consist principally of looking at problems in a new way.

Contraction of Focus

Nietzsche has a propensity to probe issues of value by the construction of types. Types are abstractions, simplifications, and intensifications of individuals exemplifying certain values. Even when the opportunity presents itself for an investigation of exceptional concrete individuals, his preference is to consider types. For example, in *The Anti-Christ* he is more interested in considering the type of the redeemer than any actual historical figure. "What *I* am concerned with is the psychological type of the redeemer" (A 29). Essentially the same point holds for his consideration of Paul. Nietzsche makes the following observation about *Beyond Good and Evil,* again illustrating the propensity to think in terms of types, and the passage is only one of many that could have been selected: "This book (1886) is in all essentials a *critique of modernity,* the modern sciences, the modern arts, not even excluding modern politics, together with signposts to an antithetical type who is as little modern as possible, a noble, an affirmative type" (EH X:2). Putting mere preference in thinking style aside, types have a useful role to play in the investigation of values. One could investigate the degree to which people are actually altruistic in the vast and ever changing complexities of life, but this would make altruism difficult to evaluate, and may miss important aspects of it. On the other hand, if we construct the type of the altruist, a person exclusively oriented toward the well-being of others, then we have certainly abstracted, simplified, and intensified mundane reality, but we have also gained a far more tractable intellectual object. Among other things, types furnish useful instruments for assessing the impact on aggregate value of certain modes of living. Types are important precisely because they are an aid to global assessments of value.

Types furnish an intellectual framework where issues can be pursued that could not be pursued when confronted with the full complexities of the real world. To take an example; to be exclusively oriented toward the well-being of others means that the well-being of others is placed before one's own. In the framework of the type, we can ask, What kind of person would place the well-being of others before their own? What possible justification could there be for one person always putting the well-being of others before their own? What self-conception must a person have who always places the well-being of others ahead of their own? Of course, the questions go on. These are important questions to pose, and the answers are bound to increase the understanding of altruism. The investigation of such types can furnish insights into values that cannot be gained independently.

The use of types is favored by Nietzsche in other cases as well. In the consideration of Christianity there is the exploitation of the type of a being exclusively oriented toward another world, and this again furnishes the basis for a range of thought provoking questions. What kind of being would place an imaginary world ahead of this world? What possible justification could there be for placing an imaginary world ahead of the real world? Who benefits from such a placement? Nor are types used merely negatively; the *Übermensch* is itself a type embodying positive values. Critics may claim that types are limited cases that never occur in the real world, and hence that it is pointless to consider them. But to my mind exactly the opposite is the case; their nonoccurrence in the real world can make investigation of them all the more revealing. It is parallel to investigating motion on frictionless planes and perfectly elastic collisions. A narrowly empirical stance against the use of types would find itself ravaging science as well.

There is a further point worth noting. Moral philosophy in the English-speaking world has been heavily oriented toward a consideration of moral judgments, moral rules and actions, including the status of moral judgments, the status of rules, the nature of the antecedents and the nature of the consequences of actions. The same attention has not been paid to what is valuable about persons.[6] The latter considerations embrace the virtues to which some attention has been paid, but one can hardly call the amount of attention great. This is something of a puzzle. If it is possible to discuss intelligently the value of actions, then it ought to be possible to discuss intelligently values pertaining directly to persons. It is in such discussions that reasoning about types can be useful.[7] Nevertheless, one must acknowledge that however inventive Nietzsche may be here, this kind of thinking is not entirely novel. He might not have relished the comparison, but Plato's *Republic* already contains exemplary cases of thinking involving types, and is a testament to the fruitfulness of doing so.

To sum up, investigating types is a distinctive strategy employed in the service of revaluation, but its impact in general is harder to assess. One can hardly expect the strategy to yield mathematical certainty. Reasoning about types can, of course, be challenged, but the only really effective challenge is better reasoning about types. However, this much can be said, to abstract, simplify, and intensify where no one has done this before always has the potential to reveal new connections and lead to new valuations. Whenever we look at an issue from a new perspective the prospect of changing views is always present. Indeed, types furnish assistance in global assessments of value in a way investigations into the concrete and the particular cannot. This is an important strategy, and constitutes a further illustration of the point that there is more to revaluation than the mere pitting of one substantive value system against another.

Expansion of Focus

This strategy is the inverse of the previous one; the context of inquiry is expanded rather than contracted. A question such as "What is the value of justice?" immediately calls forth a host of questions such as "What is the origin of justice?" "What was justice originally intended to achieve?" "What is the function of justice now?" "How effective is it in fulfilling its function?" "Who benefits from the advocacy of justice?" "Who is harmed by the advocacy of justice?" "Does society as a whole benefit from the advocacy of justice?" "Is justice beneficial to the human species?" and so on. What warrants this expansion of focus and makes these questions relevant is the rejection of the absolute theory of truth in favor of perspectivism. Perspectives need to be assessed on broader grounds than claims to absolute truth, since a key point about perspectives is that they are framed to serve the interests of the perspective framers.

The genealogical method falls into this broad category. Nietzsche's most explicit resort to the genealogical method is in the *Genealogy of Morals*, and this is how he conceived of the task in the preface: "Let us articulate this *new demand:* we need a *critique* of moral values, *the values of these values themselves must first be called in question*—and for that there is needed a knowledge of the conditions and circumstances in which they grew, under which they evolved and changed (morality as consequence, as symptom, as mask, as tartufferie, as illness, as misunderstanding; but also morality as cause, as remedy, as stimulant, as restraint, as poison), a knowledge of a kind that has never yet existed or even been desired" (GM Preface, 6). Naturally, this involves every aspect of the origin, growth, development, function, and effects of morality. The expansion of focus is dramatic. If my observations in chapters 3 and 4 are correct, then this is not a purely value-neutral, theory-neutral enterprise. Valuation and explanation will be parts of the enterprise throughout its course, although straightforward historical investigations will also be included (GM Preface, 7). But there is no general method here that can be pursued independently of Nietzsche's theoretical and valuational commitments. The rules for the conduct of such an inquiry are unfortunately not given. We largely have to be content with whatever can be gleaned from the individual examples of genealogical investigation left behind.[8]

Believers in the view that value judgments are candidates for absolute truth may argue that the majority of these questions concerning genealogy are simply irrelevant and have no bearing on the soundness of values. They may claim that such an expansion of focus is a journey into irrelevance. There are three points to be made. First, these questions are themselves highly relevant to the issue of whether value judgments are in fact candidates for absolute truth. Second, even if justice, for example, has some intrinsic objective value, its benefits and disbenefits in actual practice are facts about it that must be taken into account in an overall assessment of its value. Finally, even if there are objective values, what the objective values are can surely only be determined by assembling all the information surrounding them. Merely sweating with conviction is not a method for determining which values are the correct values, even if values are completely objective. Let me take one of these points. Suppose there was a watertight rational case that retributive punishment, where the punishment is in direct proportion to the suffering caused, is the morally right course. Further, suppose that punishing on this basis doubles the crime rate compared to not punishing at all. Quite independently of the intrinsic rightness of retributive punishment, if indeed it is such, the conjectured disastrous consequences of its application are certainly relevant to its overall evaluation.

Thus, this strategy has the potential for the revaluation of values even in a completely objectivist framework. But as in the previous case, it is difficult to generalize about its impact. Expanding the context of inquiry in which the value questions are considered certainly has the potential to reveal warrants for changes in our judgments, but, by the same token, it may leave the judgments exactly as they are. Once again, the strategy does not just rely on pitting one fixed set of values against another, although there is no reason why other values cannot figure in its employment.

Relocation of Focus

Here the center of attention shifts independently of any contraction or expansion of viewpoint. What was called functional recategorization in chapter 4 is a case in point. It is not uncommon to conceive of the primary function of religions as stating truths about the universe from which values are held to flow. According to Nietzsche, the primary function of religion is the advocacy of values;[9] the ontological claims are only secondary defensive operations. In the former conception, since the values are held to depend on the facts, the facts are the principal objects of focus. Furthermore, the ontological claims themselves may preclude considering the consequential values on their merits. If the values are seen as primary, then they can be focused on directly and undividedly, and it ought not to be surprising if this leads to new conclusions. This is an important instance of the relocation of focus, but it is only one of several.

Nietzsche does not regard the actions of persons as ontologically independent occurrences (GM I:13). As a result, there is a shift of focus from considering the value of individual actions to value issues concerning the agent. The question "What is the value of an altruistic act?" is transposed into "What is the value of being an altruist?" Of course once this relocation of focus has taken place the other strategies mentioned can be applied. The new location can provide the center to which the strategies of both focus contraction and focus expansion can be applied. Of course the strategy of the relocation of focus can also be reapplied after the initial shift. Thus, "What is the value of an altruist to society?" constitutes another shift, and "What is the value of a society of altruists to life?" is another. Nor need these strategies be the only ones applied. As a consequence, an issue can be looked at from a multiplicity of new points of view.

The relocation of focus from act to agent is closely paralleled by another kind of relocation that occurs frequently in Nietzsche. This is a relocation of focus from abstractions to agents. For example, "What is the value of knowledge?" is transposed into "What is the value of knowledge for human beings?" At first glance it may appear that the shift of focus is not very significant, but I do not think that that is so. The first question orients us to seeking characteristics intrinsic to knowledge, while the second question orients us to the very opposite. It is hardly necessary to elaborate that changing the object of search often leads to seeing what is otherwise missed. Furthermore, relocation of focus does not always require that we abandon an old way of looking at a problem; what it demands is that we add a new one.

As in the case of the previous two strategies, it is impossible to generalize about the consequences of the application of this strategy. The potential for altering our valuations is there, but there is no inevitability this will take place. Here again, we have a strategy that does not question-beggingly oppose one substantive set of values to another.

A New Emphasis

The body has approximately the same primacy and centrality in Nietzsche's later thinking that the soul has in Plato's. "Is there a more dangerous aberration than contempt for the body?" (WP 1016); he clearly thought not. For Nietzsche, what is good about human beings, enthusiasm for life, dynamism, creative capacity, and so on, all originate from the body:

> But the awakened, the enlightened man says: I am body entirely, and nothing beside; and the soul is only a word for something in the body.
> The body is a great intelligence, a multiplicity with one sense, a war and a peace, a herd and a herdsman.
> Your little intelligence, my brother, which you call "spirit," is also an instrument of your body, a little instrument and toy of your great intelligence.
> You say "I" and you are proud of this word. But greater than this—although you will not believe it—is your body and its great intelligence, which does not say "I" but performs "I." (Z I:4)

The "mind" or "soul" is an expression of the body; the body in its full complexity produces and fashions the "mind" or "soul." The body is more ontologically basic than the "mind" or "soul." In Plato's case, the soul is more ontologically basic than the body, and this imposes a valuational order; the benefit of the soul is more important than the benefit of the body. For Nietzsche, the situation is slightly more complex. The benefit of the body is vital, but since "mind" and "soul" are also aspects of the body an issue arises of balance between the two aspects, and this issue will shortly be taken up.

For Nietzsche, Christianity's contempt for the body is one of the most telling points against it: "Christianity, which despised the body, has up till now been mankind's greatest misfortune"(TI IX:47). Whether a candidate value benefits or harms the body is always an important question about it. What is propounded as a value must pass the test of not being inimical to the health of the body, but it is, of course, far better for it to make a positive contribution to the health of the body.

The greater the harm to the body the worse the value, the greater the benefit to the body the better the value. Promotion of the health, strength, and vitality of the body is one of the important aspects of the higher-order value of invigoration.

There is no problem in this new emphasis on the body in normal circumstances. However, the interpretation of this new emphasis is not entirely free of difficulties. The principal complication is posed by the rejection of dualism. If "spirit" is body too, then what do we do when "spirit" and body naively understood conflict? Suppose that we have a choice between two changes to human nature by genetic manipulation. Suppose that we could either double everybody's physical strength or double everybody's intelligence, but that it was impossible to do both. Which alternative ought we to pick? One choice offers more for the body naively understood; the other offers more for the "spiritualized" aspect of the body. To resolve this issue, we need to turn explicitly to Nietzsche's higher-order values. The twin cornerstones of the higher-order values are invigoration and enrichment. Indeed, the dilemma posed can be seen to raise a problem for these higher-order values; are they themselves not in conflict here?

Let me begin with invigoration. One important question is this: What increases our capacity to change the world more, a doubling of physical strength or a doubling of intelligence? There can be no doubt that the answer is intelligence. If one's physical strength is doubled, one can lift double the weight one lifted before, but with a doubling of intelligence, one can discover such things as the laws of levers and pulleys and lift weights that are a hundred times heavier than anyone has lifted before. What has enabled us to send objects that even a hundred strong men cannot lift to the moon is intelligence. Thus in a straightforward sense, there is greater invigoration if intelligence is increased than if physical strength is increased. Given the choice of doubling physical strength or doubling intelligence, the choice for Nietzsche must be a doubling of intelligence. Thus, while emphasis on the vitality of the body naively understood constitutes an aspect of invigoration, invigoration extends beyond that to the general increase of human performance capabilities. Let me now turn to enrichment. Here it is even more evident than in the previous case that the increase in intelligence furnishes the greater capacity for the creation of a multitude of things to which people can be strongly drawn, thereby yielding a significant enrichment of life. Thus the consideration of both invigoration and of enrichment supports the choice of increased intelligence rather than increased physical strength in cases where we cannot have an increase in both.

A critic may well inquire where the new emphasis on the body is in this which looks suspiciously like the old emphasis on the mind. But the impression is misleading and is the consequence of a deliberately manufactured conflict. There is in Nietzsche a genuine emphasis on promoting the well-being and vitality of the body in its most direct physical sense. The existence of situations in which his higher-order values force a choice favoring the less directly physical over the directly physical does not diminish this.

Unlike many of the previous strategies, attaching special importance to the body obviously depends on Nietzsche's values. The legitimacy of their employment in the context of revaluation has already been dealt with in chapter 1, but I will add several observations. It is important not to have too static and rigid a conception of the process of revaluation. Once some values are revalued the results can be brought to bear on values not yet considered. The initial products of revaluation need not lie inert outside the process until it is completed but may themselves be employed in it. Thus it by no means follows that whenever he employs values in his revaluation he must have embraced those values prior to the process of revaluation.

It is possible to harbor the suspicion that no more than a purely subjective response is expressed in the importance accorded to the body. But this is not the case. The valuational importance of the body is a consequence drawn naturally from the ontological and causal primacy of the body. The response in his case is no more purely subjective than is Plato's, when he draws quite different consequences from the supposed ontological primacy of the soul. The drawing of these consequences from the ontological order is subject to challenge in either case, but reason favors the drawing of these consequences in the first instance.

General Observations

A number of clusters of values have been identified. These included the cognitive value cluster, the moral value cluster, the religious value cluster, the aesthetic value cluster, and the political value cluster. Indeed, this inquiry has proceeded in this framework. At the time, the question of what means could be employed to determine the relative worth of these clusters was noted. One crucial point about Nietzsche's higher-order values is that they fall outside these clusters entirely or else only partially overlap with them. Nietzsche has propounded values that are more basic than the values in these clusters, values in terms of which these clusters themselves can be evaluated and ranked. This embodies a conception that ought to be taken seriously. It is surely possible that the compartmentalized way we have traditionally looked at values is a mistake and that there really are more basic values that ought to be our primary concern. Nietzsche certainly thought so, and the possibility warrants continued investigation.

To return to the central theme, in revaluing all values we appear to be confronted with a dilemma. If we do not use values in the revaluation, how can we *revalue* at all? And if we use values in the revaluation, some values appear not to be being revalued. In any event, what warrants their employment in revaluation? What right do we have to take *their* side? The answer has already been outlined in chapter 1, but this survey of strategies has filled in that outline. A significant number of strategies do not rely on substantive values. Where substantive values are employed they need not be plucked from thin air but can themselves be the products of seeking to accommodate and account for the phenomena of valuation or be the products of previous steps in revaluation. Further, while it is true that not all strategies work against all values, there are no values that escape all strategies. Thus revaluing all values, and hence by implication revaluing the highest values, is an intelligible enterprise, and it ought to be possible in principle to carry it out.

However, there are possible impressions I wish to counter. Talk of strategies may suggest that there are routine methods for revaluing values. This is certainly not the case. In most instances, an original and creative mind was required to invent the strategies and a penetrating and imaginative mind is required to apply them. Strategy in chess is perhaps the best parallel. The invention of a novel strategy requires genius, and even after its invention the same strategy will fare differently in the hands of a grand master than it fares in the hands of an ordinary club player. I make no claim to have unearthed all the strategies Nietzsche employs in his revaluation, but I hope to have dealt with a good sampling of the major ones. But whatever the totality is he actually avails himself of, it ought not to be regarded as a closed list. There is no reason why the inventive ought not to add to it.

Conclusion

Nietzsche's Project and Its Outcome

The plan to revalue all values is magnificent in sheer boldness and scope. Knowledge, morality, religion, art, and even political values fall within its ambit. There is a fierce determination to call every sacred cow to account. By the same token, the level of detail at which the inquiry is often pursued cannot fail to impress. The execution is penetrating, vigorous, and imaginative. When we turn to an assessment of the success of the enterprise there are two issues to consider. The first concerns the success of what was done; the second concerns the question whether anything of major importance was not done that could have been done. As far as the attempted revaluations are concerned, there will always be argument about how successful they are, but there is no denying their inventiveness and capacity to stimulate. In the enterprise of revaluing values, what Nietzsche accomplished was a dramatic and fertile beginning to a process that can have no end.

This study has concentrated more on the revaluation *potential* of the strategies Nietzsche employs than on their actual revaluation *effect*. But I have sought to indicate which strategies are effective and which ones are not. At times, where he intends to kill, he merely wounds; but in this enterprise, wounds are also successes. However, the enterprise of revaluation leaves far more than the debris of damaged and discarded values. In the attempt to carry out his plan he has produced a feast of interesting methods and challenging solutions to fundamental problems. From among the positive contributions I single out his higher-order values, his theory of value, and his conception of the maximally affirmative attitude as creations of enduring importance. The notion that there are higher-order values in terms of which values in the traditionally separated clusters of values are to be assessed and ranked is particularly significant. To be sure, both the methods and the solutions are further starting points rather than end points, and I regard this not as a drawback but as a virtue of the way Nietzsche does philosophy. Seekers of final proofs will find Nietzsche disappointing, but those willing to be provoked to thought are bound to find their reward.

Keeping in mind that Nietzsche's revaluations are a beginning, it is still possible to inquire whether there are any major gaps in his enterprise. Toward the end, he scaled down the scope of the enterprise, but there is really no satisfactory answer to the point raised. Anyone who approaches him with any degree of sympathy will feel there are issues they would have liked him to have dealt with more extensively. Some may feel this about political issues, others about economic issues, still others about environmental issues, and so on. But there is little point in focusing on what has not been done while there is so much richness in what has been done.

While there may be difficulty in seeing Nietzsche's project as complete, even as an initial venture, such reservations cannot alter the fact that his philosophy is one of the great philosophies of activity, change, and power. He is the outstanding modern Heraclitean. It is a philosophy hard to rival for its capacity to challenge and stimulate. He is impressive in attack, and the critical examination of values has been permanently altered by his presence. Yet his is one of the great naturalistic philosophies of affirmation, and his positive contribution to thinking about values is of an importance that demands attention. What incompleteness there is in the execution of his enterprise is a challenge to go further.

Notes

The German edition of Nietzsche's works used is the *Kritische Studienausgabe* in 15 volumes, edited by G. Colli and M. Montinari. The German edition of the letters used is the *Kritische Studienausgabe* in 8 volumes, edited by G. Colli and M. Montinari. However, I have chosen to utilize existing translations for the purposes of quotation in my text. The translations are by Walter Kaufmann and R. J. Hollingdale. Where there has been a choice between the translations of Kaufmann and Hollingdale, I have preferred those of Hollingdale.

Introduction

1. Walter Kaufmann in *Nietzsche: Philosopher, Psychologist, Antichrist,* in his chapter on Nietzsche's method observes, "Thus Nietzsche is, like Plato, not a system-thinker but a problem-thinker" (82), and goes on to characterize Nietzsche's approach as aphoristic and experimental, citing as an advantage of this approach that one does not have to begin with unproved assumptions as does a system-thinker. I have reservations about the application of this distinction to Nietzsche. But accepting what there is in it, even a problem-thinker cannot begin with an intellectual vacuum. What means, what methods does Nietzsche the problem-thinker use when he investigates his problems? With what intellectual instruments does he perform his experiments? These are some of the issues that I propose to pursue.

2. The same view has not prevailed outside the English-speaking world. Deleuze makes the following observation: "It is clear that modern philosophy has largely lived off Nietzsche." See Deleuze, *Nietzsche and Philosophy,* 1. While this may well be true of the philosophy of which Deleuze speaks, it would not ring true to most philosophers in the English-speaking world.

3. Karl Jaspers, *Nietzsche,* 10. For an assessment of Jaspers's interpretation, see Kaufmann, "Jaspers' Relation to Nietzsche," in *Philosophy of Karl Jaspers,* 407–36. For Jaspers's rejoinder see 857–63 of the same volume.

4. Some have found interesting parallels between Nietzsche and Wittgenstein. For example, see Erich Heller, "Wittgenstein and Nietzsche," in *The Importance of Nietzsche,* 141–57, and Tracy B. Strong, *Friederich Nietzsche,* 78–86. I also allude to a similarity in more than style in chapter 6.

5. René Descartes, "Meditations on First Philosophy," in Descartes, *Philosophical Writings.*

6. In Descartes, *Philosophical Writings.*

7. It is unlikely that Nietzsche himself would have been so modest. He thought that he had a thing or two to teach Descartes about doubt even in the realm of facts, particularly in regard to claims about the "self."

8. Hollingdale sees Nietzsche's stance on truth as the most important feature of his philosophy in general (Hollingdale, *Nietzsche,* 1).

9. For an account of Nietzsche's views that gives greater attention to this aspect of his thought than is usual, see Strong, *Friederich Nietzsche.* There is also a useful chapter in Ofelia Schutte, *Beyond Nihilism,* 161–88.

10. This applies to religion in particular. Comparison with Hume is revealing. Few can rival Hume for devastating critical thrusts at religion. Yet Hume did not want his *Dialogues Concerning Natural Religion* to be published until after his death; his own position is difficult to discover in the Dialogues, and to this day there is uncertainty about whether he was an atheist or not.

Chapter 1: Value and Power

1. There is no single entirely satisfactory term that can be used here, but I take "goal" to be the least misleading provided that the following points are understood: a goal does not have to be a static end state, an activity may also constitute a goal; and it can be a goal to attain something and a goal to avoid something.

2. For the sake of simplicity I omit the qualification required in the case in which the inner power repels us from something.

3. Mackie takes the queerness of such characteristics as a telling point against them. See J. L. Mackie, *Ethics,* 38–42.

4. John Stuart Mill, *Utilitarianism,* chap. 4.

5. Theories of this kind have been held to commit the naturalistic fallacy. I am not raising the issue here of whether it is a genuine fallacy; I am simply raising the issue of whether Nietzsche's theory is structurally parallel to theories that have been accused of having committed such a fallacy.

6. "The study of whole economic systems aggregating over the functioning of individual economic units. It is primarily concerned with VARIABLES which follow systematic and predictable paths of behaviour and can be analyzed independently of the decisions of the many agents who determine their level." G. Bannock et al., *Dictionary of Economics,* 266.

7. To pursue the parallel with macroeconomics, the implementation of a macroeconomic policy such as increasing the money supply does not carry with it any prescriptive or normative force regarding the behavior of individuals, although it is natural to suppose that individuals will adjust their behavior accordingly.

8. I leave this qualification out in what immediately follows, but what follows should be read with this qualification in mind.

9. What is being presented is only one interpretation of the status of the will to power in Nietzsche's philosophy. It seems to me the most plausible interpretation; it is well supported by the quotes in the text and in this note. "This world is the will to power—and nothing besides! And you yourselves are also this will to power—and nothing besides!" (WP 1067).

10. W. V. O. Quine, *Word and Object*, 3.

Chapter 2: Cognitive Values

1. On this issue, John T. Wilcox, *Truth and Value in Nietzsche*, is useful. But the best discussion I know of is in Richard Schacht, *Nietzsche*, 52–117. Maudemarie Clark's *Nietzsche on Truth and Philosophy* is formidable, contains a nice review of major interpretations, but I do not accept key assumptions that drive her own interpretation.

2. Certainly, views of truth in line with Nietzsche's thoughts on the matter have been quite widely embraced, to the delight of some and to the despair of others.

3. Alexander Nehamas challenges whether Nietzsche's view on truth is pragmatist in any sense, and cites as a ground the fact that Nietzsche sometimes speaks of truth as dangerous and hard to bear, and notes some disparaging remarks about "utility" ("Will to Knowledge, Will to Ignorance, and Will to Power in *Beyond Good and Evil*," in *Nietzsche as Affirmative Thinker*, ed. Y. Yovel, 90–108, esp. 97–98). But for Nietzsche, "consequences" have to be understood in terms of increased power and this may well be accompanied by increased pain and increased danger. Furthermore, one needs to distinguish between "short term consequences" and "long term consequences"; what has great short term disutility may well have greater long term utility. Pragmatism by no means implies that every pill is sugarcoated.

4. Nietzsche thought he had a sufficient case that introspection could not be a source of absolute truths (see BGE 16).

5. This kind of argument is traceable to Immanuel Kant. For Kant's most lucid statement of the position see "General Observations on Transcendental Aesthetic," in *Critique of Pure Reason*, 82–91.

6. Nietzsche and Kant differ in that while both embrace the claim that all knowing is conditioned, Nietzsche specifically denies the existence of "things-in-themselves." But to deny the existence of "things-in-themselves" and to reconcile such a denial with the conditioned nature of all knowing are separate matters, and whether Nietzsche has succeeded in the latter task is a matter of legitimate doubt.

7. The issue is considered in Ruediger Hermann Grimm, *Nietzsche's Theory of Knowledge*, in a section titled "The Paradoxes of Nietzsche's Notion of Truth," 26–29. The discussion is useful, but to my mind the problem can also be put in more pressing forms.

8. If a correspondence theory of truth is to be identified simply with the fulfillment of Tarski's Convention T, then it is compatible with any verification model whatever. For arguments that nontrivial correspondence theories cannot simply be identified with the fulfillment of Convention T see Wilfrid Sellars, "Truth and 'Correspondence,'" in *Science, Perception, and Reality*, 197–224, and D. J. O'Connor, *The Correspondence Theory of Truth*, 91–111. For Tarski's more informal version of the original technical paper, see Tarski, "The Semantic Conception of Truth," *Philosophy and Phenomenological Research* 4 (1944), reprinted in *Readings in Philosophical Analysis*, ed. Herbert Feigl and Wilfrid Sellars, 52–84.

9. For example, Nicholas Rescher, *Coherence Theory of Truth*, 1–31.

10. The problem has remained so refractory that now even a logician is suggesting that here—and not only here—we should embrace and enjoy contradictions as a natural part of our cognitive life. See Graham Priest, *In Contradiction*.

11. Maudemarie Clark exploits some of this technical sophistication in her study. For those wishing to savor this level of technical sophistication directly see Hilary Putnam, "Models and Reality," *Journal of Symbolic Logic* 45 (1980), reprinted in Putnam, *Realism and Reason*, 1–25, and comments on Putnam's views by David Lewis in "Putnam's Paradox" for stimulating illustrations.

12. This theme begins explicitly with the early *On the Uses and Disadvantages of History for Life* (UM II); it recurs regularly thereafter, although contrary themes are also expressed (BGE 39).

13. This point will be taken up in more detail in chapter 4.

Chapter 3: Moral Values

1. The failure to recognize that by "moral values" and "moral judgments" Nietzsche had, at times, narrower categories in mind than we typically have when we use those terms, that he recognized a broader category of values and value judgments, and that his search was precisely for values that were more soundly based than "moral values" furnishes the basis for some easy point scoring against Nietzsche. For example, see Kai Nielsen, "Nietzsche as a Moral Philosopher," esp. 203–5.

2. There is already strong support for the position in Mackie, *Ethics*.

3. Slave morality and herd morality are not always clearly distinguished by Nietzsche, but his discussions imply that there are important differences.

4. These two are among the strongest candidates for inclusion in a definition of morality as such. Thus, insofar as Nietzsche attacks them, he is not merely attacking a particular morality, he is attacking morality in general. For a discussion of definitions of morality see G. Wallace and A. D. M. Walker, eds., *Definition of Morality*.

5. The most substantive philosophical work on altruism in the recent past,

treating it as part of an investigation into the basis of morality, is Thomas Nagel, *Possibility of Altruism*. But the concept of altruism presented there is so formal and attenuated that Nagel admits it to be compatible with the kinds of substantive value judgments that Nietzsche espouses and that are themselves standardly regarded as running counter to more "commonsensical" conceptions of altruism (127).

6. This type is close to, but by no means identical to, the type Richard Dawkins calls "sucker." See Dawkins, *Selfish Gene*, 198–202.

7. The reason why Nietzsche operates with such conceptions will be considered in chapter 7.

8. For the classic paper on the issue see Robert L. Trivers, "Evolution of Reciprocal Altruism."

9. It is arguable that "reciprocal altruism" is a misnomer, and that "enlightened self-interest" would be more apt for the phenomena intended. Either way the issues raised are of direct relevance to Nietzsche's views.

10. Of course this is only an illustration. For an excellent discussion of the underlying model and the conditions under which "reciprocal altruism" could arise, see Robert Axelrod, *Evolution of Cooperation*.

11. For one of the rare but nevertheless stimulating attacks on universality, see Michael Stocker, "Agent and Other."

12. Of course, to form any secure judgment on the matter the analogy would have to be investigated in greater detail; but as long as the conformity to moral rules does not require a more extreme level of conformity than does the conformity to linguistic rules, Nietzsche's case does not look promising.

13. It seems that the stronger position is being put in GM I:13, namely, that it is impossible to go against nature, and hence, by implication, impossible to adhere to universal moral rules. Of course this would make a morality enjoining such behavior pointless; but, by the same token, it would also be pointless complaining about the deleterious effects of such a morality.

14. Nietzsche himself uses the term "automaton" in regard to duty in A 11 and in regard to adherence to moral rules in WP 346. There is a witty exploitation of the theme of "moral" automata in Michael Frayn's *The Tin Men*.

15. Those seeking to combine the views that moral considerations are overriding and that morality is universal need to give some attention to the issue of what it is that can make an individual's life worthwhile.

16. Just as adherence to linguistic rules may constitute necessary conditions for the attainment of the highest cultural values.

17. This theme is touched on in Fyodor Dostoyevsky, *Letters from the Underworld*: "For my part, I look upon undivided love of prosperity as something almost indecent; for to cause an occasional catastrophe, come weal come woe, seems to me a very pleasant thing to do. Yet I am not altogether for adversity, any more than I am altogether for prosperity; what I most stand for is my per-

sonal freewill, and what it can do for me when I feel in the right mood to use it" (41). Nietzsche indicates in a letter to Heinrich Köselitz (Peter Gast) that he had read this work in a French translation. See *Sämiliche Briefe,* VIII, no. 814, March 7, 1887.

18. The legitimacy of the transformation is briefly argued for in Thomas Nagel, *View from Nowhere,* 156–62.

19. See also BGE 225.

Chapter 4: Religious Values

1. Nietzsche was not alone in possessing such attitudes at this time. "As for religion, I believe it useless to speak of it or to search for its relics, since to give oneself the trouble of denying God is the sole disgrace in these matters." Charles Baudelaire, *Intimate Journals,* 21.

2. Schacht, *Nietzsche,* 119–30.

3. For example, J. P. Stern, *Study of Nietzsche,* 147.

4. Immanuel Kant, *Critique of Practical Reason,* 220–29.

5. Given that it is not difficult to be swept along by the vigor of Nietzsche's case, there is point in pausing to raise an awkward example. Leibniz thought of this world as the best of all possible worlds, of God as the most active of all possible beings, and of every monad necessarily being different from every other monad. There is not a trace of either world-weariness, world-denigration, or the desire to reduce everyone to the same mold in this conception. Indeed, a more world-glorifying, activity-glorifying, diversity-glorifying position is hardly conceivable. Is Leibniz really the extraordinary exception that on Nietzsche's view he must be held to be? For a brief statement of Leibniz's own views see "Principles of Nature and of Grace, Founded on Reason" (1714), reprinted in *Leibniz, Philosophical Writings,* ed. G. H. R. Parkinson, 195–204.

6. For example, Ninian Smart in *World Religions: A Dialogue.* The summary of the case is given on 30–31.

7. There is a connection between the magnitude of this threat and the anti-nature character of the slave morality. The greater the external threats and the more potent the measures required to coerce people to act in a certain way the more that way must deviate from what are natural modes of behavior for human beings (GM II:22).

8. The idea of exact literary reduplication is exploited by Jorge Luis Borges in an interesting way in "Pierre Menard, Author of the Quixote," in Borges, *Labyrinths.*

9. The one work in English that arguably matches the intensity and passion of Nietzsche's opposition to Christianity, and not on entirely dissimilar grounds is D. H. Lawrence's *Apocalypse.*

10. This structure is built up in Nietzsche's works basically from *Thus Spoke Zarathustra* on. A substantial part of it is given in the Epilogue to *The Case of*

Wagner. Of course, the form given here is not the form in which Nietzsche presents the matter, but the concepts, the claims, and their interconnections are unquestionably his.

11. It seems that Nietzsche was a Quinean before Quine.

12. See W. V. O. Quine, "Two Dogmas of Empiricism."

13. The whole issue of whether facts entail values simply collapses in the absence of a satisfactory criterion for the identity of meaning. The questions, "Does 'good' mean the same as 'maximizes happiness'?" or "Does 'good' mean the same as 'is commanded by God'?" and so on, simply lapse into unintelligibility. But of course this still leaves one free to defend "the good is that which maximizes happiness," or "the good is that which is commanded by God" as a thesis, and in whatever way one is able.

14. I call this "a kind of Quinean holism" because I do not explicitly wish to saddle Quine with the conception involved. In one of the few places where Quine writes directly on the matter he appears to believe that a fact/value distinction can be successfully drawn. See W. V. O. Quine, "On the Nature of Moral Values."

15. "The periodic submersion of the ground by the Nile, with the consequent loss of boundary marks, led to the art of land measurement by surveyors or 'rope stretchers,' an art which later, in the hands of the Greeks, became the science of deductive geometry." William Cecil Dampier, *Shorter History of Science*, 11.

16. It is also worth noting in relation to the discussion that is to follow in chapter 7 that what finally did force a revaluation of its status was simply the invention of coherent alternatives.

17. Adolf Grünbaum, *Geometry and Chronometry.*

18. Ibid., 14.

19. Ibid., 27.

20. For example, Hilary Putnam, "An Examination of Grünbaum's Philosophy of Geometry," and Graham Nerlich, *Shape of Space*, 155–86.

Chapter 5: Aesthetic Values

1. For an argument that while this three-part division is important, it still fails to do full justice to the complexity of Nietzsche's thoughts on the matter see Peter Pütz, "Nietzsche: Art and Intellectual Inquiry," trans. Roger Hausheer, in M. Pasley, ed., *Nietzsche: Imagery and Thought*, 1–32.

2. Shuichi Kato, *Form, Style, Tradition*, 4.

3. In what follows I will simply refer to it as the representation theory.

4. For a perceptive treatment of the major traditional theories of art see H. Gene Blocker, *Philosophy of Art.*

5. Quoted in *Artists on Art: From the 14th to the 20th Century*, compiled and edited by Robert Goldwater and Marco Treves (New York: Pantheon Books, 1945), 54.

6. Aristotle, *Poetics of Aristotle*, IV, 15.

7. Heidegger lists five statements as capturing the essence of Nietzsche's views on art. They are: (1) Art is the most perspicuous configuration of the will to power, (2) Art must be grasped in terms of the artist, (3) According to the expanded concept of "artist," art is the basic occurrence of all beings; to the extent that they are, beings are self-creating, created, (4) Art is the distinctive countermovement to nihilism, (5) Art is worth more than "the truth." I agree with two and five. I disagree with four since I see the *Übermensch* and the eternal recurrence playing at least an equal role in the movement against nihilism. One and three raise matters of interpretation that are not central to my enterprise. See Heidegger, *Nietzsche: Volume 1*, 69–76.

8. A quite unflattering picture of artists is presented in GM III:5, but I believe that these apparently conflicting views can be reconciled. Usually when Nietzsche is expressing a poor opinion of artists it is actual artists that he has in mind: when he is expressing a high opinion of artists it is ideal artists that he has in mind. It is ideal artists that are assigned to an elevated position in art.

9. This is cited simply to show how Nietzsche thought of love, and not to demonstrate the connection between love and art. The latter connection is made explicit in WP 808.

10. This observation does not occur in a direct discussion of art. But the remark is general, it is characteristic, and its application to art appears inevitable.

11. Plato, *Republic*, bk. 10, 602–8.

12. "The pure judgment of taste is independent of charm and emotion. Every interest vitiates the judgment of taste and robs it of its impartiality." Immanuel Kant, *Critique of Aesthetic Judgement*, 64.

13. "The intrinsic problem of the metaphysics of the beautiful can be stated very simply: how is it possible for us to take pleasure in an object when this object has no kind of connection with our desires." Arthur Schopenhauer, "On Aesthetics," in *Essays and Aphorisms*, 155.

14. Aristotle, *Poetics*, VI.

15. "Through this, when an aesthetic perception occurs the will completely vanishes from consciousness. But will is the sole source of all our troubles and sufferings. This is the origin of the feeling of pleasure which accompanies the perception of the beautiful." Schopenhauer, *Essays and Aphorisms*, 155.

16. Leo Tolstoy, *What Is Art? and Essays on Art*, 119–26.

17. R. G. Collingwood, *Principles of Art*, 105–53.

18. Ibid., 117–21.

19. For a useful survey of theories of play see Michael J. Ellis, *Why People Play*.

20. Herbert Spencer, *Principles of Psychology*, vol. 2, pt. 8, IX, "Aesthetic Sentiments," 627–48. Nietzsche does criticize Spencer's views on altruism and

makes a number of other references to him, but to my knowledge he does not refer directly to his views on art.

21. That art concerns primarily the "spiritualized" aspects of the body is the interpretation that appears to be adopted by Heidegger. See *Nietzsche: Volume 1*, 92–106. He is taken to task for this interpretation by Michel Haar, who argues that for Nietzsche art primarily concerns the "nonspiritualized" aspects of the body. See "Heidegger and the Nietzschean 'Physiology of Art,'" in D. F. Krell and D. Wood, eds., *Exceedingly Nietzsche*, 13–29. I see the point in both views. For Nietzsche, art arises from and acts on both the "spiritualized" aspects of the body and the "nonspiritualized" aspects of the body. The two quotations that follow in the text lend support to this view.

22. However, excessive focus on Nietzsche's view of Wagner can lead to distorted conceptions of Nietzsche's musical judgment, and to regard that judgment as idiosyncratic. Reading section five of *David Strauss, the Confessor and the writer* (UM I) is a useful corrective, and reveals how fundamentally sound Nietzsche's musical judgment was.

23. The diversity of art is well brought out by Morris Weitz in "The Role of Theory in Aesthetics," 27–35. But I do not accept Weitz's argument that this diversity precludes the possibility of general theories of art.

24. Weitz, ibid., distinguishes between a "descriptive" use of the term "art" and an "evaluative" use. It is plain that Nietzsche uses the term in an evaluative sense, and his theory can be described as an evaluative theory of art rather than a descriptive theory of art. But even evaluative theories of art need to pay attention to the range of pre-theoretical paradigms of art and what they are doing.

25. George Dickie, *Art and the Aesthetic*, 113–34.

Chapter 6: New Directions

1. Magnus observes, in a related point, that there is greater agreement among interpreters on Nietzsche's destructive enterprise than on his constructive efforts. See Bernd Magnus, "Nietzsche and the Project of Bringing Philosophy to an End," in Y. Yovel, ed., *Nietzsche as Affirmative Thinker*, 39–57.

2. The *Übermensch* figures strongly in *Thus Spoke Zarathustra* and then largely disappears from sight, although there appears to be a definite reference to the *Übermensch* at the end of *Genealogy of Morals* II:24. What weight ought to be attached to the conception in a balanced account of Nietzsche's philosophy as a whole is consequently problematic, and it is not my concern to resolve this problem. I am simply concerned with the conception insofar as it forms part of a strategy for erecting new values.

3. For example, Arthur C. Danto, *Nietzsche as Philosopher*, 196–200.

4. The point is noted by Robert Nozick, *Anarchy, State, and Utopia*, 241.

5. This is a point that Nietzsche himself appears to acknowledge in WP 885.

6. Provided that one is prepared to accept the plausible contention that in the last paragraph of GM II:24 it is the *Übermensch* that is being referred to, then this is just the picture that is being presented.

7. Whomever this passage may actually be addressed to, there can be no doubting that the *Übermensch* will also have to have this hardness.

8. The underlying conception already appears to be being questioned in BGE 126: "A people is a detour of nature to get to six or seven great men.—Yes: and then to get round them."

9. The classification scheme I have chosen for the interpretations of the eternal recurrence is my own, but it differs only in a minor way from the classification in terms of the cosmological, normative, and attitude interpretations.

10. This is essentially Heidegger's position, but as such it forms only part of a more elaborate interpretation. See Heidegger, *Nietzsche: Volume 2,* esp. 198–208.

11. Deleuze incorporates this position into his interpretation and makes the following interesting connection with Kant: "The eternal return gives the will a rule as rigourous as the Kantian one. We have noted that the eternal return, as a physical doctrine, was the formulation of the speculative synthesis. As an ethical thought the eternal return is the new formulation of the practical synthesis: whatever you will, will it in such a way that you also will its eternal return." See Deleuze, *Nietzsche and Philosophy,* 68. For an assessment of Deleuze's approach to Nietzsche see Hugh Tomlinson, "Nietzsche on the Edge of Town: Deleuze and Reflexitivity," in D. F. Krell and D. Wood, eds., *Exceedingly Nietzsche,* 150–61.

12. To my mind, interpretations that see eternal recurrence basically as the recurrence of the general features of the universe, permitting variations of detail within successive cycles, are difficult to reconcile with the quotation that has just been given, especially when it is taken in conjunction with the passage from *Gay Science* given previously.

13. Some may wish to maintain that there is a middle way between these alternatives, but while I do not wish to rule such a suggestion out entirely, the intelligibility of such an alternative requires demonstration.

14. This is essentially the position adopted by Soll. See Ivan Soll, "Reflections on Recurrence," in Robert C. Solomon, ed., *Nietzsche: A Collection of Critical Essays,* 339–40.

15. For example, ibid., 340.

16. In any event, these will not be ordinary physical or material objects.

17. This is flatly opposed to the position put by Deleuze: "It is the thought of eternal return that selects" (Deleuze, *Nietzsche and Philosophy,* 69). To my mind, there is no serious doubt about Nietzsche's expecting the doctrine of eternal recurrence to have a profound effect. The real difficulty is of whether "pro-

found effect" requires a direct effect on behavior as Deleuze supposes, or whether there is a way of interpreting "profound effect" that renders it consistent with the preceding quotation.

18. Bertrand Russell appears to suggest this when recommending what attitude people ought to adopt: "He will see himself and life and the world as truly as our human limitations will permit; realizing the brevity and minuteness of human life, he will realize that in individual minds is concentrated whatever of value the known universe contains" (*Conquest of Happiness*, 145).

19. Admittedly this is no more than a personal judgment. Heidegger sees in this the culmination and completion of Western metaphysics with the combination of the Parmenidean and Heraclitian viewpoints, after which metaphysics has nowhere left to go. See Heidegger, *Nietzsche: Volume 2*, 198–208.

20. Danto brings this out well but he does not explicitly make the point that follows. See Danto, *Nietzsche as Philosopher*, 210.

21. The case for this interpretation is put very ably by Bernd Magnus in an excellent book. See Magnus, *Nietzsche's Existential Imperative*.

22. In a related, but by no means identical, interpretation Nehamas argues that the literary text constitutes a model for Nietzsche's conception of reality in general. See Nehemas, *Nietzsche*.

23. This interpretation is defended in a stimulating way by Nehamas as part of his more general interpretation. See ibid., 74–105.

24. These models are traceable back to Karl R. Popper, although initially he had only science in mind. See Popper, *Logic of Scientific Discovery*.

25. Alan White, *Within Nietzsche's Labyrinth*, 63–104, esp. 100–104.

Chapter 7: A Survey of Strategies

1. Of course, the case given is not the only one. To cite another example, the concept of "free will" is explicitly charged with contradiction in BGE 21.

2. For an elementary and clear account of Russell's Paradox and how it can be avoided in the construction of set theory, see Robert Rogers, *Mathematical Logic*, 142–65.

3. Tarski, "Semantic Conception," 59–60. Tarski's solution has now been shown to be flawed, requiring recourse to other solutions. See Saul Kripke, "Outline of a Theory of Truth."

4. Of course it is being assumed that altruism here is something containing a genuine level of self-denial. There is absolutely no inconsistency in the selfish advocacy of "reciprocal altruism," for it is itself essentially based on self-interest.

5. One model of theory replacement that is quite congenial to Nietzsche's way of conceiving matters is that of Thomas S. Kuhn. See Kuhn, *Structure of Scientific Revolutions*. But Nietzsche is not sufficiently methodologically explicit to warrant categorically the attribution to him of a single specific model of theory replacement.

6. For a survey of the moral philosophy of the recent past in the English-speaking world that neatly illustrates this, see W. D. Hudson, *Century of Moral Philosophy.*

7. In recent times there have been a number of calls for a complete reform of moral philosophy. What I am suggesting is far less ambitious.

8. For a more extensive treatment of the issue, see Michel Foucault, "Nietzsche, Genealogy, History," in *The Foucault Reader,* ed. Paul Rabinow (New York: Pantheon, 1984), 76–100, and David C. Hoy, "Nietzsche, Hume, and the Genealogical Method," in Y. Yovel, ed., *Nietzsche as Affirmative Thinker,* 20–38.

9. Wittgenstein essentially repeats this part of the functional recategorization of religion, but what is somewhat ironic is that while for Nietzsche this was a stepping stone to a critical attack on religion, religiously inclined followers of Wittgenstein saw this as a rescuing of religion from the onslaught of reason. For Wittgenstein's view see *Lectures and Conversations,* ed. Cyril Barrett, 53–72.

Bibliography

Aristotle, *The Poetics of Aristotle*, trans. S. H. Butcher. London: Macmillan, 1895.

Axelrod, Robert, *The Evolution of Cooperation*. New York: Basic Books, 1984.

Bannock, G., R. E. Baxter, and E. Davis, *Dictionary of Economics*. London: Penguin, 1972.

Baudelaire, Charles, *Intimate Journals*, trans. Christopher Isherwood. London: Picador, 1990. This translation was first published in 1930.

Blocker, H. Gene, *Philosophy of Art*. New York: Charles Scribner's Sons, 1979.

Borges, Jorge Luis, *Labyrinths*, trans. and ed. Donald A. Yates and James E. Irby. New York: New Directions, 1964; Harmondsworth: Penguin, 1970.

Clark, Maudemarie, *Nietzsche on Truth and Philosophy*. Cambridge: Cambridge University Press, 1990.

Collingwood, R. G., *The Principles of Art*. London: Oxford University Press, 1938.

Dampier, William Cecil, *A Shorter History of Science*. New York: Meridian, 1957. First published by Cambridge University Press in 1944.

Danto, Arthur C., *Nietzsche as Philosopher*. New York: Macmillan, 1965.

Dawkins, Richard, *The Selfish Gene*. Oxford: Oxford University Press, 1976.

Deleuze, Gilles, *Nietzsche and Philosophy*, trans. Hugh Tomlinson. London: Athlone Press, 1983.

Descartes, *Philosophical Writings*, trans. and ed. E. Anscombe and P. T. Geach. London: Thomas Nelson, 1954.

Dickie, George, *Art and the Aesthetic: An Institutional Analysis*. Ithaca: Cornell University Press, 1974.

Dostoyevsky, Fyodor, *Letters from the Underworld*, trans. C. J. Hogarth. London: Dent, 1913.

Dürr, Volker, Reinhold Grimm, and Kathy Harms, eds. *Nietzsche: Literature and Values*. Madison: University of Wisconsin Press, 1988.

Ellis, Michael J., *Why People Play*. Englewood Cliffs, N.J.: Prentice-Hall, 1973.

Feigl, Herbert, and Wilfrid Sellars, eds. *Readings in Philosophical Analysis*. New York: Appelton-Century-Crofts, 1949.

Frayn, Michael, *The Tin Men*. London: Collins, 1965.

Gillespie, Michael Allen, and Tracy B. Strong, eds. *Nietzsche's New Seas: Explorations in Philosophy, Aesthetics, and Politics*. Chicago: University of Chicago Press, 1988.

Grimm, Ruediger H., *Nietzsche's Theory of Knowledge*. Berlin: Walter de Gruyter, 1977.

Grünbaum, Adolf, *Geometry and Chronometry in Philosophical Perspective*. Minneapolis: University of Minnesota Press, 1968.

Heidegger, Martin, *Nietzsche*, 2 vols. Pfullingen: Neske, 1961.

———. *Nietzsche: Volume 1: The Will to Power as Art*, trans. David Farrell Krell. New York: Harper & Row, 1979.

———. *Nietzsche: Volume 2: The Eternal Recurrence of the Same*, trans. David Farrell Krell. San Francisco: Harper & Row, 1984.

———. *Nietzsche: Volume 4: Nihilism*, trans. Frank A. Capuzzi, ed. David Farrell Krell. San Francisco: Harper & Row, 1982.

Heller, Erich, *The Importance of Nietzsche: Ten Essays*. Chicago: University of Chicago Press, 1988.

Hollingdale, R. J., *Nietzsche*. London: Routledge & Kegan Paul, 1973.

Hudson, W. D., *A Century of Moral Philosophy*. London: Lutterworth Press, 1980.

Hume, David, *Dialogues Concerning Natural Religion*. Harmondsworth: Penguin, 1990. First published in 1779.

Jaspers, Karl, *Nietzsche: An Introduction to the Understanding of His Philosophical Activity*, trans. Charles F. Wallraff and Frederick J. Schmitz. Chicago: Regnery, 1965.

Kant, Immanuel, *Kant's Critique of Aesthetic Judgement*, trans. James Creed Meredith. Oxford: Clarendon Press, 1911.

———. *Kant's Critique of Practical Reason*, trans. Thomas Kingsmill Abbott. London: Longmans, Green and Co., 1873.

———. *Kant's Critique of Pure Reason*, trans. Norman Kemp Smith. London: Macmillan, 1961. First published in 1929.

Kato, Shuichi, *Form, Style, Tradition: Reflections on Japanese Art and Society*, trans. John Bester. University of California Press, 1971; Tokyo: Kodansha, 1981.

Kaufmann, Walter, *Nietzsche: Philosopher, Psychologist, Antichrist*, 4th ed. Princeton: Princeton University Press, 1974.

———. "Jaspers' Relation to Nietzsche." *The Philosophy of Karl Jaspers*, ed. P. A. Schilpp. New York: Tudor, 1957.

Krell, David Farrell, and D. Wood, eds. *Exceedingly Nietzsche: Aspects of Contemporary Nietzsche-Interpretation*. London: Routledge, 1988.

Kripke, Saul, "Outline of a Theory of Truth," *Journal of Philosophy* 72 (1975): 690–716.

Kuhn, Thomas S., *The Structure of Scientific Revolutions*, 2d ed. Chicago: University of Chicago Press, 1970.

Lawrence, D. H., *Apocalypse*. Harmondsworth: Penguin, 1974. First published in 1931.

Leibniz, G. W., *Philosophical Writings*, ed. G. H. R. Parkinson. London: Dent, 1973.

Lewis, David, "Putnam's Paradox," *Australasian Journal of Philosophy* 62 (1984): 221–36.

Mackie, J. L., *Ethics: Inventing Right and Wrong.* Harmondsworth: Penguin, 1977.

Magnus, Bernd, *Nietzsche's Existential Imperative.* Bloomington: Indiana University Press, 1978.

Mill, John Stuart, *Utilitarianism.* London: Fontana-Collins, 1962.

Nehamas, Alexander, *Nietzsche: Life as Literature.* Cambridge: Harvard University Press, 1985.

Nagel, Thomas, *The Possibility of Altruism.* Oxford: Clarendon Press, 1970.

———. *The View from Nowhere.* New York: Oxford University Press, 1986.

Nerlich, Graham, *The Shape of Space.* Cambridge: Cambridge University Press, 1976.

Nielsen, Kai, "Nietzsche as a Moral Philosopher," *Man and World: An International Philosophical Review* 6 (1973): 182–205.

Nietzsche, Friedrich Wilhelm, *The Anti-Christ,* trans. R. J. Hollingdale. Harmondsworth: Penguin, 1968.

———. *Beyond Good and Evil,* trans. Walter Kaufmann. New York: Vintage, 1966. Also trans. R. J. Hollingdale (Harmondsworth: Penguin, 1973).

———. *The Birth of Tragedy and The Case of Wagner,* trans, W. Kaufmann. New York: Vintage, 1967.

———. *Daybreak,* trans. R. J. Hollingdale. Cambridge: Cambridge University Press, 1982.

———. *Ecce Homo,* trans. and ed. W. Kaufmann. New York: Vintage, 1969. Also trans. R. J. Hollingdale (Harmondsworth: Penguin, 1979).

———. *Gay Science,* trans. W. Kaufmann. New York: Vintage, 1974.

———. *Human, All Too Human,* trans. R. J. Hollingdale. Cambridge: Cambridge University Press, 1986.

———. *Kritische Studienausgabe* [works], ed. G. Colli and M. Montinari in 15 volumes. Berlin: de Gruyter, 1980.

———. *Kritische Studienausgabe* [letters], ed. G. Colli and M. Montinari in 8 volumes. Berlin: de Gruyter, 1986.

———. *On the Genealogy of Morals,* trans. W. Kaufmann and R. J. Hollingdale. New York: Vintage, 1969.

———. *Philosophy in the Tragic Age of the Greeks,* trans, M. Cowan. Chicago: Henry Regnery, 1962.

———. *The Portable Nietzsche,* trans. and ed. W. Kaufmann. New York: Viking, 1954.

———. *Thus Spoke Zarathustra,* trans. R. J. Hollingdale. Harmondsworth: Penguin, 1961.

———. *Twilight of the Idols,* trans. R. J. Hollingdale. Harmondsworth: Penguin, 1968.

———. *Untimely Meditations,* trans. R. J. Hollingdale. Cambridge: Cambridge University Press, 1983.

———. *The Will to Power,* trans. W. Kaufmann and R. J. Hollingdale, ed. Kaufmann. New York: Vintage, 1968.

Nozick, Robert, *Anarchy, State, and Utopia.* New York: Basic Books, 1974.

O'Connor, D. J., *The Correspondence Theory of Truth.* London: Hutchinson, 1975.

Pasley, Malcolm, ed. *Nietzsche: Imagery and Thought: A Collection of Essays.* London: Methuen, 1978.

Plato, *The Republic of Plato,* trans. Francis MacDonald Cornford. London: Oxford University Press, 1941.

Popper, Karl R., *Logic of Scientific Discovery.* New York: Basic Books, 1959.

Priest, Graham, *In Contradiction: A Study of the Transconsistent.* Dordrecht: Martinus Nijhoff, 1987.

Putnam, Hilary, "Models and Reality." *Realism and Reason: Philosophical Papers,* vol. 3. Cambridge: Cambridge University Press, 1983.

———. "An Examination of Grünbaum's Philosophy of Geometry." *Philosophy of Science: The Delaware Seminar,* vol. 2, ed. B. Baumrin, 205–55. New York: Interscience Publishers, 1963.

Quine, Willard Van Orman, "On the Nature of Moral Values." *Values and Morals: Essays in Honor of William Frankena, Charles Stevenson, and Richard Brandt,* ed. Alvin I. Goldman and Jaegwon Kim, 37–45. Dordrecht: D. Reidel, 1978.

———. "Two Dogmas of Empiricism," *Philosophical Review* 60 (1951). Reprinted in Quine, *From a Logical Point of View.* New York: Harper and Row, 1963.

———. *Word and Object.* Cambridge: MIT Press, 1960.

Rabinow, Paul, ed. *The Foucault Reader.* New York: Pantheon, 1984.

Rescher, Nicholas, *The Coherence Theory of Truth.* Oxford: Clarendon Press, 1973.

Rogers, Robert, *Mathematical Logic and Formalized Theories.* Amsterdam: North-Holland, 1971.

Russell, Bertrand, *The Conquest of Happiness.* London: Allen & Unwin, 1930.

Schacht, Richard, *Nietzsche.* London: Routledge & Kegan Paul, 1983.

Schopenhauer, Arthur, *Essays and Aphorisms,* trans. R. J. Hollingdale. Harmondsworth: Penguin, 1970.

Schutte, Ofelia, *Beyond Nihilism: Nietzsche without Masks.* Chicago: University of Chicago Press, 1984.

Sellars, Wilfrid F., *Science, Perception, and Reality.* London: Routledge & Kegan Paul, 1963.

Smart, Ninian, *World Religions: A Dialogue.* Harmondsworth: Penguin, 1966. First published by S.C.M. Press, 1960.

Solomon, Robert C., ed. *Nietzsche: A Collection of Critical Essays.* Garden City, N.Y.: Doubleday Anchor, 1973.

———, and Kathleen M. Higgins, eds. *Reading Nietzsche.* New York: Oxford University Press, 1988.

Spencer, Herbert, *The Principles of Psychology,* 2 vols., 2d ed. London: Williams and Norgate, 1872.

Stern, J. P., *A Study of Nietzsche*. Cambridge: Cambridge University Press, 1979.

Stocker, Michael, "Agent and Other: Against Ethical Universalism," *Australasian Journal of Philosophy* 54 (1976): 206–20.

Strong, Tracy B., *Friedrich Nietzsche and the Politics of Transfiguration*. Berkeley: University of California Press, 1975.

Tolstoy, Leo, *What Is Art? and Essays in Art*. London: Oxford University Press, 1930.

Trivers, Robert L., "The Evolution of Reciprocal Altruism," *Quaterly Review of Biology* 46 (1971): 35–57. Reprinted with some omissions in Arthur L. Caplan, ed., *The Sociobiology Debate: Readings in the Ethical and Scientific Issues Concerning Sociobiology* (New York: Harper & Row, 1978), 213–26.

Wallace, G., and A. D. M. Walker, eds. *The Definition of Morality*. London: Methuen, 1970.

Weitz, Morris, "The Role of Theory in Aesthetics," *Journal of Aesthetics and Art Criticism* 15 (1956): 27–35.

White, Alan, *Within Nietzsche's Labyrinth*. New York: Routledge, 1990.

Wilcox, John T., *Truth and Value in Nietzsche: A Study of His Metaethics and Epistemology*. Ann Arbor: University of Michigan Press, 1974.

Wittgenstein, Ludwig, *Lectures and Conversations on Aesthetics, Psychology, and Religious Belief*, ed. Cyril Barrett. Oxford: Basil Blackwell, 1970.

Yovel, Yirmiyahu, ed. *Nietzsche as Affirmative Thinker*. Dordrecht: Martinus Nijhoff, 1986.

Index

and enrichment of life, 81; conformity toward, 82, 215*nn12,13;* and highest values, 83–86; and the meaning of life, 83–86; mentioned, 201. *See also* Moralities; Morality; Moral judgments; Moral value-model; Moral values

Moral value claims. *See* Moral judgments

Moral value-model: to be replaced by aesthetic value-model, 82–83, 85, 97; and highest values, 83; and the meaning of life, 85; and universality, 85; and religion, 97

Moral values: as human products, 59–60, 63; elements in evaluation, 60; and characteristics of producers, 63; function of, 63–64; revaluation of, 69; and false presupposition, 191; as restricted category, 214*n1;* mentioned, 6, 92, 196, 207. *See also* Moralities; Morality; Moral judgments; Moral rules; Moral value-model

Multiplier effect: and eternal recurrence, 167–73 passim; and positive values, 174

New emphasis: and the body, 205–7; as a revaluation strategy, 205–7

New scales: as a revaluation strategy, 199

New values: and power, 6; and higher-order values, 64, 152; need for, 64, 152–53; and theory of value, 152; and *Übermensch,* 152–65 passim; and replacement solution, 155–57; and value crisis, 156–61 passim; and imposition model, 160; acceptance of, 182–83; and whole person, 182; advocacy of, 186

Objectivity: definition of, 23; denial of, 25; and objectivity, 135, 150; and value judgments, 192–94; and genealogical method, 203

Ontology: and Nietzsche's theory of value, 8; associated with absolute theory of truth, 24; associated with religious belief systems, 94–98 passim, 204

Pain: status of, 91–92; and utilitarianism, 91–92; and higher-order values, 92; as ineliminable, 99; and eternal re-

currence, 169–70; and affirmative attitude toward life, 177–80; as a means, 195; and pragmatism, 213*n3*

Parasite model of nonautonomy, 89–90

Personal identity: and eternal recurrence, 167, 170–72, 180–81; and memory, 170

Perspectivism: and absolute theory of truth, 23, 24, 29–33, 37–46 passim, 53, 59, 202; better and worse views, 26, 27, 28, 38, 42, 45, 59; relation to pragmatism, 26; relation to relativism, 26–28; and new perspectives, 28; and absolute truth, 29–32, 37–41, 45, 59; and concepts as creations, 36; and problems of self-refutation, 37–46; and rational choice, 42, 43; and irresolubility, 45; and the value of truth, 53; relation to morality, 56, 58; and subjectivity, 56–58, 124–25; and reason, 59; and altruism, 68, 70; and universality, 78–79; and eternal recurrence, 175–76, 184; and expansion of focus, 202

Phenomena of valuation: and conceptual network, 113; role in revaluation, 20–21

Play theory of art, 144–45

Pleasure: and truth, 27; status of, 91–92; and utilitarianism, 91–92; and higher-order values, 92; and eternal recurrence, 169–70; as a means, 195

Polytheism, 101–2

Post-survival: definition of, 14; and enhancement of life, 14, 16; as higher-order value, 16–17; and will to power, 17

Power: feelings of, 1–2, 26, 71, 146; and attraction, 2–6 passim, 11; and celebration of life, 2, 16; in the individual, 2–14 passim; and repulsion, 2–6 passim, 212*n2;* and value, 2–11 passim; and goals, 3–10 passim, 15, 16; network relations of, 4; and groups, 6–8, 11, 12–13; and ultimate value, 8–10; as activity, 9–10; and enhancement of life, 13; and higher-order values, 14–17; and artworks, 54; as abstract concept, 111; against petty use of, 160; mentioned, 25, 210

Pragmatic theory of truth: basic verifica-

E. E. SLEINIS was born in Germany of Latvian parents. He was educated at the University of Melbourne and the University of Sydney in Australia, and Johns Hopkins University in the United States. After teaching briefly at the University of Illinois in Champaign he took up a position at the University of Tasmania in Australia, where he is currently located.